TALBIS IBLIS

(Delusion of the Devil)

TALBIS IBLIS

(Delusion of the Devil)

Vol. I

By
Abu'l Faraj Ibn Jauzi

Translated into English by
D.S. Margoliouth

Edited by
N.K. Singh

kitab bhavan

NEW DELHI-110 002. [INDIA]

KITAB BHAVAN

Publishers, Distributors, Exporters & Importers
1784, Kalan Mahal, Darya Ganj,
New Delhi - 1100 02 (India)

Phones : (91-11) 23277392/93, 23274686, 32906494
Fax : (91-11) 23263383

Website : www.nusratalinasri.com

Email : nasri@vsnl.com
: nusrat@bol.net.in

1ˢᵗ Edition 2003
3ʳᵈ Edition : 2011

ISBN : 81-7151-322-0 (Set)
ISBN : 81-7151-323-9 (Vol. I)

Laser Typesetting at:
Laser Track
Darya Ganj, New Delhi - 1100 02

Printed & Published in India by :
Nusrat Ali Nasri for KITAB BHAVAN
1784, Kalan Mahal, Darya Ganj,
New Delhi - 1100 02 [India]

CONTENTS

Chapter   VI

The way wherein the devil deludes Savants in different departments

Chapter   VII

Chapter   VIII

Chapter IX

Chapter X

Chapter XI

Preface

Praise be to God, who has committed the balance of justice to the hands of the inteliigent, and sent Apostles to promise reward and give warning of punishment; has revealed unto them the Books which explain wrong and right has established Codes that are perfect without fault or flaw. I praise Him as one who knows that he is the Causer of causes, and I attest His Unity, as one who is sincere in his intent and undoubting; and I testify that Muhammad is His Servant and His Envoy, sent at a time when infidelity had let down its evil over the face of faith, so that he cleared away darkness by the light of guidance, and revealed to him, and elucidating the difficulties of the Book: "leaving them on the white highroad, wherein is no pitfall and no mirage."

God be gracious unto him and all his household and Companions, and their successors, favouring them until the Day of Judgement and Reckoning: and may he give them perfect peace. The greatest benefit conferred on man is Reason, since that is the instrument whereby he acquires knowledge of God Almighty, and the else whereby he arrives at belief in the Apostles, Only in-as much as it is insufficient for all that is required of a man, Apostles were sent and Books revealed. So the Code is like the sun, and the reason like the eye, which, if sound, when it is opened, sees the sun. When the veracious sayings of the Prophets are assured to the reason by the evidence of miracles, is surrenders to those Prophets, and relies of them for what is hidden from itself.

When God bestowed reason on the human world, he commenced with the Prophet hood of Adam; he kept instructing them according to God's inspiration, and they went right till Cain followed his selfish passion and slew his brother. Thereupon different passions swayed mankind, which sent them astray in the wilds of error, so that they worshipped idols and adopted divers beliefs and courses of action, disagreeing therein with the Prophets and their own reasons, and following their lusts, inclining to their customs and imitating their magnates.

The Devil was confirmed in his opinion of them, and they followed him, all but a party of Believers. You are to know that the Prophets furnished adequate instruction, and met the ailments with certain remedies; they agreed in pursuing an invariable course. Satan proceeded to mingle doubts with the instruction, and poison with the medicine: misleading tracks with the plain road. Nor did he cease playing with their intellects so that they worshipped idols in the Sacred House, tabooed the sa' ibah, bahirah, wasilah, and ham, approved of burying girls alive deprived them of inheritance, with other forms of error suggested to them by the Devil. Then God Almighty sent Muhammad, who abolished the atrocities, and enjoined what was profitable. His Companions walked with him and after him in the illumination of his light, immune from transgression and its deceit. Only when the light of their existence was withdrawn the clouds of darkness came on. Passions once more generated innovations, narrowing a path which had always been wide; most people became schismatic and sectarian.

The Devil proceeded to delude and beguile, to separate and combine. He can only play the robber in the night of ignorance; were the mourn of knowledge to break on him, he would be discredited. I thought, it may duty to warn against his wiles, and point out his traps, since to indicate a danger involves warning against falling into it. Now the two *Sahih* contain the following Tradition recorded by *Hudhaifah* people used to ask the Prophet about the good, whereas I would ask him about the bad, fearing lest it should overtake me. And indeed we have been informed by Abû'l-Barakat Sa'd Allâh b. 'Ali al-Bazzâr by a chain of authorities leading up to Ibn 'Abbâs that the latter said. By Allâh may thinks there is no-one on the earth's surface whose death would give greater pleasure to Satan than mine.—He was asked. How so? He replied: He starts an innovation in East or West, and someone brings it to me. When it gets to me, I confute it with the Sunnah, and it is returned to him as he issued it.

The main purpose of the composition of this work is to warn against his enticements, and instilling fear of his temptations disclosing what he would hide and exposing his hidden guile. God in His bounty helps all hones endeavour. This title has been compiled in two Volumes which in their entirety will dispel his delusions, and the understanding of which will make clear to the intelligent his falsification. First Volume has been divided into eleven following chapters:

i. Let him hide himself with God's veil.

ii. The way wherein the devil deludes those who believe in miracles wrought for the glory of Saints.

iii. The way wherein the devil deludes the believers in "Shrines."

iv. The way wherein the devil deludes the Dissidents.

v. The way wherein the devil deludes the Jews.

vi. The way wherein the devil deludes savants in different departments of knowledge.

vii. The way wherein the devil deludes Governor and Sovereigns.

viii. The way wherein the devil deludes devotees and their devotion.

ix. The way wherein the devil deludes ascetics and devotees.

x. The way wherein the devil deludes the Sûfis.

xi. The way wherein the devil deludes the Sûfi in the matter of purification.

About the Author

Jamal al-Din Abû'l-Faraj 'Abd al-Rahman b. Ali, popularly known as Ibn al-Jaûzi, 510 A.H.--- 599 A.H. (A.D. 1116 - A.D.1200), was the author of a vast number of works—theological, historical, biographical, medical, philological, and entertaining—of which several have been printed in recent times. He was famous as a preacher and the traveller Ibn Jubair gives an enthusiastic account of two of his sermons heard in Baghdād.

We learn from this notice that he was court-preacher, and indeed devoted some of his eloquence to eulogy of the Caliph and the imperial household; which seems inconsistent with his repeated warnings to the learned against association with princes. His father, he tells us, died when he was very young, and his mother paid him no attention. Nevertheless he was brought up in luxury, so that his first attempts at abstinence produced an illness as this interfered with his devotions, he returned to a less ascetic diet.

From his earliest years, he had a passion for the acquisition of knowledge, all departments of which he aspired to master. He claims to have read more than 20,000 volumes, Ibn Khallikān calls him the most learned man of his time. Specimens of his homilies are to be found in his collection of Miscellanies, called *al-Mudhish*. Ibn Jûbair's account of their effectiveness bears out what the author records on the subject. He was instrumental in bringing more than 200,000 Muslims to repentance and converting more than 200 members of other communities to Islam. On one occasion he found himself preaching to a congregation of more than 10,000 persons, all of whom had either softened hearts or weeping eyes.

The legal system followed by Ibn al-Jaûzi was the Hanbalite, which about a century later produced an equally voluminous writer in Ibn Taimiyyāh, and has owing to the rise of Wahabism acquired fresh importance in our time. This school was vehemently opposed to the Shi'ah; early in the fourth century we read cf their interfering with visitors to the tomb of Husain and Miskawaihi preserves a letter of the Caliph Radi in which they are rebuked for stirring up strife and threatened with punishment.

One of the bulkiest of Ibn Taimiyyah's works is a refutation of the Imami sect of the Shi'ah. Since both Shi'ah and Sûfis practised rites which could not easily be attested of the early Muslims, a follower of the Hanlative system would naturally be out of sympathy with opinions and practices which he felt justified in branding as "innovations". Moreover, though clearly a man of conspicuous piety and learning, Ibn al-Jaûzi was also a man of the world, convinced that wealth was a good thing, and that the needs of the body could no more be neglected than those of the soul. In his *Said al-Khātir* he repeatedly gives expression to these convictions.

Translator's Note

The work of which a translations is here offered is directed against the sins of contemporary society, which it traces to "delusion by the Devil." Its title *(Talbis Iblis)* of which those words are a rendering, had been previously selected by Ghazali for a work of similar scope which he contemplated. Ibn al-Jaûzi, though he handles Ghazali severely, adopted it by far the greater part of the book is criticism or censure of the Sûfis, who, owing to the establishment of Orders by

Ibn al-Rifa'i and 'Abd al-Qadir âl-Gilani in the sixth century of Islam, were beginning to render them, especially in North Africa, a political factor.

Since the attitude of European writers on Sûfism, such as Prof. Nicholson, Prof. Han Palacious, and Miss Margaret Smith, is usually sympathetic and favourable, it seemed desirable for the study of Islamic Culture to render accessible the views of a hostile writer, whose eminence as an Islamic scholar and theologian is indisputable. He claims indeed that his hostility is confined to what he regards as the aberrations of "the moderns," of the earliest ascetics arid Sûfis he speaks with respect and even admiration. Like Tanukhi, the author of the *Table-talk of a Mesopotamian Judge, he is a laudator temporis action.*

The work does not apparently contain any statement which would furnish an exact date for its composition. It is however, mentioned several times in the author's *Said al-Khãtir,* in which the latest date introduced is 575. 'Works of his own to which reference is made in *the Talbis* are *Minhaj-al-wusul ila 'ilm al-usul* and *Dhamm-al-Hawa.*

The text translated is the printed edition of the year 1340, issued from the Sa'adah Press, Cairo by Muhammad Amin al-Khanji and Muhammad Munir al-Dimishqi. Personal and geographical names have been verified in such sources of information as are now accessible to students and corrected accordingly; and the same has been done with passages cited by the author from accessible works. For his quotations from the last work of al-Naubakhti held has been obtained from the reproduction of these from the Talbis in Dr. H. Ritter's edition of the same writer's work on the Sects of the Shi'ah.

Many lines of the text are occupied with *Isnads, i.e.,* series of persons through whom traditions have ultimately reached the writer. Few of the Readers of these translation would wish to have these reproduced. It has seemed sufficient to mention the first and the last link in each chain.

Meaning and Misrepresentation of Delusion

Misrepresentation is exhibiting what is false in the form of truth, and delusion is a form of ignorance which makes one believe the unsound to be sound, and the bad good; and the cause of it is the existence of a semblance which produces that effect. The Devil only enters into people to the extent of his ability, and his power over them increases or diminishes in proportion to their vigilance or negligence, their knowledge or ignorance. The heart is like a fortress surrounded with a wall, which has gates and breaches; its inmate is reason, and the angels pay recurrent visit to that fortress, besiege which there is a suburb wherein is lust, and thither the demons pay called unhindered. War is incessant between the people of the fortress and those of the suburbs. The demons ceaselessly go-round and round the fortress, looking out for a time when the watcher is off guard and they can pass in by a breach. The watchman ought to known all the gates of the fortress of which he is incharge, and all the breaches, and ought not to slacken vigilance for a moment, for the enemy does not slacken. Some one said to al-Hasan al-Bāsri: Does the Devil ever sleep?— He said: Where he to sleep, we should have repose.

Now this fortress is illuminated by the Record, and sparkles with faith; therein is a polished mirror wherein appear the figures of whatever passes by. The first thing which darkens the walls of the fortress, and rusts the mirror. Perfect meditation removes the smoke, and the polishing of remembrance clears the mirror. The enemy makes divers assaults: at one time he attacks and enters the fortress but is charged by the watcher and driven out; at other he enters and does mischief, and remains owing to the negligence of the watcher. At times too the wind which disperses the smoke is still, so that the walls are blackened and the mirror rusts. Satan unnoticed passes in, and sometimes the negligent watcher is wounded and captured, made to serve and set to devise schemes for aiding and abetting lust.

At times he becomes a kind of expert in evil. One of the men of former time said: I saw Satan and he said to me: I used to meet people and instruct them; now I meet them and learn of the— Often Satan assails the man of keen intellect, bringing with him lust as a bride whom he has unveiled, and the sight of whom diverts and captivates the sage; the strongest fetter wherewith captives can be secured is ignorance; intermediate in strength is lust; the weakest negligence. So long as the cuirass of faith is on the Believer, the enemies' shafts will hit no vital place. Al-Hasan b. Salih said: Satan opens to a man ninety-nine gates of good, meaning thereby one gate of evil. Al-A'mash said: A certain man used to hold converse with the Jinn; they said; No one is harder for us to deal with than the man who follows the Sunnah; as for the lustful, we simply play with them.

Account of the way wherein he deludes the Sophists : These people are called after a man named Sofista; they hold that things have no reality, and that what we witness may be as we witness it or otherwise than as we witness it. Men of learning traversed this by of saying to them: Has this assertion of yours reality, or not? If you say it has no reality, and so allow that it may be falls, how can you want people to accept that which has no reality? You seem by this statement to confess that your statement by Abû Muhammad al-Hasan b. Musa al-Naukakhti, The Book of Opinions and Religions. He says: I have noticed that many metaphysicians have committed a serious mistake in the matter of these people.

They argue and debate with them, and endeavour to refute them by pleading and discussion; but, as they do not admit reality, or accept the evidence of the senses, how can you talk to one who says "I do not know whether you are talking to me or not" and how can you argue with one who states that he does not know whether he exists or not, and how can you address one who professes that addressing is no more expressive than silence, and that the unsound is on a level with the sound? Further, he says, discussion can only be conducted with one who admits necessity, or confesses to something, the truth of what he denies. If a man does not admit that, arguing with him is waste of time.

The author observes: This statement was traversed by Abû'l-Wafa b, Aqil, who says: "Certain persons say: How can we talk to these people, when the utmost which the debater can effect is to approximate the noumenon to that which is perceived by sensation?" He uses that which is present as evidence whereby he infers the absent.

But these people do not admit sensations, so how is it possible to talk to them?—This, says Abû'l-Wafa, is too narrow a view. One ought not to despair of treating these people, for what has befallen them is no more than a delusion, which we ought not to despair of treating, as they are the victims of some indisposition. The case of ourselves and then might be compared to that of a man to whom there is born a son with a squint, who always sees two moons in lieu of one, and so has no doubt that there are two moons in the sky. His father tells him that there is only one moon; the mischief, he says, is in your eyes; close your squinting eye and look. The lad does so, and then says: I see one moon because I have closed one of my eyes, so one of the moons is out of sight. This produces a second difficulty, so the father says to him: "If it be as you say, then close the sound eye. The lad does so and sees two moons, and knows the truth of what his father says."

The following was narrated by Muhammad b. Isa al-Nazzam: A son of Salih b. 'Abd al-Quddus died, and there came to him Abû'l-Hudhail, accompaniment by al-Nazzam, who was a young lad, sympathizing. Finding Salih distressed Abû'l-Hudhail said to him: I know of no reason for you grief it men are in you opinion like plants. I am grieving over him, replied Salih, because he never read The Book of Doubts. And what, asked Abû'l-Hudhail, is the Book of Doubts?— a book, he replied, composed by me, whose reader will doubt whatever has been, so that he will even fancy that he has never existed, and what has not been, so that he will think it has been. Then, said al-Nazzam to him, doubt that your son has died and suppose him to be not dead; and, if he is dead, doubt next that he may have read the book, even if he did not do so.

Abû'l-Qasim al-Balkhi relates how a certain sophist used to visit a certain metaphysician. One day he came to him and began to argue with him. The metaphysician ordered his slave to take the sophist's horse. When the latter was leaving he could not find the animal, so he came back to the metaphysician and said to him: You have stolen my horse. The metaphysician replied: Nonsense perhaps you did not come riding. The sophist said, No, I did, —The metaphysician said to him: Think, He said: This is a matter of which I am certain.

The metaphysician began to say to him, Reflect. He said: Nonsense this is no case for reflecting, I do not doubt that I came riding. The metaphysician said: Then how do you profess that there is no reality in anything, and that the waking state is like the sleeping state?—The sophist was nonplussed and abandoned his doctrine. Naubakhti says: One of the agnostic sects hold that things have no essential reality, but that their reality is relative to people's beliefs about the. For they say, one with yellow bite finds honey bitter, whereas others find it sweet. So, likewise, they say, world is eternal with those who believe in its eternity, freshly created with those who believe that it is so. Colour, too, is a body for those who believe it to be an accident. So, if we were to fancy that there were no believers, things would depend on the existence of some believer.

These are a kind of sophists, and we may say to them: Is you statement true?— they will say: it is true for us false for our opponent.—Then we say: You claim that your statement is true is refuted, and your admission that your doctrine is false for your opponent testifies against you. Admitting that your doctrine is false from one point of view you save your opponent the trouble of demonstrating its falsity. Further, a question that may be put to them is this. Do you maintain that sensation is of reality? If they say No, then they are in the case of the former set of sophist: if they say, It's reality is relative to the believer, then they deny its essential reality, and may be dealt with as the former.

Naubakhti proceeds: To this group there belong those who assert that the world is in a state of flux, and that a man cannot ponder on one thing twice, owing to things constantly changing, You can ask them: How is this known, when you deny the persistence of what can produce knowledge? Possibly the one who gives the reply may be different from the person questioned.

Account of the way wherein he deludes the Materialists: The Devil has put it into the minds of many that there is no God and no Maker, that these things came into existence without a producer. Such persons, not having perceived the Maker by sensation, or employed reason to reason doubt the existence of a Maker? For it a man were to pass by a plot whereon was no building, and presently see a wall built there, he would know that there must certainly have been a builder to build it. So then this floor that is laid and this roof that is raised and these marvellous buildings, and the laws which are so wisely in force,—do not they point to a Maker? It was a fine saying of an Arab: the dung indicates the camel. So a lofty structure that is so subtle, a deep foundation that is so solid—do not they point to a subtle expert? If a man was to ponder on himself, that would be a sufficient guide, and satisfy all thirst for information.

For this body of ours contains evidences of wisdom such as no book could contain. Let a man consider the teeth sharpened so as to cut, the molars rounded so as to grind, the tongues to turn over what is masticatised, the liver controlling digestion, and sending to each member the necessary amount of nourishment, the fingers with their joints enabling them to close and open, and to works, not made hollow on account of the work which they have to do since if they were hollow, any hard thing which attacked them would break them of different lengths so that they close evenly and how there is secreted in the body that whereon it depends, the soul with whose departure ruin overtakes the reason which guides to what is profitable. Each one of these things cries out: It there any doubt about God?

The atheist flounders because he seeks Him by the avenue of Sensation: some however deny Him because, though admitting His existence generally, they do not perceive Him particularly, and so come to deny it altogether had such a person exercised his thought, he would have known that we have things only generally perceived, such as the soul and the reason, yet no-one would decline to assert their existence. And is our purpose more than to assert creation generally? And how can one ask, How is He or What is He, seeing that He has neither mode nor quiddity?

A convincing proof of His existence is that the world is contingent, as is shown by its not being free from contingencies; and that which is not free from contingencies is contingent; whence the coming about of this contingencies: and that which is not free from contingencies is contingent; whence the coming about of this contingent must have someone to cause it, and that is the Creator, praised be He! The heretics proudly object to our saying: The Artifice must have an Artificer; saying. In this you rely upon and appeal to what is actually seen. So we say: Just as the Artifice must have an Artificer, so the form which is impressed by the Artificer must have matter on which the form can be impressed, such as wood for the form of a door or iron for the form of an eye. So the argument whereby you established the Maker involves eternity of the world.—Our reply is that we do not require matter; on the contrary we assert that the Maker things. For we know that the form and the figures which confine themselves in bodies, e.g., that of horses, have no matter; God created them, and they must have a former. So we have shown you a form which is a thing, that has come from nothing, whereas you cannot show us an artifice which has come without an artificer.

Account of the way wherein he deludes the Physicists: When the devil saw that there was little agreement with him in denying the Maker, because men's reason testifies that the made thing must necessarily have a Maker, he suggested to some people that these creations are the work of nature; saying that nothing is created except by the coming together of the four natures therein, indicating that those are the doer. In reply to this we say they coming together of the natures is proof of their existence, not of their action; further it is established that the natures only act by coming together and intermingling; this is contrary to their nature and indicates that they are coerced.

Further they admit that the natures are not alive nor knowing nor powerful, and it is known that continuous and orderly action can only proceed from a being that is knowing and wise; how then can one that is neither knowing nor powerful act? If they say: Were the agent wise, there would occur no flaw in his building, neither would these mischievous animals exist, whence it is known that it must be by nature. We reply; This is turned against you by the orderly and elaborate things which proceed thence, the like of which could not proceed from nature. As for the flaw to which you point possibly it is for the sake of trial or repression or punishment; or there may be hidden therein certain advantages unknown to us.

Next, how does the work of nature stand in relation to a such which rises in April over divers sorts of berries, moistening the grape and the date, but parching and drying the grain? If the sun acted by nature, it would either have derived them all or moistened them all; hence nothing is left but to admit that the selecting agent employed the sun by will dry the one for storage, and ripen the other for plucking. What brings dryness does so through coverings without contact with the berry itself, whereas what moistens comes in contact with the berry. Further the sun whitens the poppy-flower, and reddens the anemoned, sours the pomegranate and sweetens the grape, the water being the same. The Lord alludes to this in the verse: irrigated with the same water, yet We make some of them superior to others for food.

Account of the way wherein he deludes the Dualists: These are people who make of the Maker of the world two: the Doer of evil Darkness. Both are eternal, always have been and always shall been mighty, sentient, hearing, seeing. These two differ in essence and form and are contrary in action and administration. The substance of Light is excellent, beautiful, luminous, pure, clean, sweet-smelling, fair to look upon, and its soul is beneficent, generous, is, profitable, the source of good, pleasure, joy prosperity: in it there is nothing bad nor harmful. The substance of Darkness is contrariwise, foul deficient, ill smelling, ugly, and its soul is wicked, miserly, stupid, stinking, mischievous, the source of evil and corruption. This is what Naubakhti records concerning them, adding: now some of them assert that Light has always been above Darkness, whereas others say that on the contrary they are collateral.

Most of them hold that Light has always been aloft in the northern region and Darkness depressed in the Southern, each of the two having always been separate from the other. Naubakhti proceeds: they assert that each of the two is five sorts, four of them bodies and a fifth the spirit. The bodies of Light are four: Fire, Wind, Earth, Water; and its spirit breeze, which has always been moving in these bodies. The bodies of Darkness are four: Burning, Darkness demons and 'Light has no power for evil, which is impossible for it: whereas Darkness is in the like case with good. Various doctrines are recorded as there is in respect of Darkness, and foolish works, such as that it is their duty not to store more than one day's food; some hold that a man should fast a seventh of his life, should eschew lying, greed, sorcery, idolatry, sexual sin and thrift, and should not inflict pain on anything possessed of spirit; with certain curious doctrines which they invented in their insipid wickedness. Yahya b. Bishr al-Nihawandir [Not the famous heretic, whose name was Ahmad b. Yahya b. Ishaq. The Daisaniyyah were a Christian (gnostic) sect] states that some of them called Daisaniyyah held that the nature of the world was a fair nature, copying the body of the Creator, who is Light, for a time; that he was annoyed thereby and when he grew weary thereof he decided to remove it from him, plunged into it and mingled therewith and thence there was composed this world of light and of darkness; so that which is of the aspect of corruption is from the darkness.

These persons waylay men and strangle them, asserting that thereby they are delivering the light from the darkness. Foolish doctrines! What suggested this to them was that they found evil and discord in the world, and said that two discordant things could not spring from the same root,' just as fire cannot produce both cold and heat. Learned men have refuted their assertion that the creator is two beings: for, say they, if He were two, those two would either be both powerful or both weak or one of them powerful and the other weak. Both could not be weak, since weakness would prevent the ascription of divinity, neither could one of the two be weak: it remains that both must be supposed to be powerful, and we must imagine that one of the two may wish to move this body at a time when the other wishes to kept it still. The wishes of the two could not them possibly be fulfilled.

If the wish of one of the two be fulfilled, then the weakness of the other must be admitted. They also refuted the doctrine of this sect that Light does good, and darkness evil. For if one who was wronged fled and hid in darkness, this would be a good springing from an evil. It is needless to waste breath in debating with these people, for their system is fabulous.

Account of the way wherein he deludes the Philosophers: The Devil only succeeded including the philosophers from their relying exclusively on their theories and their reason, and adopting the conclusions of their thoughts without paying attention to the Prophets. Some of them take the view of the Materialists that the world has no Maker—as is recorded of them by Naubakhti and others. Nihawandi states that Aristotle and his school assert that the earth is a star in the middle of this sphere, and that there are worlds in all the stars similar to what is on this earth, with rivers and trees. They deny the Creator, though most of them hold that the world has a primal cause.

Further he asserted the eternity of the world, which had always existed with God, being indeed caused by Him, but consequent not later than He in time, just as the caused is consequent to the cause and the light to the sun in essence and order, not in time. It may be said to them: Why do you deny that the world may have come into existence by a pre-existent will which caused it to come into being at the time when it came? If they say: this would involve a period of time between the existence of the Creator and the creatures, we reply: Time is a creature, and there was no time before time. Then there may be said to them: God Almighty could have made the altitude of the upper sphere a cubit more or a cubit less than it is. If they say he could not, that is declaring in impotent, and if a thing cannot be greater, or smaller than it is, its being in its state is necessary not contingent, and the necessary is independent of a cause. They do indeed conceal their doctrine by the assertion that God is the Creator of the world; but this is with them a figurative expression, not a reality, for a doer wishes what he does, and according to them, the world appeared of necessity, not because God made it. One of their doctrines is that the world is to last forever, its existence having no end as it had no beginning, because they say, it is caused by eternal causation, and the caused coexists with the cause.

But the world be contingent, then it is neither from eternity nor caused. Galen said: If the sun, for example, were capable of annihilation, some decay would have appeared therein in all this long period. It may be said to him that a thing may perish suddenly of itself, without decaying. And besides how do they know that it is not decaying, when according to them it is about a hundred and seventy times the size of the earth? It were to lose the amount of a mountain, this would not appear to the sense. Besides we know that gold and the ruby are liable to corruption though they endure for years, and no diminution is perceptible. No, creation and annihilation are by the will of the Mighty One, and the Mighty One changes not in Himself, neither acquires any fresh attribute. Operation is not changed by a will which has existed from eternity.

Naubakhti in his *Book of Opinions and Religions* relates that Socrates held that the origins of things are three: an active cause, the element, and the form. God Almighty, he said, is the Agent: the element is the primal substratum of being and corruption; and the form is substance for the body. Another of them said; God is the active cause; the element is the passive: and another said: reason ordered things as they are arranged. Another said: nature did it.

Yahya b. Bishr b. 'Umair al-Nihawandi relates that certain philosopher said: Since we witness the world combining and separating, moving and quiescent, we know that it has had a beginning, and must necessarily have had a starter. Then we see how a man falls into the water not knowing how to swim, or into the fire, and calls for help to that Creator and Director, but He does not help him; whence we know that Creator has no existence. These philosophers, he says, were divided into three sects on the question of the non-existence of the Creator-director. One asserted that having completed the world, he was satisfied with it and afraid lest he might add to it world is without him, and the rulings (of fate?) Go on between his creatures animate and inanimate anyhow. The second of these sects say: No, discord appeared in the substance of the Creator and kept on attracting his power and his light until the power and the light came into that discord, which constitutes the world; the light of the Creator deteriorated, and all that remained of it was "a eat" (deriving Sinnaour (eat) from sa'anur (light deteriorated).

They hold however that he light will be attracted from the world to him, so as to be again as He was, and to weaken His creatures' portion. He has neglected them, and in consequence injustice is life. The third of these sects say: no, wherein the Creator had perfected the world. His parts were spread over it, so that all His power is in the world, that power being of the substance of divinity.

The statement of Nihawandi is in a copy in the Nizamiyyah written some two hundred years ago. Were it not that such things had been said and transmitted and that the mention of them shows what the Devil has done in the matter of deluding, it would have been better to avoid mention of them out of reverence for God Almighty: we have however explained the advantage to be got from their being recorded.

Most of the philosophers take the view that God Almighty knows Himself, but nothing else; it is admitted that the creature knows both himself and his Creator; hence the rank of the creature must be superior to the Creator's.

This in my opinion is too clearly horrible to be worthy of discussion; only look at the traps set by the Devil for these fools for all their profession of consummate intelligence. Avicenna differs from them on this point, holding that God knows Himself, and knows Universal, but not particulars. This doctrine was learned from them by the Mu'tazils, who seem to have thought knowledge of both too much. Praise be to God who had made us of those who reject from Him ignorance and deficiency, and believe in His word *Knoweth He not whom He hath created* and *He knoweth what is on land and sea, and there falleth not a leaf but He knoweth it.* And they took the view that God's knowledge and power are His substance, in order to avoid making two eternals. The reply to them is to say that He is one eternal possessing attributes.

Further the philosophers reject the resurrection of the bodies and the return of the spirits into the bodies, and the existence of material Heaven and Hell. They assert that these are figures used for the sake of the common people who reject spiritual reward and punishment. They hold that the soul endures after death eternally either in indescribable pleasure—such being perfect souls or indescribable pain—such being polluted souls. The degrees of suffering very with different people and the pain will be removed from some and cease. To them it may be said; We do not deny the existence of the soul after death, and its return is in consequence called restoration: nor that it is to have felicity or damnation; only what prevents the resurrection of the bodies?

Why should we reject bodily pleasures and pains in Paradise and Hell, when the Code affirms them? We believe in a combination of the two felicities and damnation, the spiritual and the bodily. Your treating realities as figures is arbitrary, having no evidence. If they say: Bodies are dissolved, devoured, and changed: we answer: Nothing can stand before Might. Further, man is man and, supposing a body were to be made for him from would other than that whereof he was made he would not cease to be himself, as indeed his parts change from youth to age and to emaciation and obesity. If they say: The body is not a body until it ascend from one state to another till it becomes flesh and veins: we reply that the bodies will grow in the graves before resurrection.

There is a tradition, traced to Abû Hurairah that the Prophet said: Between the two blasts there are but forty. They said: O Abû Hurairah, forty days?—He said; I decline.—Forty years?—He said: I decline. Then God will send down water-from the heaven and they will grow like vegetables. He added: There is no part of a man but will decay except one *bone*, the so sacrum; from that he was created, and thence will mankind be recomposed on the Day of Resurrection.— The Tradition is to be found in the two *Sahih*.

Now the Devil has deluded some of our co-religionists and got at them through the door of their sagacity and intelligence, showing them that it is right to follow the philosophers, owing to their being sages, from whom there have proceeded deeds and words which indicate recorded of the wisdom of Socrates, Hypocrites, Plato, Aristotle, and Galen. These persons certainly possessed attainments in mechanics, logic and natural science, and by their sagacity they discovered hidden things. Only when they talked of theology they mixed things up, and so differed on this subject, whereas they did not differ about things of the senses and mechanics. We have recorded the confusion of their tenets, and the cause of this confusion is that human abilities do not apprehend the sciences save generally, and recourse must be had therein to the Codes.

Now these people of latter days in our community were told that those sages denied the Creator and rejected the Codes, believing them to be cunningly devised expedients; the former accepted what was told them of the latter, repudiated the badge of religion, neglected prayer, handled forbidden things, despised the precepts of the Code, and threw off the bonds of Islam. The Jews and Christians are more excusable than they, because the former do hold to Codes proved by miracles. The religious innovators are also more excusable, because they profess to study the evidences. Whereas these have no support for their unbelief except their knowledge that the philosophers were sages. Do you suppose they do not know that the Prophets were sages and something more?

What has been told these philosophers about the denial of the Creator is abuser: for most people affirm the existence of the Creator, and do not reject prophecies, only have neglected to study them; a few of them are exceptional and follow the materialists, whose minds are simply corrupt. We have seen among the philosophers of our own community a number whose philosophizing has gained for them nothing but bewilderment. They act neither according to its precepts nor those of Islam. Nay, there are some of them who fast during *Ramadan,* and say their prayers, and then start objecting to the Creator and the prophecies, and in their talk reject the resurrection of the bodies. Scarcely any of them are to be seen who are not afflicted with poverty and injured thereby. Such a person spends most of his time in railing at fate and objecting to the Disposer; indeed one of them said to me: I quarrel only with Hirn who is above the sphere, he composed many verses on this theme. One of them was about this world :

Without a craftsman is it work of craft?

Without an archer possibly a shaft?

Strange this existence, with no option brought to us beforehand and no knowledge taught! This like some labyrinth from which no skill Can rescue, no, nor wisdom nor strong will. We grope in darkness which no sun makes bright. Nor moon nor fire stick gives a ray of light. Bewildered, dazed, held fast in her embrace by ignorance, with frown upon her face. What is wrought therein is doubtless work: But what is said thereon is idle talk.

Since both philosophy and monasticism were near in time to that of our law, some of our co-religionists stretched out their hands to take hold of the one and others to take hold of the other. So you will find many foolish people when they study doctrine philosophize, and when they study asceticism become eremites. We pray God to kept us steadfast in our religion and safe from four enemy. Truly, He is one who answers.

CHAPTER I

Let Him Hide Himself Without God's Veil

We have been told by Abû Bakr b. Habîb, a Tradition going back to Muhammad b. Ahmad an-Najjâr according to which the latter said: 'Alî b. Bâbawayhi was one of the Sûfis; one day, having bought a piece of meat, which he wished to carry home,[1] being ashamed before the people in the street, hung it to his neck, and carried it in that way.

I would observe: One may well be amazed at people who demand of themselves the obliteration of nature's traces, a thing which is neither possible nor the intention of the Code. Now it is implanted in man's nature not to like to be seen otherwise than decently attired, and to be ashamed of being naked or having his head uncovered, and this sentiment is not disapproved by the Code. This man's rendering himself contemptible in men's eyes was a proceeding condemned by both the Code and the reason, and a loss of self-respect rather than an act of self-discipiine, like carrying his shoes on his head. There is a saying in the Tradition: "Eating in the street is baseness.[2] " For indeed God has honoured the human being, and provided many people with servants. It is no religious act for a man to humiliate himself in public. Certain of the Sûfis took the title *Malâmatiyyah* (Culpables) and perpetrated offences, asserting that their object was to lower themselves in people's estimation, and so escape the disasters of pride and hypocrisy. They are like a man who misconducted himself with a woman, who became pregnant, and "being asked why he had not employed contraception, said he had been told that the practice was disapproved. And have you not been told, he was asked, that

---

[1] The sense seems to require "to have it carried home by a slave".

[2] Quoted in *Majma' az-Zawâ'id*, Cairo. 1353, V. 24 from *Tabarâni*.

fornication is forbidden?—These ignoramuses have forfeited their dignity with God, and forgotten that the Muslims are God's witnesses on earth.

We have been told by Ibn Habîb a Tradition going back to Abû 'Abd Allâh b. Khafîf, according to which the latter said: I heard Abû'l-Hasan al-Madanî say: One day I went out of Baghdâd to the Yâsiriyyah canal, at one of the villages on which there was a man who was favourably inclined to our associates. Walking on the bank of the canal I observed a patched cloak lying on the ground with a sandal and a small piece of clothing. I collected these, saying to myself that they must belong to a dervish. Walking on a little I heard a murmuring and a splashing in the water, I looked, and there was Abû'l-Hasan an-Nûri who had thrown himself into the muddy water, was plunging about, and doing himself any amount of mischief. Seeing him, I felt sure that the clothes were his, and went down to him. Looking at me he said: Abû'l-Hasan, do you not see what is being done to me? Several deaths have befallen me.—He added: All you know about me is the rumour which everyone else has heard.—He then began to sob, saying: You see what is being done to me.—I endeavoured to soothe him, washed the mud off him, clothed him in his patched cloak, and carried him to the house of the man whom I mentioned. There we stayed till the afternoon, then went off to the mosque, and when the time for the first evening prayer arrived I saw people running, locking their doors, and mounting on the roof. We asked what the matter was, and they said that lions come into the village at night. Now round the village there was a vast thicket, where the reeds had been cut, the stumps of which were left standing like knives. When an-Nûrî heard this talked about, he rose up, dashed into the thicket among the stumps of the reeds which had been cut away, and called aloud: Lion, where are you?—We felt sure that either he had been torn to pieces by a lion, or impaled himself on the stumps of the reeds. Shortly before morning he came back, and threw himself on the ground, with his feet in a terrible condition. We extracted as many of the splinters as we could with pincers, but for forty days he was unable to use his feet. I asked him what the meaning of his conduct had been. He replied: When they mentioned the lion, I felt terror in my soul; so I said to my soul "I will hurl you into that of which you are afraid".

I would observe that no sensible person could fail to see that this man "floundered" before he fell into the water and the mud. What right has any man to throw himself into water and mud, and is this the act of any but a madman? Where too is reverence or respect to be found in his complaint: You see what is being done to me? How is such plainness of speech to be justified, when reverence should keep the tongue dry in the mouth. Further, what was he seeking but fame? Moreover he was transgressing the Code by going to face the lion and walking on the stumps of reeds. Has any man a legal right to throw himself to a lion? Are you to suppose that he wanted to change the nature of his soul wherein fear of wild beasts is implanted? This was not in his soul's power neither did the Code demand it therefrom. One of an-Nûri's associates heard him talk in this style, and gave him an excellent reply. We have been told by Muhammad b. 'Abdallâh b. Habîb a Tradition going back to Abû Ahmad al-Maghâzili[3] according to which the latter said: I saw an-Nûri with his head downwards and his feet upwards, saying: Thou hast alienated me from mankind, and deprived me of self, of wealth, and worldly things. With Thee there is nought save knowledge and fame.—I said to him: If you are satisfied, well and good. If not, knock your head against the wall!

We have been told by Muhammad b. Abî'l-Qâsim a Tradition going back to Abd Allâh b. 'Alî as-Sarrâj [4] according to which he said: I heard Ibn 'Alwân says: Three hundred *dinârs* were brought to Abû'l-Husain an-Nûri, the price of a dwelling house which he had sold. He then sat on a bridge and began to toss the coins one by one into the water, saying: Lord.[5] Thou wouldst fain seduce me from Thee by this sort of thing!—As-Sarrâj proceeds:'[6] Some of the people said: He would have done better to spend the money in God's path.— I (said Ibn 'Alwân) replied: If those *dinârs* distracted him from God

---

[3] Three persons with this *nisbah* are cited in the *Luma,'* two with different *kunyahs*, and the third, Ishāq without one. The text here has al-Mughāzi. which is unlikely to be correct. Probably the person named here is the Abû Ahmad al-Maghâzili noticed in *Kitāb Bughdàd* XIV, 421.

[4] The story is from the *Luma,* p. 193. end.

[5] The text of the *Luma,* is here substituted for ours, which has "Thou (feminine) hast come" etc.

[6] This with what follows is not in the *Luma'*.

for one instant, he should have tossed the whole lot into the water at once, so as to escape their seduction all the more rapidly, as God says (xxxviii, 32), *He started striking them on the legs and necks*.[7]

I would observe that these people merely reveal their ignorance of the Code and their want of intelligence. We have previously demonstrated that the Code enjoins the conservation of property and that it should only be committed to persons of discretion. The Code regards it as man's sustenance, and reason attests that it was created only for their benefit. If a man throws it away, he destroys what was meant for his welfare, and ignores the wisdom of its maker. The excuse alleged by as-Sarrâj 'is worse than an-Nûri's act; for if the man was afraid of being seduced by the money, he should have secured himself by tossing it to some indigent man. It is further a specimen of these people's ignorance how they misinterpret the Qur'ân according to their perverse ideas. He alleges the "striking of the legs and necks," thinking that this gives permission for the destruction of property; but the Code gives no such permission, for Solomon only *stroked* (not struck) the legs and necks, saying, "You are devoted to God's service." This has been explained above.

Abû Nasr as-Sarrâj records in his *Luma*[8] that Abû Ja'far ad-Darrâj said: One day when my master went out to purify himself, I took and examined his wallet, and found therein silver amounting to four *dirhams*. Now at times we ate nothing.[9] So when he came back I said to him: There are so many *dirhams* in your wallet, and we are starving.—What, he asked, have you taken it? Give it back.—Presently, he told me to take it and buy something with it.—I said to him: I adjure you by Him Whom you worship, tell me the story of these pieces.—He replied: They are all that God has bestowed upon me, in the way of worldly goods, and I wanted to order in my will that they should be buried with me, so that on Resurrection-day I could return them to God, saying: Here are the worldly possessions which Thou didst bestow upon me.

---

[7] The reference is to Solomon's treatment of some horses which he admired.

[8] Page 194. line 5 from the end.

[9] The text has been corrected from the *Luma'*.

We have been told by Ibn Habîb a Tradition going back to Abû 'Abd Allâh' al-Husri according to which he said: Abû Ja'far al-Haddâd (the Smith) went on twenty years working for a *dinār* a day, which he would spend on the poor, while fasting himself; in the twilight he would go and beg for some breakfast at the doors.[10] I would observe that if this man had known that begging is unlawful for one; who is able to earn, he would not have acted in the way described. And even if we were to assume it to be lawful, where does self-respect come into the humiliation of mendicity?

We have been told by Hibat Allâh b. Muhammad a Tradition going back through Ahmad b. Hanbal to 'Abd Allâh b. 'Umar, according to which the last said: The Prophet said: Mendicity will not leave one of you alone till he meets God without a morsel of flesh on his face.[11]

Ahmad also produced another Tradition going back to az-Zûbair b. al-'Awwâm, according to which the Prophet said: It would be better for a man to take a cord and gather fire-wood, bring it to the market, sell it and so render himself independent, expending the proceeds on himself, than to beg of people whether they give or refuse.

I would observe that Bukhâri only has this last Tradition, whereas the two agree in regard to the former one.[12]

Further, in the Tradition of the Prophet recorded by 'Abd Allâh b. 'Amr the Prophet is reported to have said: The alms may not be given to a wealthy person or one in sound condition possessing *mirrah,* — a word meaning strength, being derived from coiling the strands of a rope, and referring in this Tradition to strong build and bodily health enabling a man to endure toil and fatigue.[13] Ash-Shâfi'i says: The alms may not be given to one who has sufficient strength

---

[10] Another story of this person's fasting is told in *Luma.'* p. 332.

[11] The form in which Ahmad b. Hanhal reports this Tradition in the *Musnad* I. 338, etc. is somewhat different.

[12] *Bukhâri,* ed. Krehl, II, 10; has this, but it is repeatedly cited in the *Musnad.*

[13] Tradition quoted from Tirmidhî, Abû Dàwûd, and Ibn .Hanbal (Ibn Taymiyyah, *al-Muntaqa* II,144.)

to enable him to earn.

We have been told by 'Abd ar-Rahmân b. Muhammad al-Qazzâz a Tradition going back to Yunus, son of Abû Bakr ash-Shiblî, according to which he said[14]: One night my father rose and placed one foot on the roof and the other on the rick, and I heard him say: If you close your eyes I will throw you down into the court.—He remained in this posture till morning, when he said to me: My son, I have heard no-one mentioning God this night, save a cock worth two *dânaq*.

I would observe that this person combined two illegalities: one, endangering his life, since, had he fallen asleep and fallen, he would have been assisting his own ruin; undoubtedly had he thrown himself down he would have perpetrated a serious offence, and his exposing himself to the risk of falling was an offence. A second, his depriving his eyes of their share of sleep; for the Prophet said: Thy body has a claim on thee, and so has thy wife, and so has thine eye.—He said besides: If anyone of you feels sleepy, let him sleep.'[15]—Passing by a cord which had been stretched by Zainâb, to take hold of when she felt weak, he ordered it to be slackened. He also said: Let one of you pray strenuously, but if he feels lazy or slackens, let him sit down.[16]—These traditions have been cited above.

We have been told by Muhammad b. Nãsir a Tradition going back to Abû'l 'Abbâs al-Baghdàdî[17] according to which the latter said: In our youth we associated with Abû'l-Hasan son of Abû Bakr ash-Shibli; one night he offered to entertain us, but we stipulated that he should not bring his father into the company. He promised that he would not. We went into his house, and after the repast in comes ash-Shiblî, with a candle between each two of his fingers, eight in all. He sat down in our midst and we were in awe of him. He said: Gentlemen, regard me as your candelabrum— He then asked where his attendant Abû'l-'Abbâs was. When I came forward he

---

[14] The story is from *Kitâb Baghdâd* XIV, 354, whence the text has been corrected.

[15] Bûkhari, ed. Krehl, I, 65. where "while praying" is added.

[16] Muslim 1, 217. where the story of Zainab is told.

[17] In *Kitāb Baghdād* XIV, 419, there is an account of a person so named, associate of Bishr al-Hâfi who died 227.Shibli's life lasted 247-334. The narrator of the story in the text can scarcely be the same.

said to me: Sing the song which you used to sing:

My camel's driver when he reached al-Hîrah knew not what
to say: I bade him loose my saddle there, nor mind if others
went their way.

I sang it; he changed colour and left the room.

We have been told by Ibn Nâsir a Tradition going back to al-
Husain b. Ahmad b. 'Abd ar-Rahmân as-Saffâr, according to which
the latter said: One feast-day ash-Shibli came out having shaven
his eyelashes and eyebrows, with a ribbon round his head, reciting
the verse:

Others breakfast and make merry

I alone am solitary.

We have been told by 'Abd al-Rahmân b. Muhammad a Tradition
going back to Abû'l-Hasan 'Alî b. Muhammad b. Abî Sàbir ad-Dallâl,
according to which the latter said:[18] I stationed myself near ash-
Shiblî in the Poets' Dome in the Mosque of al-Mansûr, where the
people were gathered round him; the circle was joined by a
handsome lad, named Ibn Muslim, whose beauty was unsurpassed
in Baghdâd at the time. Ash-Shibli said to him: Go away,—but he
would not move. Again ash-Shiblî said to him: Go away from us,
you demon!—But the lad would not move. Then ash-Shiblî, said to
him for the third time: Go away, else I will tear to pieces all that you
have on you.—-Now the lad had on him exquisite garments worth a
great sum. The lad then moved away, and ash-Shiblî recited:

On Aden's, two peaks to the hawks

They threw meat, then the hawks they did chide.

But why, is the question I ask,

Were the leashes that held them untied?

If people had thought of our good,

Thy beautiful face they wouldhide.

Ibn 'Uqail observes that the man who says this has missed the
path of the Code, for what he means is that God created this person

---

[18] The story comes from *Kitāb Baghdàd*, XIII. 95.

merely to lead us into temptation. But that is not so, the purpose of such a creation is to make us reflect and examine just as the sun was created to give night, not to be worshipped.

There is a Tradition going back to Ahmad b. Muhammad al-Nahawandi, according to which he said: When a grandson of ash-Shibli died, his mother shore her head for him. Ash-Shiblî had a long beard, and ordered it to be shaven off. Being asked his reason for this, he replied: She has shorn her hair for one who is lost; why should not I shave off my beard for one who is found?

There is also a Tradition going back to 'Abd Allâh b. 'Alî as-Sarrâj according to which he said:[19] At times ash-Shibli used to wear costly raiment then doff it and put it over the fire. It is recorded, too, that he once took a piece of ambergris and fumigated an ass's tail therewith. Further some one stated that he had visited ash-Shibli and seen him with almonds and sugar in front of him which he was burning in the fire. As-Sarrâj asserts that he only burned them because they were distracting him from the remembrance of God. (On which I would observe that as-Sarrâj's excuse, is more extraordinary than the act). He goes on to say that ash-Shibli sold a dwelling house and then distributed the proceeds, giving nothing to his own family. Also[20] that, hearing a Qur'ân-reader recite *be silent therein and address me not* (xxiii. 110), he said: Would that I were one of them![21]

I would observe that the man thought that the speaker addressing them was God; but God will not address them;[22] moreover if He were to address them contemptuously, why should anyone desire it? As-Sarrâj proceeds to record that one day ash-Shiblî said in a discourse: God has servants who could extinguish Hell-fire by spitting on it.

This, I would observe, is similar to what we have related of Abû Yâzid, the two are of a piece.

There is also a Tradition going back to Abû 'Alî ad-Daqqâq

---

[19] From the *Luma'*, p. 400.
[20] *Luma'*, p. 406.
[21] i.e., the damned.
[22] Sûrah iii, 71.

according to which he said: I have been informed that ash-Shiblî used to rub his eyes with a certain quantity of salt to practice keeping vigil and not falling asleep.—This, I would observe, is an evil practice; no Muslim has a right to inflict pain on himself, and blindness would be the result. Neither is constant sleeplessness permissible, since it is depriving the soul of a right. It is clear that constant sleeplessness and insufficient food were what induced these states and actions.

There is a Tradition going back to Abû 'Abd Allâh ar-Râzî according to which he said: I had been given a woollen garment by some one, and seeing a cowl on ash-Shibli's head which would suit the woollen garment, I felt a desire to possess it. When ash-Shibli rose to leave his lecture-room he turned towards me—as it was his custom to do when he wanted me to follow him—and I followed him. When he entered his house he bade me doff the woollen garment, which I did; he proceeded to fold it, then flung the cowl upon it, called for fire and burned the two.

I would observe that Abû Hâmid al-Ghazâli[23] narrates how ash-Shibli took fifty *dinârs* and flung them into the Tigris, saying: No one has ever honoured you but has been humiliated by God.[24]

Abû Hâmid astonishes me more than ash-Shibli, by recording this by way of eulogy instead of disapproval; where is there any sign here of jurisprudence?

There is a Tradition going back to Husain b. 'Abd Allâh 'al-Qazwîni according to which he said: I was told by a man who frequented the company of Bunân[25] that the latter said: One day I had no means of subsistence, and was in great straits. Seeing a piece of gold lying in the road I wanted to take it, but then, saying to myself that it was "a find"[26], I left it; presently, recollecting the Tradition, "If all the world were blood freshly shed, the Muslim could

---

[23] The reference would seem to be to III, 49, 2 from end, where however, Shibli is not mentioned.

[24] In *Ihya* III, 175, 'last line, this is quoted as a saying of al-Hasan.

[25] Abû'l-Hasan b. Muhammad b.Hamdân, died, 316; account of him in *Kitâb Baghdâd* VII, 100-2.

[26] A find of lost property should be advertised for a year before possession can be taken.

lawfully take sustenance therefrom," I picked it up, put it into my mouth, and walking on a short distance, found myself in a group of lads, whom one of them was addressing. He was asked by one of them: When does a man feel the reality of veracity?—He replied: When he throws the morsel from his lips.—Then I took the piece of gold out of my mouth and threw it away.

I would observe that the jurists are all agreed that his throwing it away was unlawful, and it is amazing that he should have done so owing to something said by a lad who did not know what he was saying. Abû Hâmid al-Ghazâli[27] narrates how Shaqîq al-Balkhi[28] came to the ascetic Abû'l-Qâsim, with something packed into a corn of his garment. Being asked what it was, he replied: Some nuts given me by a brother who said he wanted me to breakfast with them. Abû'l-Qâsim said to him: What, Shaqîq, do you imagine that you will last till tonight? I will never again speak to you.—He went inside and locked the door in the man's face.

I would observe: Consider this legal subtlety—-shunning a Muslim for an action that was not only lawful, but commendable, since a man is commanded to prepare for himself food with which to break his fast, and preparation in advance is prudence. Hence God says *Make ready for them all ye can of force* (viii, 62). The Prophet stored up a year's provisions for his women-folk. 'Umar brought half his wealth and hoarded the remainder-without incurring disapproval. Sheer ignorance is what has perverted these ascetics.

There is a Tradition going back to Ahmad b. Ishâq al-'Umânî according to which he said: I saw in India a shaikh known as "the Patient, aged a hundred years, one of whose eyes was closed. I said to him: Patient one, to what lengths has your patience gone? He replied: I desired to look on the lustre of the world, but was unwilling to take my fill thereof, so have kept one eye closed for eighty years, never opening it. Of another we have been told that he tarred one of his eyes, saying that to look on the world with two

---

[27] *Ihyä* IV. 356. line. 22 The name of the ascetic there is Abû Hâshim ar-Rummâni, whose name according to Sam'âni, p. 258 b was Yahyâ b. Dînâr.

[28] Died 135. Notice of him in *Shajarät al-Dhahab* i. 341 and at length in *Tadhkirät al-Auliyä* I. 196 -202.

eyes was excess.—I would observe: Apparently his purpose was to look on the world with a single eye! We pray God for sound minds.

Yusuf b. Ayyub al-Hamadhâni[29] narrated how his teacher 'Abdallâh al-Jawni used to say: I have procured this empire not out of the sanctuary, but out of the privy. I used to look after it as servant, and one day when I was sweeping and cleaning it, my soul said to me: Is it in this that you are spending your life?—Do you, I replied, disdain the service of God's servants?—So I enlarged the top of the pit, jumped into it, and began putting the filth into my mouth. Then people came, drew me out, and washed me.

I would observe: Notice how the poor wretch regarded his followers crowding round him as "empire," and believed that he had procured this "empire" by jumping into filth and putting it into his mouth! Thereby, he supposed, he had acquired virtue for which he was rewarded by a crowd of followers. Yet his action was a transgression meriting punishment. In general we may say that these people through lack of knowledge flounder about.

There is a Tradition going back to Muhammad b. 'Ali al-Kattâni[30] according to which he said: Al-Husain b. Mansûr[31] came to Makkah at the beginning of his career, and we strove hard to get hold of his cloak. As-Sûsî[32] says: we got out of a louse which weighed half a *dânaq,* so strenuous had he been in his asceticism... On this I would observe: Notice how ignorant this man was about that cleanliness which the Code recommends. It permits the pilgrim, who is forbidden to shave his head, to do so when troubled with lice, and make up for the breach of the rule by an expiatory act.[33] Still more ignorant was the man who regarded this as ascetic discipline.

There is a Tradition going back to Abû 'Aba Allâh b. Muflih, according to which he said: There was with us in the mosque a

---

[29] Ascetic and preacher, 440-535. Accounts of his in Ibn Khallikān IV. 412, and *Shajarāt adh-Dhahab* IV, 110-11.

[30] *Died* 322. Notice of him in *Kitāb Baghdād* III, 74-76.

[31] Generally known as al-Hallāj.

[32] Yûsuf b. Hamdân; there is a notice of him in *Nafahāt al-Uns,* p. 144, without date.

[33] Such as fasting or almsgiving; Bukhāri, ed. Krehl, I, 453.

poor Sûfi, who at one time was starving, and said, Lord, either give me food, or let a pinnacle of the place of worship fall upon me. Thereupon, there came a raven, which posted itself on the pinnacles, and a tile from under its foot fell upon the man, who began to bleed and wipe away the blood, saying: What carest Thou if the world is done to death? — In my opinion God caused this man's death and did not preserve him alive in recompense for this audacity.[34] Why could he not set about earning or begging?

Among the Sûfis there are people called *Malâmatiyyah* (Culpables), who perpetrate crimes, asserting that their purpose is to abase themselves in people's eyes, and so be immune from pride. They have indeed abased their pride in the eyes of the Deity by disobeying the Code. He[35]adds that some of them make a display of conduct which is worse than the reality, and conceal their best Paralogims:[36]. Now this is most reprehensible for the Prophet whose commits any of these abominations, Let him hide himself with God's veil[37] and concerning Ma'iz he said; My friend, why didst thou not conceal it with thy garment?[38]—One of the Companions of the Prophet passed by him when he was talking to Sâfiyyah his wife, and the Prophet said to him. "It is Sâfiyyah"; and indeed people know how much any act which excites suspicion is disliked, since the Believers are God's witnesses on earth. Hâdhayfah on his way to the Friday prayer saw people coming back from it, and concealed himself for fear people might think ill of him. These cases have already been adduced. Abû Bakr al-Siddiq said to a man who told him he had caressed and kissed a woman "Repent unto God and tell no-one about it," A man came to the Prophet and said that he had relations with a strange woman which fell short of fornication. The Prophet said: Did you not pray with us?—The man replied: Yea, O Apostle of God.—The Prophet said: Did you not know that two (successive) prayers atone for anything done between them?[39]

---

[34] The text has been corrected.

[35] Abû Hamid al-Ghazalî, from whose Ihyã (III, 217, line 8) the previous sentence is taken.

[36] An example given by Ghazâli is that of a man who drinks a lawful beverage in a vessel which makes it look like wine.

[37] Qastalànî on Bukhàri IX, 50, quotes this from al-Hakim; it does not appear to be in the Six Books.

[38] Mu'izz b. Malîk was stoned by the Prophet's order for immorality; only after he had insisted that he had committed the offence.

[39] This doctrine is stated at length in a Tradition quoted in *Majma' az-Zawà'id* I, 297.

A man said to one of the Companions: Verily I have committed such and such sins.—The Companion said: Verily God has concealed them for you, if only you would conceal them yourself.— Yet these Sûfis disobey the Code and wish to eradicate what is innate in the soul.

Further, some antinomians have insinuated themselves into the Sûfi community, and aped them, in order to preserve their lives; and of these there are three classes.

Class I are unbelievers, some of whom do not acknowledge God, whereas others acknowledge Him, only reject prophethood, holding that the Prophets' utterances are absurd. Wishing, however, to indulge their passions they saw no means of saving their lives, shielding themselves, and compassing their lusts, comparable with he Sûfic system; hence they enter it ostensibly, whereas secretly they are unbelievers; for these miscreants there is nothing but the sword.

Class II are believers in Islam, and of two subdivisions; one consisting of persons who imitate their shaikhs in their conduct, without following up any evidence or any paralogism; they simply do what their shaikhs tell them and what they see them doing. (*The account of the second subdivision is missing.*)

Class III are persons to whom paralogisms'[40] have occurred, and who act in accordance with their implications. The source whence these paralogisms arose is that, busying themselves with the study of religious systems they were deluded by the devil into supposing that paralogisms can oppose (sound) arguments, that it said: is hard to distinguish between them, that the object of the inquiry is to sublime to be attained by knowledge and that its acquisition is a born bestowed on a human being, not procured by study. Thus the devil closed against them the door of salvation, which is the search after knowledge, and they came to detest the name of knowledge as much as a *Râfidî* detests that of Abû Bakr or "Umar. Knowledge, they say, is a screen, and those who possess it are thereby screened from the real object. If a learned man objects

---

[40] This word suits the author's argument somewhat better than "false reasoning" of which it is the equivalent.

to this, they tell their adherents that the man secretly agrees with them, and only makes show of the contrary to their doctrine before the weak-minded populace; if he persists in contradicting them, they assert that he is stupid, fettered by the bonds of the Code, screened from the real object. They proceed then to act according to the paralogisms which have entered their minds, yet, had they understood, they would have known that their acting according to the paralogisms is a case of knowledge.[41] Hence their disapproval of knowledge is futile, and I will now record and expose their paralogisms, God willing.

These are six in number,

1. They assert that if things are predestined, and some persons destined to bliss and others to damnation, so that the former will not be damned, nor the latter saved; further if actions are required not for their own sake, but for the acquisition of bliss and the avoidance of damnation, and the actions have anticipated us in existence: why should we trouble ourselves about action? Let us not restrain ourselves from what gives pleasure, seeing that which is written in destiny will certainly come about.

The reply to this paralogism is to tell them that this is a repudiation of all the Codes, an abrogation of all the enactments of the (sacred) books, and a confutation of the messages of all the Prophets. For when the Speaker in the Qur'ân says "Maintain prayer," someone will ask, Why? If I am destined to bliss, to bliss I shall go, and if I am destined to damnation, to damnation I shall go; what will the maintenance of prayer profit me? Similarly when the Speaker says: Neither have ought to do with fornication, some one will say: Why should I deny myself a pleasure when bliss and damnation are predestined and settled? So Pharaoh might have talked to Moses when the latter said to him (lxxix, 18) *Hast thou a mind to purify thy-self?* Next, such a reasoner will mount to the Creator and ask: What is the use of Thy sending messengers, when that which Thou hast predestined is to be-fall?—Now any process which leads to the repudiation of the Books and the stultification of

---

[41] The meaning must be that any course of action which is not instinctive, but based on reasoning. assumes the possession of knowledge; but the expression is not felicitous.

the Prophets is sheer absurdity. And this was refuted by the Prophet when his Companions asked, Shall we not rely?, and he answered,[42] Work for each man is helped to that for which he was created.— You should know that man has the power of "earning," *i.e.*, choosing, and on this choice falls reward or punishment. When a man disobeys, it is clear that God has predestined such disobedience, but punished the man for the disobedience, not for his destiny. For this reason a murderer is executed, and destiny is not accepted as an excuse.

The Prophet turned their attention from consideration of destiny to work, only because commands and prohibitions are plain and manifest, whereas what is predestined therein is hidden; and it is not for us to neglect the ordinances which we know on account of something foreordained of which we are ignorant. The Prophet's words, "each man is helped to that for which he was created" are a reference to the predestined causation; when it is foreordained that a man shall know, the search after, the love of, and the understanding of knowledge are made easy for him; when it is ordained that he shall be ignorant, the love of knowledge is withdrawn from his heart. Similarly if a man is destined to have children, marriage is made easy for him; but not if he is destined to be childless.

Paralogism 2. Their assertion that God is independent of our actions unaffected by them whether they be acts of obedience or disobedience so that we ought not to trouble ourselves uselessly.

We reply to this in the first place by the previous answer, *viz.*, that this is repudiation of the enactments or the Code; it is like saying to the apostle and His sender "There is no use in what you command us." Next in reply to the paralogism we shall say: Whosoever imagines that God Almighty profits by an act of obedience or suffers from one of disobedience, or attains any object thereby, has no knowledge of God, who is far removed from accidents and objects, from profit and loss. The profit of the actions redounds on ourselves as the Deity says (xxiii, 6) *Whoso striveth striveth only for himself* and xxxv, 19) *Whoso purifieth himself purifieth himself only for himself.* The physician prescribes a diet for the patient for the patient's benefit not for his own: and just as the body has benefits and injuries

---

[42] The Tradition occurs in several forms; the citation here comes near the form in which Ahmad b. Hanbal (I. 29) records it.

from foods, so the soul has things that profit it and things that hurt it, such as knowledge, ignorance, belief, action. The Code is like the physician, who knows best about the remedies which he prescribes.[43] This is the doctrine of those who assign purpose to God's acts; most of the learned, however, hold that they are without purpose. Another reply is that if God is independent of our actions. He is independent of our knowledge of Him; but He has enjoined us knowledge of Him, and likewise obedience to Him. We must look then to His command, nor to the purpose of His command.

Paralogism 3. Their assertion that the vastness of God's mercy is ascertained that it is not inadequate for us, whence there is no reason why we should deny ourselves what we desire.

The answer to this is similar to the first answer: for this assertion involves repudiation of the threats conveyed by the divine messengers, and belittlement of what they so earnestly warn against, and the punishment for which they so powerfully describe. The delusion here can be cleared away by the reflexion that just as the Deity describes Himself as merciful, so too he describes Himself as severe in punishment. Further, we find saints and Prophets tried with disease and hunger and punished for lapses; nay more, He is feared by those whose salvation is assured. The Friend (Abraham) on the Day of Resurrection will say Myself myself,[44] and the Interlocutor (Moses) will say myself. Our own 'Umar said: Woe to 'Umar if he be not forgiven!

You should know that one who hopes for mercy must apply himself to the means whereby it is to be obtained, among which is repentance of lapses, just as one who hopes to reap must sow. God says (ii, 215) *Verily those that have believed and those that have migrated and striven in the path of God they hope for God's mercy,* meaning that hope is fitting for these whereas the hope of those who persist in sin and hope for mercy is unlikely to be realised.

---

[43] A selection comprising pp. 391-97 of the Arabic original.

[44] *i.e.,* I myself require an intercessor, so cannot intercede for chapters. This comes from a Tradition quoted in the *Ihyā* IV, 412, according to the commentator (x. 489) from second-rate authorities. A part of it is cited in *Majma' az-Zawā'id* X. 342.

The Prophet said:[45] Sagacious is he who examines himself and works for what shall be after death; and incompetent is he who lets his soul pursue its lusts and wishes for many things from God.— Ma'rûf al-Karkhî said: Thy hoping for mercy from One whom thou dost not obey is calamity and folly.

You should know that there is nothing in the acts which proceed from the Deity that authorizes one to feel safe from His punishment; what they contain only prevents despair of His mercy. And just as despair is improper owing to the kindness which He displays in His creation, so presumption is improper owing to the evidence which it furnishes of His resenting and avenging. For since He amputates the most precious member of the body for the theft of a quarter of a dinâr, there is no guarantee that His punishment hereafter will not be on a similar scale.

Paralogism 4. It has occurred to some of them that the object is discipline of the soul whereby it may be freed from ruinous stains; having disciplined them for a time, and finding purification impossible, they say: Why should we trouble ourselves over a thing which is unattainable by humanity? and so they abandon the effort. This delusion is dispelled by the reflexion that they suppose the object of the Code to be the suppression of certain internal attributes of humanity, *e.g.* lust, anger, etc., whereas this is not the object of the Code, neither is the eradication of the natural propensities conceivable. No, the propensities were created for some utility; were it not for the desire for food, the human being would perish; were it not for the desire for marriage, the race would come to an end; were it not for anger no man would repel annoyance. Likewise love of property has been implanted in the nature, because its possession enables these desires to be gratified. What is meant by discipline is restraint of the soul from what is harmful in all this, and reducing it to moderation. God praises (xxix, 40) *him who restrains the soul from passion;* now it can only be restrained from something which it seeks: if the seeking had been eradicated from its nature the man would not need to restrain it. And God says (iii, 128) *and the suppressors of wrath,* not "those who lack wrath". The word here

---

[45] Tradition cited in the *Ihyâ* IV, 309. line 14, according to the commentator from Tirmidhî. Ibn Majah, and Ibn Hanbal.

used for "to suppress" means properly "to send back,"used of an animal sending up the cud into its throat. The Deity here praises him who restrains his soul from acting in accordance with an outburst of anger. One who claims that discipline is alteration of the nature makes an absurd pretension. The aim of discipline is to refrain the vehemence of the soul's lust or wrath, not to eradicate them: the disciplined man is like the prudent dietist,[46] who when food is presented takes what is good for him and abstains from what will harm him. The undisciplined is like a stupid boy who eats what he likes, not troubling about the consequences.

Paralogism 5. Some of these people after maintaining their discipline for a time suppose themselves to be stabilized, and say: Now we need not trouble what we do; commands and prohibitions are formalities for the vulgar herd, from which they would be exempted if they were stabilised. The purport of prophethood is reducible to wisdom and welfare, its object being to keep the vulgar herd in order; we are not of the vulgar herd, so as to be within the confines of the ordinances, for we are stabilised and know wisdom. In these people's view a result of their stabilisation is that they are devoid of jealousy, so that according to them the stage of perfection is only attained by one who feels no horror when he sees his wife with a stranger; if he feels horror he is attending to his personal share, and is not yet perfect: had he been perfect, his lower self would be dead; "lower self" is the term whereby they designate jealousy, "perfection of faith" that whereby they designate that imperturbability which is the character of the impotent, Ibn Jarir in his *History* [47] records how the Rawandis used to practice licence, one of them inviting a number to his house, giving them food and drink, and letting them cohabit with his wife.

This paralogism is dispelled by the observation that so long as there are individual beings in existence it is not possible to discard the manifest forms of obedience to the divine will, since these were established in the interest of mankind. The purity of the heart may at times overcome the foulness of nature, only such foulness sinking

---

[46] The text has "physician," which cannot well be the author's meaning.

[47] Tabari III, 418.

to the bottom keeps quiet so long as there is persistence in goodness, but the slightest thing will stir it, like a clod which falls into water with a bed of clay. This nature can only be compared to water which bears the ship of the soul along, with the reason acting as a tow-rope; though the tow-rope had been pulling for a whole league, if it be let go, the ship will begin to descend again. One who claims that his nature alters lies; and one who asserts that he can look at the beautiful without passion being aroused does not speak the truth. Indeed, if these people miss a morsel or are maligned by someone, they display vexation; where then is the effect of the reason when they are led away by passion? We have seen some of them giving women the handshake, whereas the Prophet, who was immune from sin, would nor give one of them the handshake. We have been told that a number of them fraternise with women and sit privately with them, but claim safety, *i.e.*, hold that they are safe from wrongdoing—which is far from being the case. Where is the "safety" from the guilt of forbidden privacy, and prohibited gazing, or security against the onset of evil thoughts? 'Umar b. al-Khattâb said: If two decaying bones were to meet in private, one of them would have a desire for the other—referring to an old man and an old woman.

There is a Tradition going back to Ibn Shâhin[48] according to which he said: There are Sûfis who allow promiscuity under the profession of fraternity, one of them saying to a woman: Fraternise with me on condition of waiving all opposition between us.—I would observe that we have been told by the physician Abû 'Abd Allâh Muhammad b. 'Alî al-Tirmidhî in his book *Discipline of the Soul,* [49] that he had been told how Sahl b. 'Alî al-Marwazî used to say to his brother's wife, who lived in the same house. Hide yourself from me for a time; presently he would tell her to be as before. Tirmidhi states that the former injunction was when he felt concupiscent.—I would observe that the disappearance of the instinct is inconceivable so long as the man lives; it only weakens. Men who are physically

---

[48] Umar b. Ahmad b. Uthmān, died 385. Account of him in *Kitāb Baghdâd* XI, 265-68.

[49] Mentioned by Hājji Khalîfah, who gives the author's death date 255. He is in Qushayri's list of Sûfis, (I, 16).

incapable still desire to touch and to gaze. But let it be supposed that all this has been eradicated, does not the Code forbid gazing, and indeed without exception? And the power to do that remains. We have been told by Ibn Nâsir a Tradition going back to Abû 'Abd al-Rahman as-Sulamî, according to which the latter said: Abû Nasr[50] al-Nasrābādî, being told how some people sat with women, declaring themselves safe from temptation when they looked at them, said: So long as persons remain in existence, commands and prohibitions remain, and the laws of licit and illicit are binding on those to whom they are addressed; and only those venture on what is doubtful who expose themselves to the commission of what is illicit. Abû 'Alî ar-Rudhbâri,[51] being asked about some one who said he had arrived at a stage wherein he was unaffected by the change of states, said: He has indeed arrived, only at the infernal region.—Al-Jurayri[52] is recorded to have said: I heard Abû'l-Qâsim al-Junaid say to a man who, speaking of cognition, said: The cognisant of God arrive at the abandonment of motions which belong to the cateyory of charitable works and modes of approaching the Deity. This is the language of people who talk of the discarding of actions,[53] which is to my mind atrocious. The thief and the adulterer are in a better case than those who talk thus. Those who are cognisant of God take the actions from Him, and render them to Him. Were I to last a thousand years I would not reduce my acts of charity by an atom, unless prevented, for it confirms my cognisance of Him, and strengthens my state.

There is also a Tradition that Abû Muhammad al-Murta'ish said: I heard Abû'l Hasan an-Nûri say:[54] If you see a man claiming to have with God a dignity which removes him from the limits set by knowledge of the Code, do not come near him; and if you see a man claiming a hidden character which is not indicated nor attested by something manifestly recorded, suspect his orthodoxy.

---

[50] The author should have said Abûl-Qâsim, kunyah of Ibrāhim b. Muhammad al-Nasrābādī, died 367, of whom this story is told in the *Risālah Qushayriyyah* II, 144-

[51] Ahmad b. Muhammad, died 322 or 323. This story comes from the *Risâlah Qushayriyyah*, 190.

[52] Abû Muhammad Ahmad, died 321. Notice of him in the same work. I. 172. The story here comes from I. 142.

[53] *i.e.,* being no longer bound by the legal liability to perform them.

[54] This comes from the *Risālah Qushayriyyah* I, 150.

Paralogism 6. Certain of them have gone to such lengths in discipline that they have seen something resembling a kind of miracle, or veridical dreams, or have come into possession of fine phrases the fruit of reflexion and isolation, and, believing themselves to have arrived at the goal, discard actions none the less adorning their exterior with the patched cloak, the prayer-carpet, the dance, and emotion, and employing the phraseology of Sûfism about cognisance, emotion, desire: the reply to them is the same as that given to the last.

Ibn 'Uqâyl says: people have strayed away from God and abandoned the enactments of the Code for their own inventions. Some of them worship some one other than God, thinking Him too great to be worshipped; such other beings they suppose to be intermediaries.[55] Some are monotheists, only discard acts of devotion, asserting that they were only appointed for the vulgar herd, through their want of cognisances. This, however, is a form of polytheism: for God, knowing that cognisance of Himself is profound and sublime, and those who were not cognisant were unlikely to take heed, bade them fear the Fire, because people know how it stings whereas to the cognisant He says (iii. 27). *Now God bids you beware of Himself.* Knowing too that most cults require familiarity with symbols, establishment of regions and localities, buildings, stones for religious rites, direction for turning, explained the realities of faith in Himself, saying (ii. 185) *It is not righteousness that we turn your faces eastward and westward: nay righteousness is believing in God;* and (xxii. 38) *their flesh and their blood reach not God:* teaching that the important thing is the purpose, and that mere cognisance will not suffice without obedience, as the heretical Bâtinîs and the Sûfi visionaries hold, relying thereon.

There is a Tradition going back to Abû'l-Qâsim 'Alî b. al-Muhassin at-Tanûkhi after his father according to which the latter said: We have been told by a number of learned persons that there is in Shîrâz a man known as Ibn Khafîf of Baghdâd, head of the Sûfi community there, to whom men gather and who talks to them about "imaginations" and "suggestions". Thousands attend his circle and

---

[55] This story is from *Table-talk of a Mesopotamian Judge*, part ii, p. 227.

he is regarded by them as highly expert. He has perverted the weak-minded to this system. One of his followers died, a Sûfi who left a Sûfi widow. There was a gathering of Sûfi women, who were a multitude, and no one besides them attended the mourning. When they had finished the interment, Ibn Khafîf with his intimate associates, also a multitude, entered the dwelling, and he began to console the widow in Sûfi language, after which she said: I feel consoled.—He then said to her: Is any other there?—No-one, she said.—Then, said he, what is the sense of our souls hugging the vexations of grief and being tortured with the torments of sorrow? Why should we neglect amalgamation, so that the lights may meet, that the spirits may be purified, the substitutes fall, and the blessings descend?—The woman said: If you will. The two companies "amalgamated" for the whole night, and when morning they came, the men were dismissed.

The expression "Is any other here"? means "Is there anyone here who does not agree with the system?" "Amalgamation" has an obscene sense. "That the lights may meet" refers to their principle that in everybody there is a divine light. The "substitutes" refers to the doctrine that every married woman has a substitute for the dead or absent mate.

I (say Tanûkhi) regard this as atrocious; had I not been told it by a number of persons whom I regard as unlikely to lie, I should not have repeated it, as too atrocious and unlikely to occur in an Islamic country. I was told that this and similar occurrences became so notorious that they reached the prince 'Adud ad-Dawlah, who arrested a number of the persons, scourged them, and by scattering the groups put a stop to the proceedings.

The Sûfis knowing little about the Code, illegal acts and utterances have proceeded from them, similar to that which has been mentioned; then they have been imitated by persons who are not of their community, but have taken their name, and from them similar things have proceeded to what we have narrated. Pious men among them were rare; they have been severely censured by the learned and even by their own leaders.

CHAPTER II

The Way Wherein the Devil Deludes those who Believe in Miracles, Wrought for the Glory of Saints

Some of them say: The Lord is generous, pardon is ample, and hope is part of religion; hope is the name which they give to their desire and deception, and it is this which has ruined most criminals. Abû 'Amr b. al-'Alã said: I have been told how al-Farazdaq was once sitting with people who were conversing about the mercy of God, he being the most hopeful among them. They asked him why he slandered chaste women. He replied: Tell me, were I to sin against my parents as I have sinned against God, would they be satisfied with hurling me into a furnace filled with coals of fire?— No they said: they would pity you, —I, said he, am more confident of God's mercy than to theirs.

This, I would observe, is sheer ignorance. For God's mercy is not softheartedness, since were it so, not a sparrow would be killed, not an infant put to death, nor would anyone be made to enter Hell.

There is a Tradition going back to 'Abbãd according to which he said: Al-Asmã'i said: I was with Abû Nuwãs in Makkah, where we saw a beardless lad kissing the Black Stone. Abû Nuwãs said to me: By Allãh, before I go I shall kiss him by the Black Stone.— I said: Wretch, fear God, as you are in the holy place and by His holy House. —He said: It must be so. —Then approaching the Stone, as the lad was about to kiss it, he put his cheek on the lad's, and kissed him, while I was looking on.— Wretch, I said, in God's sanctuary!—None of that, he said: my Lord is merciful. Then he recited the lines.

Two lovers with cheek meeting cheek

Hard by the Black Stone which is kissed;

In innocence met they, those two,

As though they were meeting by tryst.[1]

I would observe: Consider the audacity of looking for mercy and forgetting the terrible punishment for violation of that sanctity! We recorded at the beginning of this book how a couple who had misconducted themselves in the Ka'bah were turned into stone. Visitors to Abû Nuwâs in his last illness bade him repent to God: would[2] you frighten *me*, was his reply, I was told by Hammad b. Salaman after Yazid al-Raqashî[3] after Anas that the Prophet said: Every Prophet has the right of intercession, and I have reserved my intercession for those of my community who commit capital offences.

I would observe that this man erred in two ways. One in looking to the side of mercy and not looking to the side of punishment; the second, in forgetting that mercy is only for the penitent, as God says (xx. 84) *Verily I am forgiving to him who repents* and (vii. 155) *My mercy embraces everything and I shall write it for those that fear.*

Now this delusion is what ruins numbers of the unlearned, and we have dispelled it in our account of the believers in license.

Among the unlearned there are those who say: These learned people do not observe the ordinances, so-and-so does one thing and so-and-so another; my own case is similar.—This delusion is dispelled by the observation that the ignorant and the learned are equally bound by the ordinances, and the fact that passion gets the better of the learned is no excuse for the ignorant.

Some of them say: What does my sin matter that I should be punished? Or, Who am I that I should be reprimanded? My sin does not hurt Him, neither does my piety profit Him, and His pardon is greater than my offence. As one of them says:

Who am I before God in heaven

That sins of mine be not forgiven?

---

[1] From the *Diwân* of Abû Nuwâs, Cairo, 1898, whence the citation has been corrected.

[2] Died 167: account of him in *Tahdhib* III. 11-16.

[3] Yazid b. Abân Abû 'Amr al-Basri, died between 110 and 120. Account of him *ibid.*, XI. 309 -11. Abû Nuwâs lived 146-98.

Now this is consummate folly, as they seem to believe that only an opponent and an equal will be reprimanded. They do not know that by disobedience they virtually become opponents, Ibn 'Uqāyl, hearing a man ask: Who am I that I should be punished? said to him: You are the person to whom, if God were to slay all mankind, leaving you sole survivor, His words *O ye people* would be addressed.

Some of them say: I will repent and make good. Many a man over-confident in his hope has been snatched away before realization by death. It is no prudent course to hasten the wrong and await the right; repentance may not be feasible, may not be sincere, may not be accepted, and even if it be accepted the shame of the crime is indelible. It is easier to expel the evil thought so that it departs than to labour over repentance till it is accepted.

Some repent and then cancel their repentance. To such a person the devil obtains access by his wiles, knowing how irresolute he is. There is a tradition going back to al-Hasan according to which he said: If Satan, when he looks on thee sees thee disobedient to God, he seeks thee[4] time after time; but if he finds thee constant in obedience to God, he gets tired of thee and discards thee. But if he sees thee at one time so, and at another so, he has hopes of thee.

One of the delusions which he exercises on them is pride in some noble pedigree; a man says I am a descendant of Abû Bakr, or of Ali, or a *Sharif*[5] being a descendant of al-Hasan of al-Husain or closely related to some man of learning or some ascetic. They argue on two suppositions; one, that one who loves some man will also love his family and descendants the other that these persons have the right of intercession, and that their families and descendants have the best right to their intercession. Both these suppositions are erroneous: for God's love is not is like that of human beings: He only loves those who obey Him: Jacob's descendants, the People of the Book, did not profit by their parentage. Moreover, if love for the father extended itself, it would extend collaterally also[6]. And as for intercession. God says (xxi. 28) *They shall not intercede save for those whom He accepteth.* When Noah wanted to convey his son in

---

[4] Conjectural emendation of the text.

[5] Our author apparently does not distinguish between a *Sayyid* and a *Sharif.*

[6] This is probably the meaning, but the original is obscure.

the Ark, he was told (xi. 46) *Verily he is not of thy folk.* Abraham could not intercede for his father, nor our Prophet for his mother. Indeed the Prophet said to the blessed Fātimah. "I cannot avail thee with God at all." One who thinks he shall be saved through his father's salvation is like one who thinks his hunger will be satisfied by his father's eating.

One of the delusions which he exercises on them is a man's being satisfied with the display or some virtuous quality, and not troubling what he does afterwards.

Some among them say: I am a follower of the Sunnah, and followers of the Sunnah are safe—and then fail to keep clear of transgressions. This delusion is to be dispelled by telling such a man that orthodoxy is an obligation, and abstention from transgressions another obligation: and one of these obligations will not do instead of the other. Similarly the Rāfidis say: We shall be protected by our attachment to the members of the (Prophet's) house. —This assertion is false, since only piety can give protection.

Some among them say: I regularly attend the congregation and do good, and this will protect me. —The reply to this is similar to the preceding.

To this category belongs his deluding the brigands who take people's property. They are called "fine fellows" and assert that a "fine fellow" does not commit immorality, nor lie, guards the honour of women and never violates their privacy; but with all that they have no scruple about taking people's property, forgetting how keenly people feel about their property; and they call their system "gallantry". At times one of them takes an oath by his gallantry and neither eats nor drinks, and they make investiture of one who joins their community with trousers similar to the Sūfis' investiture of the neophyte with the parched cloak; yet one of them may hear some false scandal about his daughter or sister, probably from some scandalmonger, and puts her to death, calling this gallantry. At times too one of them boasts of his endurance of torture.

There is a Tradition going back to 'Abd Allāh b. Ahmad b. Hanbal according to which he said: I used often to hear my father say: May God have mercy on Abū'l Haytham!—I asked him who Abū'l-Haytham was. He said: Abū'l-Haytham the smith. When I stretched out my hands for punishment and the scourges were produced, I found a man was pulling my garment from behind. He asked me if I knew who he was and I said I did not. Then he said: I am Abûl-Haytham, brigand, robber, cutpurse, about whom it is written in the records of the Prince of Believers that I have been beaten 18,000 stripes on various occasions, and endured it all in obedience to Satan for the sake of this world; so do you endure in obedience to the Merciful One for the sake of religion.

I would observe that this Abû'l-Haytham's name was Khālid, and his endurance was proverbial. Al-Mutawakkil asked him how far his endurance went. He replied: I fill a sack with scorpions and introduce my hand into it: it gives me the same pain as it would give you. I feel the same pain from the last stroke of the scourge as I do from the first; were I to put a rag in my mouth while I am being scourged, it would be burned by the heat of my breath. Only I have trained myself to endurance.—Al-Fath[7] said to him: Tell me, what induces you, who have such a tongue and such an intellect, to follow so false a course as yours?—Desire for leadership, was his reply.— Al-Mutawakkil said: We are Khulaydis,— Al-Fath said: I am a ' Khulaydi.[8]

A man said to Khālid: Your people, Khālid, are not flesh and blood, so as to be affected by blows.—He said: On the contrary they do affect us, only we have a determination to endure which you have not.— Dāwûd b. 'Ali[9] said: When Khālid was brought in, I was anxious to see him, and went to him, when I found him seated unaffected by the loss of the flesh of his *séant* by the blows. There were lads round him, and they began to say: So-and-so has been beaten. Something has been done to so-and-so. He said to them: Do not talk about other people; do something yourselves so that others will talk about you.

I would observe: See how Satan makes game of these people so that they endure terrible pain in order to gain renown. If they would endure a little piety, they would obtain reward. It is surprising that they should suppose eminence and excellence attach to their condition when coupled with the perpetration of crimes.

---

[7] Al-Fath b.Khàqàn, vizier of al-Mutawakkil.

[8] Apparently "a poor creature in Khālid's lines," though the ordinary diminutive is different.

[9] Probably the founder of the Zahiris, 201-70.

There are among the unlearned people who rely on supererogatory acts and neglect the obligatory. Thus a man enters the mosque before the call to prayer and performs supererogatory devotions, and when he prays behind a leader tries to anticipate him. Some fail to appear at the times of the obligatory prayers, but jostle others on the twelfth of Rajab[10]. Some practice devotion with weeping, yet persist, in immorality; if talked to they say: A good deed and a bad deed: God is forgiving, and merciful. A number of them practice devotion according to their own ideas, doing more harm than good. I have seen one of them who knew the Qur'ān by heart, practised asceticism, and proceeded to castrate himself. This act is the worst of atrocities.

The devil has deluded many of the unlearned into attending religious meetings and weeping, satisfying themselves therewith on the supposition that the object of religion is attendance with tear-shedding, they having heard of the excellence of attendance at religious meetings. If they only knew that the object is action, and if a man does not act in accordance with what he hears, his hearing is further evidence against him! I know people who have attended such meetings for years, shedding tears and displaying humility, not one of whom deviates from his practice of usury, deceiving his customers, ignoring the canons of prayer, maligning the Muslims, and being undutiful to parents. Such people have been deluded by the devil, who has persuaded them that attendance at the meetings and shedding tears will save them from the guilt which they contract, and persuaded some that they will be saved by associating with learned men and saints.

He has kept others busy with postponement of repentance, until they delay too long. He has set others to entertain themselves with what they hear, while omitting to act according to it.

The devil has further deluded the wealthy in four ways.

(1) *In the mode of earning.* They care not how they acquire their wealth: usury pervades most of their transactions: indeed so habitual is the practice with them that most of their transactions are transgressions of the consensus. Abū Hurairāh recorded that the Prophet said: "A time will come when a man will not trouble about the source of his money, lawful or unlawful."[11]

---

[10] Celebration of the Conception of the Prophet.

[11] An-Nasâi II. 212.

(2) *In the matter of stinginess.* Some of them pay no alms, confident of forgiveness. Some employ an expedient for nullifying the obligation, *e.g.,* giving the money before expiry of the year and then reclaiming it. Another expedient is to give a poor man, a garment which he values for the purpose at ten dinars, whereas its real value is only two; thinking ignorantly that he has cleared himself. Some give bad articles in lieu of good; some give the alms to men whom they employ throughout the year, so that the alms are in fact wages. Some pay the alms as they should, and then the devil tells them they are under no further obligation, and dissuades them from spontaneous charity through love of money, so that the man loses the reward of the charitable, and the money becomes provision for someone else. There is a tradition going back to Ad-Dahhāk according to which Ibn 'Abbās said: The first time a *dirhām* was coined the devil took it, kissed it, put it on his eye and on his navel, and said: By thee I will make men malefactors and unbelievers; I prefer a man's loving the *dinār* to his worshipping me.—There is another going back to al-A'mash[12] after Shaqiq[13] after 'Abd Allāh that the last said: Verily Satan stalks a man by every means, and when the man outwits him he makes his bed in the man's money and prevents him from spending any of it.

(3) *In the pride of wealth.* The rich man thinks himself superior to the poor man; this is ignorance, for superiority lies in the excellences of the soul which adhere to it, not in the collecting of stones winch are not connected with it as the poet says,

Wealth of mind, so sages hold.

Better is than wealth of gold;

In the soul is excellence,

Not in state and circumstance.

(4) *In expenditure.* Some squander their money at times in unnecessary building, decoration of walls, ornamentation of the rooms, and painting of pictures; at times in attire which makes its wearer look proud and ostentatious; at times in luxurious food; actions whose perpetrator is liable to do something that is either forbidden

---

[12] His name was Sulaiman b. Mihrān, died about 148. Notice' of him in *Tahdhib* IV, 222-26.

[13] Ibn Salāmah al-Asadi, died between 87 and 100. Notice of him *ibid.* IV, 361-63.

or disapproved, and he will be held responsible for everything. There is a Tradition going back to Anas b. Mālik according to which the Prophet said: Son of Adam, on the Resurrection-day thy feet shall not depart from the presence of God until thou shalt have been asked about four things: thy life, in what thou hast passed it: thy body in what thou hast worn it out: thy wealth, whence thou hast acquired it, and wherein thou hast spent it.

Some of them spend money on the building of mosques and bridges, only for ostentation, fame, and the preservation of their memory. Such a man inscribes his name on his building; if his work had been for God, he would be satisfied with God's knowledge. If he were given the task of building a wall without inscribing his name, he would not do it.

To this category belongs their production cf candles at the illuminations in Ramadān with the view of gaining renown. Their mosques remain in darkness throughout the year, because to supply a little oil each night would not affect their reputation as much as supplying a candle in Ramadān. It would have been better to help the poor with the price of the wax. At times these lights are supplied in such numbers as to involve illicit extravagance, only ostentation will have its way. Ahmad b. Hanbal used to go to the mosque with a lamp in his hand, which he set down when he prayed.

Some, when they bestow charity, give it to the poor in public, combining the desire for people's praise with humiliation of the poor.

Some take with them on such occasions *dinārs* of light weight, two *qirāt* or thereabout,[14] or indeed bad money, which they bestow in public exposed, so that people may say X has given Y a whole *dinār!*—Contrary to this was the practice of many early saints, who would wrap in paper a heavy *dinār,* weighing more than a *dinār* and a half, and hand it secretly to the poor man, who when he saw a scrap of paper would suppose it to contain a fragment,[15] but on touching it and finding it round like a *dinār* would rejoice, only when he opened the paper would suppose it to be of light weight, then when he found it to be heavy would suppose it to be nearly as heavy as a good *dinār,* but when, weighing it, he found it to be heavier than one,

---

[14] It the *dīnār* at this time weighed 20 *qirāt,* such coins must have been "light" indeed.

[15] There are frequent allusions to the breaking up of coins.

would rejoice exceedingly. The divine reward would increase proportionally with these acts.

Some give charity to strangers, but have no gifts for their relations, who have the better claim. There is a Tradition going back to Salmān b. 'Amir[16] according to which he said: I heard the Prophet say: Alms given the poor are alms: given to relations are both alms and cementing of relationship.

Some of them, though aware of the virtue of bestowing on relations, owing to some bad blood between them connected with worldly affairs refrain from giving help, albeit conscious of the relative's poverty; had such a person given assistance he would have earned reward for alms-giving, for helping a relation, and for resisting passion. It is recorded that Abû Ayyub al-Ansari[17] said: The Prophet said: The best alms are what is given to a relation who is at enmity.

Such alms, I would observe, are only accepted[18] and described as excellent because of the resistance to passion. For if the man bestows on a relative whom he likes, he will have been following his inclination.

Some of them give in charity and stint their families. It is recorded that Jābir b. 'Abd Allāh said: The Prophet said: The best charity is that which comes from the back of wealth, and begin, with those whom you have to support.[19]

There is a Tradition going back to Abû Hurairah according to which the Prophet said: Give alms.—A man said: I have a *dinār*.—The Prophet said: Bestow it on yourself.

The man: I have another.

The Prophet: Bestow it on your wife.

The man: I have another.

The Prophet: Bestow it on your son.

The man: I have another.

The Prophet: Bestow it on your servant.

The man: I have another.

---

[16] Ad-Dabbi died in the reign of Mu'āwiyah. Notice of him in *Tahdhib* IV. 137.

[17] Khālid b. Zayd. Died 50 or 55. Notice of him in *Tahdhib* III, 90-91.

[18] Doubtless as earning reward.

[19] Bukhāri, ed. Krehl, I, 361.

The Prophet: You know best what to do with it.[20]

Some of them spend money on pilgrimage, the devil deluding them with the idea that pilgrimage is a pious act, whereas the man's object is ostentation, amusement, and to be praised. A man said to Bishr the Barefoot: I have prepared two thousand *dinārs* for a pilgrimage.—Bishr asked him if he had already made one; when he replied that he had, Bishr said to him: You should pay some one's debts.—The man said: I have no inclination except to pilgrimage. Bishr said: You want to ride and when you come back be called the Hājji.

Some of them spend on "times"[21] and dancing and throw clothes upon the singer; Satan deludes such a man into thinking that he is gathering poor people and feeding them; we have shown how this leads to corruption of the heart.

Sometimes one of them, when fitting his daughter out for marriage, has a silver couch fabricated for her, supposing this to be a pious act. Or he may have a gathering for the completion of the reading of the Qur'ān, when silver censors will be produced. Some learned men may be present, and neither will he think this proceeding extraordinary nor will they censure it; following the custom.

Sometimes one of them does injustice in his will, depriving his heir, supposing that the property is his own to dispose of as he likes, forgetting that it is allotted by the law,[22] and that the heirs have definite claims upon it. There is a Tradition going back to Abû Umāmah according to which the Prophet said: Whoso is treacherous in his will shall he cast into Wabā (a *wādi* in Gehenna).— There is also, one going back to al-Amash after Khaythamah according to which the latter said: Satan says: However much a man may overcome me he will never do so in three matters: I shall bid him take money from an improper source, spend it on an improper object, and withhold it from those who have a claim to it.

The devil also deludes the poor, some of whom only make a

---

[20] An-Nasāi I, 351.

[21] For the sense "entertainment" assigned to this word see above.

[22] The text has been amended.

show of poverty being rich; if such a person adds to this mendicancy
and accepting from people, he is increasing the fire of Gehenna. We
have been told by Ibn al-Husain a Tradition going back to Abû Hurairah
according to which the Prophet said: Whoso asks people for their
money to increase his own is only asking for coals of fire, so let him
do it as little or as much as he chooses.[23]—If such a person does
not accept anything from people, his object being merely by making
a display of poverty to get people to say: There is an ascetic! he is
a hypocrite. If he conceals God's bounty to him, making a display of
poverty so as not to have to spend, his miserliness involves
complaining against God. We have previously recorded how the
Prophet, seeing a man, in appearance a Bedouin, asked him if he
possessed any property. When the man replied that he possessed
some, the Prophet said: Then let God's bounty appear on you.

If the man be genuinely poor, his proper course is to conceal his
poverty, and make a show of easy circumstances. Among the
ancients there was a man who used to carry about a key, to make
people suppose that he possessed a house, when really he passed
his nights in mosques.

A delusion which the devil exercises on the poor is his fancying
himself superior to the rich as abstaining from the things which the
rich man likes. This is an error, since superiority does not consist in
having or not having but is something beyond that.

The devil has further deluded the great mass of the unlearned
in the matter of proceeding according to custom. This indeed is the
most frequent cause of their ruin. Thus they imitate their fathers
and ancestors in the matter of religion, adhering to that in which
they were brought up. You may see one of them live fifty years
according to his father's system never considering whether he was
right or wrong. To this category belongs the Jewish, Christian, and
pagan imitation of their ancestors: and likewise Muslims follow
custom in their prayer and devotions. You may find a man living for
years and praying in the style wherein he has seen people pray,
perhaps unable to say the *Fātihah* correctly, and ignorant of what
is obligatory; nor is it easy for him to learn this, such contempt has
he for religion. If he wanted to trade he would ask before travelling
what goods were marketable in the country to which he was going.

---

[23] Ibn Mājah I. 289, and others.

You will see one of them make the inclination or the prostration before the leader in prayer, not knowing that by doing so he conflicts with the leader in a constituent element: if he rises before the leader he conflicts with him in two elements, and his prayer is null and void. I have also seen a number of people utter *salām* simultaneously with the leader, when they have still some part of the obligatory creed to recite; this is a matter which the leader cannot tolerate, so his prayer becomes null and void. At times one of them omits an obligatory devotion and increases one that is supererogatory. At times too he omits to wash part of a member. *e.g.,* the heel, or having on his hand a ring which fits the finger tightly he does not turn it round at the time of ablution so that the water does not get to what is covered by the ring, and his ablution is invalid.

As for their buying and selling, most of their contracts are faulty, neither do they recognize the authority of the Code therein; nor does one of them readily follow the ruling of some jurist in a licence of which he avails himself, so disdainful are they of putting themselves under the rule of the Code. Rarely too do they sell anything that is not adulterated or harbouring a flaw which the vendor conceals. Polishing conceals the flaws of bad gold. Indeed a woman will put her spinning in moisture so that the wet may increase its weight. An illustration of their proceeding according to custom is a man's neglecting his obligatory prayer during Ramadān, breaking his fast on forbidden food, and backbiting people. He might be beaten with a stick, but still would decline to break his fast usually, because it is usual to find the breaking fast nauseous.[24] Some of them incur the charge of usury by hiring: a man will say: I possess twenty *dinārs*, no more. If I were to spend them, they would disappear; so I will hire a house with them and live on its rent.[25] He supposes this to be well within his competence. Sometimes he mortgages the house for a sum on which he pays interest, asserting that it was a case of necessity; very likely he may own another house and have utensils therein by selling which he could dispense with the hiring and the mortgaging. Only he is chary of his reputation,

---

[24] I am unable to illustrate this passage.

[25] Presumably the rent for which he would let the house would be larger than what he paid for the hire; hence the result would not be very different from lending money on interest.

fearing it might be said that he had sold his house or was using earthenware in lieu of brass.

A matter wherein they proceed according to custom is their reliance on the utterances of the soothsayer, the astrologer, and the diviner, a practice which is widespread, and which the greatest men constantly pursue; rarely will you see one of them start on a journey, order clothes, or go to the cupper without consulting an astrologer and acting according to his words. In everyone of their houses there is sure to be a horoscope; bur in many of them there is no copy of the Qur'ān. In the *Sahih* there is a Tradition that the Prophet being asked about the soothsayers said: They are nothing.—They said: O Messenger of God, at times they communicate something which turns out to be true.—The Prophet said: That is a word of truth which the Jinni snatches and cackles like a hen into the ear of his ally. But therewith they mingle more than a hundred falsehoods.[26]

In the *Sahîh* of Muslim it is recorded that the Prophet said: For forty nights the prayer will not be accepted of a man who goes to a diviner and consults him.[27]

Abû Dâwûd records a Tradition of Abû Hurairāh according to which the Prophet said: Whoso goes to a soothsayer and believes what he says is alienated from what God has revealed to Muhammad.[28]

A further matter wherein they proceed according to custom is their multiplicity of false oaths, most of which, though they are unaware of it, are equivalent to the formula of divorce,[29] they constantly say in their oaths something "will be unlawful for me if I sell,—Among their customs is the wearing of silk, and gold rings; at times one of them abstains from wearing silk, only puts it on once in a way like the preacher on a Friday. Among their customs too is to refrain from censuring what should be censured; a man will even see his brother or neighbour drinking wine or wearing silk, and will neither censure him nor change his attitude, but associate with the culprit on friendly terms.

Among their customs is building a stone bench in front of one's

---

[26] Muslim II, 191.

[27] *Ibid.*, 192.

[28] Abû Dâwûd, Bombay ed; iv. 21.

[29] A frequent form of oath has divorce for its "sanction".

door thereby narrowing the street to passengers. At times a man lets a quantity of rain-water accumulate by his front-door, which he ought to remove; he incurs guilt by causing annoyance to the Muslims. Another custom is to enter the public bath without drawers; some indeed enter with them on, and then let them fall on their thighs, so that the sides of the man's *séant* shows, and when he gives himself over to the masseur the latter seen part of his nakedness and even touches it since the "nakedness" is all between the navel and the knee. These people then see men's nakedness and neither close their eyes nor make objection.

Another custom is to cease maintaining a wife's rights: often indeed they compel her to resign her marriage gift, the husband thinking that her resignation releases 'him from his obligation, At times two a man favours one of two wives, and divides his attentions unfairly between them; he does so without scruple, thinking that such conduct is well within his competence. Abû Hurairah recorded how the Prophet said: A bigamist who favours one of his wives unduly shall come on Resurrection day trailing one half of his body, either collapsing or leaning.[30]

Another custom is for a man to declare himself indigent before the magistrate and, when officially declared to be so, to believe that he is thereby released from all dues; he may really be wealthy, but pays no due. Sometimes a man does not quit his shop on the plea of indigence till he has amassed wealth out of the property of his customers, and put it aside[31] to spend during his retirement, supposing that such a proceeding is within his competence.

Another matter in which custom is followed is for a man to hire himself out to work the whole day, and then waste much of his time by dilatoriness or idleness or adjustment of tools, *e.g.*, a carpenter in sharpening his hatchet or a sawyer his saw; such conduct is perfidious unless it be on a small scale such as is usual. Often such a workman misses his prayer, pleading that he is in the hire of another man, not knowing that the times of prayer are not included in contracts of hire. Disloyalty in their employment is also common.

---

[30] Nasa'i II, 157.

[31] This seems to be the sense required, but the text is probably corrupt.

Among customary practices too is burying the dead in coffins, which is to be disapproved. The graveclothes should not be ostentatiously extravagant but in moderation. They bury with the corpse a number of garments, which is unlawful, as being waste of substance. Then they hold lamentation over the dead. In the *Sahih* of Muslim it is recorded that the Prophet: said: Unless the wailing woman repent before her death she shall be raised on Resurrection-day with a Tunic of pitch and a bodice of flame.[32] It is their custom too—especially that of the women —to beat themselves and tear their garments to pieces. Yet in both *Sahih* it is recorded that the Prophet said: He is not one of us who rends his garments or beats his cheeks, or utters the cries of paganism.[33] Sometimes when they see the bereaved person rending his clothes they find no fault with him, nay rather they find it with the omission of the practice, saying that the man is unaffected by the misfortune. Among their customs too is that of donning disreputable attire after a death, and continuing to wear it for a month or a year; some, too, will not sleep on a roof for this period. Another is to visit the cemeteries on the night of the middle of Sha'bān, light fires there and take dust from a revered tomb. Ibn 'Uqayl says: When the ordinances of the Code are found hard by the ignorant and the vulgar, they turn from its ordinances to the observation of others which they have invented for themselves. These are easy for them, as they are not brought under the rule of others. In my opinion, he says, they earn the name of infidels by these ordinances, such as paying reverence and honour to tombs in ways forbidden by the Code, such as kindling fires, kissing them, perfuming them,[34] addressing the dead with tablets, and writing slips containing the words "My lord, do unto me such and such a service," and taking the dust for luck. Further pouring out scent on the graves, travelling long distances to them,[35] and putting strips of stuff on trees, in imitation of the worshippers of al-Lāt and al-'Uzzā. You will not find one person among these who is conversant with any question about the alms or asks about any rule to which he is subject. According to them woe to anyone who fails to kiss the

---

[32] Ibn Mājah I, 247 has the tradition in this form; the word in Muslim I, 256 (in lieu of flame) seems to mean scab.

[33] Bukhari I, 325.

[34] Text emended.

[35] This is probably the meaning but the words might signify "attaching camels to them".

Martyrium of the Cave,[36] or to stroke a brick of the Ma'muniyyah Mosque[37] on a Wednesday, or over whose bier the bearers have not pronounced the name of Abû Bakr as-Siddiq or Muhammad and ' Ali, or whose funeral has been unaccompanied by lamentation, or who has failed to erect over his father a brick and stucco portico, or failed to rend his garment to the skirt, or to pour rose-water over the grave and bury his clothes with him.

Very many too are the delusions which the devil exercises over women. I have devoted a separate book to women, in which I have enumerated all the acts of devoutness etc. which particularly concern them. Here I will record some of the delusions which the devil exercises on them.

We have shown above how the devil only obtains power over a man in proportion to the man's ignorance; the more ignorant he is, the greater becomes the devil's power over him: the more the man knows the less control has the devil. At times a devotee sees a light or fire in the sky, and if it be in Ramadãn declares that he has seen the Night of Qadar; if it happen in another month: he declares that the gates of heaven have been opened to him. Or he may happen to obtain something which he had been seeking, and supposes this to be a miracle wrought in his honour, whereas it may have been an accident, or a case of probation, or a wile of the devil. A wiseman will not feel easy about anything of this kind, even if it be a miracle in his honour: above, dealing with devotees, we have recorded how Malik b. Dinãr and Habib al-'Ajami both said that the devil plays with Qur'ãn-readers like lads with nuts. He has led many a weak devotee astray by showing him something resembling a miracle wrought in his honor, in consequence of which the man has claimed prophethood. It is recorded that 'Abd al-Wahhãb b. Najdah al-Hawtî[38] reported

---

[36] Probably some building in Baghdãd is meant. According to Ibn Batûtah (I, 416) those who entered the Martyrium of 'Ali kissed the threshold.

[37] I am unable to illustrate the practice mentioned here.

[38] Traditionalist died 233. Notice of him in the *Tahdhib* VI, 453.

a tradition going back to 'Abd al-Rahmān b. Hassān[39] according to which the latter said: Al-Hārith the Liar was one of the people of Damascus, client of Abû'l-Julās[40] and had a father in al-Ghûtah;[41] the devil assailed him, he being a devout ascetic; had he donned a robe of gold, it would have seemed a sign of asceticism[42] in his case. When he started the formula "Praise be to God" the audience had never listened to utterance more beautiful than his. He wrote to his father: "My father, come quickly, for I have been seeing things which I am afraid may proceed from Satan." His father led him further astray,[43] writing to him: My son, go forward to that which thou art commanded for, God says (xxvi. 221) *Shall I inform you upon whom the demons descend? They descend on every guilty fabricator.* Now you are neither guilty nor a fabricator, so proceed with that which you are bidden to do.—So, he proceeded to go to the people in the mosque, one by one, tell them his experiences, and take from each man a solemn promise that if he saw what he approved, he would accept it, but if not, would conceal it. Now he would show them marvels; he would go to a marble slab in the mosque, tap on it with his hand, and it would utter the words "Glory to God"; he would give them summer fruits in winter and tell them to come out to be shown the angels, Then he would take them out to Dair Murran[44] and show them men on horseback. He won many adherents, the affair became known, and his followers became so numerous that the report reached al-Qāsim b. Mukhaymarah.[45] Hārith said to al-Qāsim; I am a prophet.[46]—Al-Qāsim said to him; You lie, enemy

---

[39] Probably the son of the poet Hassân b. Thâbit is meant. Notice of him in the *Tahdhîb* VI,162. where his death-date is given as 104.

[40] The story that follows is given by' Ibn 'Asâkir III, 443, on the same authority. He calls Abû'l Julâs al-'Abdari al-Qurashi, but gives alternatively the name of another patron. Variations of importance will be noticed. Yâqùt. *Geogr. Dict.* II, 367, also copies it.

[41] I. A. and Yaqut, al-Hûlah.

[42] The texts differ slightly, but the sense of all seems to be that anything which he did would have seemed suitable to an ascetic.

[43] This seems better than the readings of I.A. and Yâqût, which indicate how easily the Arabic script can be misread.

[44] A large monastery near Damascus.

[45] Notice of him in the *Tahdhîb* VIII, 337, where his death-date is given as 100 or 101.

[46] Instead of this, which the context seems to require, I.A. and Yâqût make him offer al-Qāsim the same conditions as the others.

of God!—Abû Idris[47] said to al-Qāsim: You have done wrong in not being gentle with him, so that we might have caught him: as it is, he will escape.— Abû Idrîs left his court and going to 'Abd al-Malik informed him of the affair. 'Abd al-Malik sent people to search for al-Hārith but was unable to arrest him. The Caliph then went on a journey and alighted at Subayrah[48] where he suspected the whole of his army of following al-Hārith's doctrine. Al-Hārith himself went off to Jerusalem, where he hid; his followers went about looking for men to bring to him. A man from Basrah who had come to Jerusalem was brought to al-Hārith,[49] who started the formula "Praise be to God," then told the man about himself and how he was a prophet and apostle. The Basran said to him: Your language is fine, but I should like to think about it.—Al-Hārith bade him do so. The Basran went away, but came again, when al-Hārith repeated his discourse; the Basran said: Your language is fine, it has impressed me, I believe in you, and this is the correct religion.—Al-Hārith now gave orders that the Basran should not be refused admittance whenever he wished to come, and the latter became a frequent caller and learned about his going out and his coming in, and whether he fled; so he got to know more about him than anyone else. Presently he asked for leave of absence; and being asked whither he meant to go replied: To Basrah, where I shall be your first missionary. —Leave was given him, and the Basran hurried off to 'Abd al-Malik who was at Subayrah; when he approached the Caliph's pavilion he cried out: Advice, advice! —The people in the camp asked what advice.—Advice, he replied, for the Prince of Believers.—'Abd al-Malik gave orders that he be admitted to his presence, and the Basran coming before the Caliph, who had his courtiers with him, cried out: Advice!—Being asked by the Caliph what his advice was, he requested a private interview at which no-one else should be present. Those who were in the apartment being sent away, he asked the Caliph to bid him approach. The Caliph, who was on a throne, bade him do so, and asked him what he had to communicate. He said: Al-Hārith.—When the Basran mentioned al-Hārith's name, the Caliph leapt to the ground from his

---

[47] "A'idh Allāh b. 'Abd Allāh al-Khawlānî *qâdi* of Damascus, died 80; notice of him in the *Tahdhib* V. 85.

[48] The texts differ as to the name; Yaqut's reading has been adopted.

[49] I. A. observed that the people of Basrah are fond of kalām (metaphysical theology), and the man was attracted by being told that al-Hārith was a *mutakallim*.

throne and asked where he was.—He is in Jerusalem, the man replied, and I know his incomings and outgoings;—he proceeded to tell the whole story and his dealings with the man. The Caliph said: You are the man's associate, and governor of Jerusalem, and governor of us here: so give me any commands you please.—The Basran asked the Caliph to send with him some people who did not understand the language. The Caliph ordered forty men from Farghānah to go with the Basran and obey any orders which he gave them. He further wrote a letter to the governor of Jerusalem to the effect that the person whom he named was to be governor over the head of the former until he left, and that the governor was to carry out any instructions which he gave.

When the Basran reached Jerusalem he gave the governor a letter, and the latter said: Give me any orders you please.—He said: Collect all the candles you can in Jerusalem, give each candle to a man and post them in the streets and corners of Jerusalem. When I say, Light up, let them all do so.—The governor accordingly posted the men with the candles in the streets and corners of Jerusalem, and went by himself at night to the house of al-Hārith, where he asked the doorkeeper to obtain admission for him to the Prophet of God. The doorkeeper said: At this hour admission to him cannot be obtained; nor till morning.—The Basran said: Tell him that I have only returned out of desire for him before reaching my destination.— The doorkeeper went in and reported the conversation to al-Hārith who bade him open the door. The Basran then cried out: Light the candles!—and this was done till they were like daylight. He then ordered his men to arrest anyone who passed by them, whoever he might be. He himself went to the place which he knew, and searched for al-Hārith, but failed to find him; al-Hārith's adherents said: It is no use your wanting to put God's Prophet to death; he has ascended into heaven. —The Basran then sought al-Hārith in a cleft which he had prepared as an underground chamber, and inserting his hand into the cellar found al-Hārith's-garment and pulled it and with it al-Hārith out. He then ordered the men from Farghānah to bind him, which they did. While they were taking him along on a mount belonging to the post, he said, (xl, 29): *Will ye slay a man for saying my Lord is Allāh?*—Then one of the foreigners from Farghānah said: This is our Coran produce your own Coran.[50] They proceeded with him till they had brought him to 'Abd al-Malik who when he heard of their arrival ordered a post to be erected to which he was tied; he then ordered someone to thrust a spear into his body. The spear struck one of his ribs which forced it back; the people began to cry out: Weapons have no power over Prophets!—One of the Muslims, seeing this, seized the spear, and approaching the man started probing till he had found a place between two ribs, where he pierced, causing the man's death.

Al-Walîd[51] added: I was told that Khālid b. Yazîd b. Mu'āwiyah went to 'Abd al-Malik b. Marwān and said to him: Had I been present, I should not have told you to put him to death.—Why? asked 'Abd al-Malik.—He was possessed by Madhhib[52] was the reply;—had you starved him, that demon would have quitted him.

It was narrated by Abû'r-Rabî'[53] a Shaikh who had known men of early times, how when al-Hārith was mounted on a post-mule, with an iron collar to which his hands were fastened round his neck, coming in sight of one of the hills of Jerusalem, he recited the text (xxxiv. 49): *Say: If I err, I only err to my own harm, whereas if I am guided aright it is through what my Lord reveals unto me.*—Thereupon the collar shook and presently detached itself from his hands and neck and fell on the ground. The guards who were with him hastily replaced the collar on him; they proceeded with him and when they came in sight of another hill he recited another text; again the collar detached itself from his hands and neck and fell on the ground; and again they replaced it. When they came before 'Abd al-Malik he imprisoned the man, and ordered some jurists and men of learning to admonish him, bid him beware of Allāh, and assure him that what had happened was from Satan. Declining to accept their views, he was tied to a post. A man came and thrust at him with a spear, but it swerved aside. The people said that such a man ought not to be put to death. Then a guard brought a thin poniard, thrust it between two of the man's ribs, shook it and caused it to penetrate. I heard someone say that when the spear swerved aside 'Abd al-Malik asked

---

[50] The text of Yâqût has been adopted. The foreignness was observable in the mispronunciation of the first letter of Qur'ân. The reading of Ibn 'Asâkir and of our text "our miracle" etc. seems pointless.

[51] One of the transmitters of the anecdote.

[52] A demon who interferes with ablution.

[53] The text has been corrected from Ibn 'Asâkir.

the man who had aimed it whether he had mentioned the name of God when doing so. The man said he had forgotten. 'Abd al-Malik bade him mention the name of God and then strike. He did so and transfixed the man.

Many people have been deceived by the semblance of miracles. We have been told with a chain of transmitters from Hasan from Abû 'Imrān that the latter said: Farqad[54] said to me: I was in trouble this morning about my tax, which amounts to six *dirhams;* the new moon has appeared, and I had nothing. I prayed, and while walking on the bank of the Tigris came upon six *dirhams.* I took and weighed them, and they were exactly six.—I said: Give them away in alms, as they are not yours.

I would observe that the Abû 'Imrān of this story is Ibrāhîm an-Nakha'î, the jurist of Kufah[55] now consider the language of jurists and how immune they are from deception: notice how Ibrāhîm explained to Farqad that this was treasure-trove, without paying any attention to the semblance of a miracle. He did not advise Farqad to advertise the find because, according the jurists of Kûfah, advertisement is not required tor a sum less than a *dinār.* He bade Farqad give the money away in alms so that it might not be supposed that he had obtained them miraculously to spend.

According to a Tradition going back to Ibrāhim al-Khurāsāni he said: One day when I was in want of water for ablution I found a jug of precious stone and a silver toothpick of which the point was softer than *khazz* (tissue of silk and wool): I used the toothpick, washed with the water, left them and went away.

I would observe that among the transmitters of this anecdote there are untrustworthy names, but if it be true it indicates the man's ignorance. Had he known the law he would have been aware that the use of a silver toothpick is illegal; not knowing this, he used it. If he supposed this to be a miracle, we may be sure that God does not miraculously put into a man's hands an article whose use He has forbidden in His Code, unless indeed He showed it to the man by way of testing him.

The historian Muhammad b. Abi'l-Fadl al-Hamdāni records how

---

[54] Probably Farqad al-Sabakhi, died 131: notice of him in the *Tahdhib* VIII, 262.
[55] Ibrâhîm b. Yazid, 46-96.

he was told by his father that the teacher of Qur'ān-reading ash-Sharmaqāni[56] used to read with Ibn al-'Allāf,[57] and used to retire to the mosque in Darb az-Zā'farani.[58] It so happened that one day he was seen by Ibn al-'Allāf going down to the Tigris when he was hungry, picking up lettuce-leaves which his fellow-students had thrown away and eating them. Ibn al-'Allāf, being grieved thereat, went to the Chief of Chiefs[59] and told him of the man's condition. This official ordered a retainer who lived near the mosque to which ash-Sharmaqānî retired to provide the door of the mosque with a lock and key, without the latter knowing, which the retainer did; he was then ordered to take thither everyday three ratls of wheaten bread, a chicken and some sweetmeat: and this he continued to do. On the first day ash-Sharmaqānî, coming to the mosque and finding these viands set down in the niche and the door locked[60] was amazed, and said to himself: This comes from Paradise, I must conceal it, tell no one about it, for a condition attaching to miracles done in honour of a saint is that they must be concealed.—He recited to me (said the narrator) a couplet:

Whoso a secret told him once betrays

Forfeits like confidence for all his days.

When he got to look well and plump, he was asked by Ibn al-'Allāf how this had come about, the latter knowing the facts and meaning to amuse himself at the other's expense. Ash-Sharmaqāni would only drop obscure hints, veiling his meaning; but Ibn al-'Allāf went on questioning him till at last the other informed him that what he found in the mosque was a miracle wrought in his honour, since no human being could produce it. Then Ibn al-'Allāf said to him: You ought to bless the son of the Muslim woman,[61] since he is the person who has done this.—This information made ash-Sharmaqānî

---

[56] His name was al-Hasan b. Abi'l-Fadl or b. al-Fadl, according to *Kitāb Baghdād* VII. 402. where his death date is given as 451.

[57] His name was 'Ali-b. Muhammad b.Yāsuf (*Ghāyat an-Nihāyah.* ed. Bergsträsser, No. 23411. Notice of him in *Kitāb Baghdād* XII, 95, where his death date is given as 396.

[58] This street is not mentioned in Le Strange's list of the streets of Baghdād.

[59] This title occurs at a later period, whence it is not clear who is meant.

[60] Presumably after he had entered.

[61] Probably he meant himself.

miserable, and he showed the signs of depression.

The wise, knowing the intensity of the devil's delusion, are on their guard against things which have the appearance of being miraculous, fearing they may be delusions wrough* by him. We have been told by a chain of transmitters going back to Abû't-Tayyib[62] a Tradition according to which he said: I heard Zahrûn[63] say: A bird talked to me. Once I had lost my way in the desert, when I saw a white bird, which said to me: Zahrûn, you have lost your way.—I said: Demon, deceive some one other than me!—It said the same a second time, and I made the same reply. The third time it sprang upon my shoulder, and said: I am no demon, you have lost your way and I have been sent to you.—Then it departed.

There is a Tradition told by Muhammad b. 'Abd Allāh al-Qurashî[64] after Muhammad b. Yahyā b. Abî Hātim after Muhammad b. 'Amr, according to which the last said: Zulfah said to me: I said to Rabî'ah: Aunt dear, why do you not admit visitors?—She replied: For what can I hope from people who, when they come to me, report about me things which I have not done?— Al-Qurashî proceeded: Another transmitter (not Ibn Abî Hātim) added; She went on to say: I am told that they say I find *dirhams* under my prayer-mat, that my saucepan cooks for me without fire; had I seen such things, I should have been alarmed thereby. I (said Zulfah) said to her: People do indeed talk much about you, saying that Rabî'ah finds food and drink in her dwelling. Do you find anything of the sort there?—Niece dear, she replied, if I were to find anything in my dwelling, I should not touch it, or set hand upon it.

Al-Qurashi proceeded: I was also told by Muhammad b. Idris'[65] after Muhammad b. 'Amr after Zulfah that Rabî'ah said: One cold morning I rose fasting, and felt an inclination for something hot on

---

[62] This would naturally mean Tāhir b. 'Abdallah al-Tabari, 348- 450, of whom there is a notice in *Kitāb Baghdād* IX, 358. But he cannot have heard Zahrûn.

[63] Notice of him in *Nafahal al-Uns,* p. 113, where he is called al-Maghribî, and said to have been a native of Tripoli. He is there made a contemporary of Muzaffar al-Kirmānshāhi whose death date seems to have been about 300.

[64] The most distinguished person of this name was a grandson of the Caliph 'Uthman, and on the mother's side of Husain b. 'Ali; according to the *Kitāb Baghdād* V. 387, he was put to death in 145: since Muhammad b. Yahya b. Abî Hātim died 252 *(Kitāb Baghdād* III, 415). This person cannot be meant here.

[65] Probably Abû Hâtim al-Hanzalî, who died 277; notice of him in *Kitāb Baghdād* II, 73 -77.

which to breakfast. I had some fat, and said: If I had onions or leeks I could dress them.—Suddenly a sparrow came and alighted on the path[66] with an onion in its beak. When I saw it, I changed my mind, fearing it might be from Satan.

According to a Tradition going back to Muhammad b. Yazid[67] he said: People used to suppose that Wuhayb was one of those destined for Paradise; when he was told of this he shed copious tears, saying: I fear this may be from Satan.[68]

There is a Tradition going back to Abû 'Uthmān al-Nîsāburi[69] according to which he said:[70] A party of us went out with our master Abû Hafs al-Nîsābûri[71] outside Nîsābûr, and sat down; the shaikh discoursed to us and delighted us, presently we saw a chamois come down and kneel before the shaikh. This caused him to shed copious tears. When he grew calmer we asked him the reason and I said: Master, you discoursed to us and delighted us, but when this wild creature came and knelt before you, it troubled you and made you sob.—Yes, he said, I saw you gather round me and how delighted you were, and the thought occurred to me: If only I could slaughter a sheep and invite you to banquet on it! The thought had not taken shape before this wild creature came and knelt in front of me, and I fancied that I was like Pharaoh, who asked his Lord to make the Nile flow for him, and his Lord caused it to flow.[72] So I said: What assurance have I but that God will give me my whole fortune in this world, and that I shall be left poor and destitute in the world to come? It is that which troubled me.

The devil has further deluded some of the later Sûfis into inventing

---

[66] Probably the word has here some different meaning from those given in the dictionaries or is corrupt.

[67] Probably the grammarian al-Mubarrad is meant.

[68] The Wuhayb of this anecdote is probably 'Wuhayb b. al-Wārd, who died 153 *(Shajarat al Dhahab* I, 236).

[69] Probably Sa'îd b. Ismā'îl is meant; though called al-Hiri he lived most of his life in Nisābûri Died 298 (*Kitāb Baghdād* IX, 102).

[70] This story is told in the *Luma',* p. 327, with slight differences.

[71] His name appears in *Kitâb Baghdâd* XII, 220, as 'Amr b. Muslim, though the father's name was doubtful. Died 265 or 270.

[72] Probably a story told to illustrate *Sûrah* xliii, 50, where Pharaoh claims possession of "these rivers which flow beneath me".

stories of miracles wrought in honour of the saints, in order, as they
suppose, to strengthen their case. The truth, however, requires no
falsehood to strengthen it, and God has exposed them through those
who are learned in transmission. We have been told by Muhammad
b. Nāsir a Tradition going back to Ahmad b. 'Abdallah b. al-Hasan al-
Ādamî according to which the latter said: I was told by my father
that Sahl b, 'Abd Allāh had said that 'Amr b. Wāsil had said—that is
the record, but the' correct form is 'Amr b. Wāsil said that Sahl b.
'Abd Allāh said: I accompanied a certain saint on the Makkah road
for three days,[73] when, being destitute, he turned aside to a mosque
at the foot of a mountain. There he found a well, with a wheel, a rope,
a bucket, and a washing-basin; by the well there was a pomegranate-
tree, with no fruit on it. He stayed in the mosque till the evening
prayer, and when the time for that arrived, there appeared forty men,
clad in sackcloth and shod with palm-leaf. Having entered the
mosque they saluted, then one of them uttered the call to prayer,
then the starting formula, and then came forward and led prayer.
When he had finished, he approached the tree, on which, there were
now forty fresh and ripe pomegranates, of which each of the men
took one, and then went away. The saint said: I passed the night in
want, and when the time arrived in which they had taken the
pomegranates, they all of them come forward. When they had prayed
and taken their pomegranates, I said: Friends, I am your brother in
Islam, and in terrible want; yet you have neither spoken to me nor
comforted me.—Their leader said: We do not speak to a man who is
screened by what he has with him. Go and cast away what you have
got behind this mountain into the valley, and then come back to us,
when you will obtain what we obtain.—I ascended the mountain, but
could not bring myself to throw away what I had got, so I buried it
and came back.—The man asked me whether I had thrown away
what I had; Yes I replied.—Then, he asked, did you see anything?—
No, I said.—Then, said he, you have not thrown anything away, so
go back and throw it into the valley.—I went back and did so, and so,
the light of sainthood covered me like a cuirass, and when I got
back, there was a pomegranate on the tree; I ate it, and was relieved
from hunger and thirst. I proceeded without further delay to Makkah,
where I found the forty men between Abraham's Station and Zamzam.

---

[73] The order of the words in the original has been altered.

They all came forward to me, greeting and asking me how I, was. I said: I can dispense with you and your conversation finally even as God caused you to dispense with mine initially. There is in me no room for any save God.

I would observe that 'Amr b. Wāsil was discredited by Ibn Abî Hātim; and al-Ādamî and his father are unknown. That the story is a fabrication is shown by their telling him to cast away what he had with him; for saints do not violate the Code, and the Code forbids waste of property. The man's saying that he was covered with the light of sainthood is also a fabrication and meaningless talk. No one who has smelt the odour of knowledge could be deceived by such a story, it can only deceive the ignorant and unintelligent.

We have been told by Muhammad b. Nāsir a Tradition going back to Muhammad b. 'Ali the Preacher' according to which the latter said: Among the things told me by one of the Sûfis[74] after al-Junaid was that the latter said that Abû Mûsā al-Daybulîs aid: I called on Abû Yazîd, and in front of him there was some water standing shaking; he bade me enter and proceeded to say: A man was asking me about modesty so I talked to him a little on the science of the subject,[75] when he began to spin round till he melted and became as you see.—Al-Junaid added that Ahmad b. Khidrawayhî stated that a little bit of the man remained, like a piece of a gem; I made of it (he said) a jewel, and each time I spoke in the language of the community or heard it spoken, it melted, till at last nothing of it remained.

I would observe that this is an atrocious absurdity, invented by ignorant people; were it not that they record it with a chain of transmitters and suppose it to be a fact, it would have been better to take no notice of it.

We have been told by Abû Bakr b. Habib a Tradition going back to 'Abd al-'Azîz-al-Baghdādî according to which the latter said: Once when I had been studying the stories of the Sûfis, mounting the roof, I heard someone say (vii, 195): *And He befriends the saints.* Turning, I saw no-one. I flung myself from the roof and stood in the air.

---

[74] Ibn al-'Allâf, died 442. Notice of him in *Kitâb Baghdād* III, 103.

[75] Qushayri has a chapter about it. III. 144 foll.

I would observe that this is an absurd falsehood, as no sensible person will doubt: but if we supposed it to be true, it would be a crime to fling himself from the roof and to suppose that God would look after one who perpetrated a forbidden action; for God says (ii, 191): *And fling not with your hands to destruction.* Flow then can the man be a saint when he violates his Lord's command? But even supposing he was one, who told him that he was one of them? We have already cited the words of Jesus who, when Satan told him to throw himself down, replied that God tries His servants, but it is not for one of them to try Him.

Certain persons have passed themselves off as Sùfîs, imitating them, have revelled in miracles and their claim to them, and shown the populace tricks whereby they have won their hearts. We have been told how al-Hallāj used to bury somewhere in the desert bread, sweets, and roast meat, then say to his followers: Suppose we go wandering,—He would then start out accompanied by a number and when they got to the place an accomplice would say to him we should like certain things.—He would then quit the company, go to the place, make a prayer of two inclinations, and bring them the things wanted. He would also stretch out his hand into the air and by legerdemain fling gold into people's hands. One of those present on one of these occasions said to him: These *dirhāms* are familiar, I will believe in you if you present me with a *dirhām* inscribed with your name and your father's. —He continued to practise legerdemain till he was executed.

We have been told by Abû Mansûr al-Qazzāz a Tradition recorded by Abû Bakr b.Thābit[76] and going back to Abû 'Umar b. Hayûyah, according to which the last said: When Mansûr al-Hallāj was led out to execution I walked among the crowd whom I jostled till I came in sight of him. He said to his followers: Do not be alarmed by this, for I will return to you after thirty days.—Hallāj's doctrine was evil; in an earlier part of this work we have expounded some of his doctrine and confused utterances, and shown how he was executed in accordance with the opinion of contemporary jurists.

---

[76] *Kitāb Baghdād* VIII. 131.

Among the later Sûfis were some who daubed themselves with ointment of mica,[77] then sat in an oven and pretended that this was a miracle.

Ibn 'Uqayl says: Ibn Shabbās[78] and his father before him had carrier-pigeons of special velocity and friends in every place. When visitors came, he would immediately despatch a bird to their village, telling his partisan there of their arrival, and asking for information about them. The partisan would write a reply, and then Ibn Shabbās would meet the visitors and tell them those news, talking to them of their affairs in the style of one who had associated with them in their own country, and then recounting to them what had happened since their departure from home and even on that very day. "Just now" he would say "such and such things have happened". They would be amazed, and returning to their district would find the facts to be as he had stated.[79] This would be performed repeatedly, and came to be regarded as irretragable evidence that the man possessed mysterious knowledge.

He proceeds: And among the things which he did was to take a sparrow and attach a string[80] to its leg, putting a minute bit of paper on the string; he would also attach a string to the leg of a pigeon but tie to the end of the string a larger paper than the other, only containing the same as the smaller one. He would then take a slave upon the roof,[81] set him in front of himself, and place the sparrow in one of his hands and the pigeon in the other. He would then let the sparrow loose, and the people would see the paper flying in the air, while the

---

[77] This supposed property, rendering the body immune from fire, seems to be attributed to mica by one of Ibn Baytar's authorities: according to *Tāj al-'Arûs* the mineral had not this property but a plant, whose juice possessed it, in the opinion of some.

[78] According to Yāqût, *Geogr. Dictionary* III. 442, a man who came to Saymarah about the year 450 where he claimed divinity, and received worship owing to the deception which he practised. See below.

[79] The mediums of our time have been supposed to obtain their information by similar methods.

[80] The word in the text which is variously written, seems unknown to dictionaries, and of no obvious etymology. It has been translated conjecturally.

[81] The text here is seriously confused, and the sentences have to be rearranged conjecturally.

pigeon would go to that village[82] where it would be taken by his friend there, who would proceed to inform him of the affairs of the village and its inhabitants. When his meeting-room was full, he would point and call out Barish (as though addressing a demon of that name) take this letter to the village of So-and-So, for a dispute has arisen among them, and endeavour to reconcile them.— He would say this in a loud voice, and then the slave who was on the watch would release the sparrow in his hand, and the letter would rise skyward in the presence of the assembly, who would see it plainly without seeing the string. When it had risen high the slave to whom the sparrow was attached would pull it, breaking the string so that it could not be seen, and sending the sparrow off to reconcile the disputants. He would do the same with the pigeon, and then tell his slave to bring the letter. The slave on the roof to whom information had come about the affairs of the village to which the visitors belonged would throw him the letter; he would then write one to the chief of the village, attach it to a string and tie the letter to the leg of a sparrow in the manner which we have described, let the sparrow fly up to the roof of the place where the letter would be taken by the slave, who would attach it to the leg of a pigeon, which would bring the letter to the village and reconcile the people of whose dispute information had reached him. The people who belonged to the village when they came out would find that the shaikh's letter had arrived, that the village chiefs had assembled and reconciled the disputants, and here has he (Ibn Shabbās) been coming and telling them! They would not doubt that he possessed mysterious information, and the populace would feel certain of it.[83] Ibn Uqayl proceeds: I have only produced such stories to make it known that these people go so far as to make a mockery of religion, and indeed how can the Code maintain itself under such conditions?

Now this Ibn Shabbās had the *kunyah* Abû'l-Hasan, his name being 'Ali b. al-Husain b. Muhammad al-Baghdādî, and he died in Basrah in the year 444. He, his father, and his father's brother were all resident in Basrah. Their doctrines were concealed from people, the prevailing view being that they followed the Imāmiyyah system of the Shî'ah, the fanatical Bātiniyyah. In my history I have recorded

---

[82] He must mean the village to which his visitors belonged.

[83] It is evident that the account of the trick is confused, and Ibn 'Uqayl's book whence it is quoted is not accessible.

how one of Ibn Shabbās's followers got to understand his treachery and fabrications, which had been kept secret till a member of the Imamiyyah-Batiniyyah sect revealed them. When this man made his revelations one of the things he stated about Ibn Shabbās was the following: One day, he said, when we were with him, he produced a roast kid, which he told us to eat, bidding us break the bone, but not break it up small. When we had finished, he told us to put it back into the oven, which he left covered; after a time he removed the cover, and we found a live kid, eating grass, neither could we see any trace of fire or ashes, nor any remains of the bone. So (said the reporter) I exercised my ingenuity till I discovered the explanation, which was that the oven opened into a cellar, separated from it by a copper plate with a screw. When he wanted to remove the fire from the oven he would give a turn to the screw, when the plate would come down and block up the oven, whereas the cellar would be opened; when he wished to exhibit the fire, he would replace the plate at the orifice of the cellar, so that the fire would be seen.

I would observe that in our own time we have seen a man point to the angels, saying: These are honoured guests, leading one to suppose that the angels had presented themselves, and that he was bidding them approach him. One of our contemporaries, finding a new jug, kept honey in it till the flavour of the honey had sunk into the earthenware. He would then take the jug with him on his travels, and when he dipped it into a river, and gave the water to his companions to drink, they found it had the flavour of honey.

Among all these people, there is not one who knows God or fears censure where He is concerned.[84]

The way wherein the Devil Deludes the Vulgar

We have shown how the devil's power of deluding is in proportion to the power exercised by ignorance; his methods of seducing the unlearned are very various, so that no exhaustive account can be given of his seductions and delusions; they are too many for that. We will only mention with God's help such of the chief categories as will indicate his general procedure.

---

[84] This phrase usually means to do right whatever people might say. Here the sense seems to be quite different.

One such is his approaching the unlearned man and inducing him to think about the nature and attributes of the Deity, so that the man begins to doubt. And indeed, according to a Tradition of Abû Hurairah, the Prophet foretold this. The 'Prophet (he related) said: "You will ask questions, even saying, this Allâh created us, but who created Allâh?—Abû Hurairah said: I swear that one day when I was seated a man from 'Iraq said to me: This Allâh created us, but who created Allâh?—I put my fingers in my ears, then cried out: The Prophet of Allâh spoke truly; Allâh the One, the Only, the Eternal, neither begetting nor begotten, neither hath He any compeer.

There is a Tradition going back to 'Ā'ishah according to which she said: The Prophet said: Verily, Satan cometh to one of you and saith: Who created thee? The man will reply: Allâh—Then he will say: Who created the heavens and the earth?—The man will reply: Allâh,—Then he will say: Who created Allâh?— When anyone of you has this experience, let him say: I believe in Allâh and His Messenger.

I would observe that this trial only comes about through the predominance of sense-perception. I mean, because the man has never seen anything which had not been made. So this unlearned man should be asked: Do you not know that time was created when no time was and space where no space was? If then this earth and its contents are not in space neither is there anything below them, yet your sense rejects this because it is familiar with nothing that is not in space, then He who is not known by sense should not be sought by sense. So consult your intellect, a sound counsellor.

At times the devil deludes the unlearned when they hear the attributes of God, which they interpret in terms of sense, and so are led to anthropomorphism.

At times he deludes them by way of fanaticism. Thus you will find the unlearned man anathematize and take up arms for a cause with whose truth he is not acquainted. The fanaticism of one may have Abû Bakr for its subject, of another 'Ali; many a war has been waged on this subject; it would take long to enumerate the cases of slaughter and incendiarism which have taken place during a long series of years between the residents in Karkh and those of the Basrah Gate on this question.[85] You will find many of these champions wearing silk, drinking wine, and committing murders—acts for which Abû Bakr and 'Ali are not responsible.

At times the unlearned man senses in himself a sort of intelligence, and the devil suggests to him to dispute with his Lord, one asking his Lord why, having foreordained, He punishes, another why He straitens the means of the pious and lavishes on the impious; while some, though grateful for blessings, when trial comes repine and become ungrateful. Some too ask where is the wisdom in demolishing these frames, punishing them with annihilation after their construction? "Some regard the resurrection as improbable. Among these are some who when their schemes fail or they are tried with misfortune become infidel, saying: I do not want to pray! It may happen that an evildoer gets the better of a believer and kills or strikes him, and the unlearned say: The Cross is triumphing, why then should we say prayers, if matters are thus?" The devil makes use of all such disasters to get these people into his power, all through their remoteness from knowledge and the learned; were they to interrogate the learned, the latter would tell them that God is wise and in control, and therewith all objections would cease.

Among the unlearned there are those who are satisfied with their own intelligence and do not mind contradicting the learned. When an opinion of the latter does not suit such a man's purpose he argues against them and insults them. Ibn 'Uqayl used to say: I have lived all these years, and if I were to meddle with the work of an artisan, he would say: You are spoiling my work. Were I to reply that I am a man of learning, he would rejoin: A blessing on your learning, only this is not your business.—Yet his business is a matter for the senses which I could understand were I to handle it, whereas my business is a matter for the intellect; yet when I give him an opinion he will not accept it.

One of the delusions which he practises upon them is their preferring those who make show of asceticism to the learned. Were they to see a woollen garment on a perfect ignoramus, they would respect him, especially if he hung down his head ,and abased himself

---

[85] Karkh was the Shi'ah quarter of Baghdâd. Both these quarters are described at length in Le Strange's *Baghdâd.*

before them. Compare this man, they would say, with that other, the man of learning, who is out for worldly gain, whereas this is an ascetic, who eats neither grapes nor dates, and has never married.— This is due to ignorance on their part of the superiority of learning to asceticism, and to their setting those who make show of asceticism above the Code of Muhammad son of 'Abd Allāh. God was merciful to them in not making them live in the Prophet's time; had they seen him marrying repeatedly, eating chicken, and partial to sweets and honey, he would have won no respect in their breasts.

A further delusion which he practises on them is their finding fault with the learned for doing things which the Code sanctions: a gross form of ignorance. Further they have a partiality for aliens, preferring the stranger to the fellow-countryman of whose ways they have had experience and of whose orthodoxy they are assured: they like the stranger better, though he may be a Bātinî. But one's confidence should be given only to one who is known by experience; God says (iv. 5): *And if ye are familiar with discretion on their part, then hand unto them their goods;* and God to Whom be praise was gracious in sending Muhammad to mankind, in that they were acquainted with his character. He says (iii. 158): *Verily God hath been gracious unto the Believers in that he raised up among them a Messenger from among themselves;* and (ii. 141): *They know him as they know their own sons.*

Respect for the professors of asceticism is carried to such a length by the unlearned that they accept the claims of the former even when they tear the Code to pieces and transgress its ordinances. You will find the hypocrite saying to the unlearned man: "Yesterday you did such and such a thing will befall you" and the man will believe him; he will say. "This man can tell one's thoughts," not knowing that the claim to mysterious knowledge is infidelity. Then they see these hypocrites doing unlawful things, such as fraternizing with women and meeting them in private, but make no objection, permitting them to do as they like.

One of the delusions which he practises on the unlearned is their abandoning themselves to transgression, and when they are reproved talking the language of atheists. Some of them say,—"I am not going to sacrifice cash for credit"— if they only knew it, it is not "cash," because it is forbidden, and there is only choice between cash and credit when both are lawful. Their case is similar to that of an ignorant man suffering from fever, who eats honey, and when remonstrated with says: "Appetite is cash and health credit!" — Further, if they knew the truth of faith, they would be aware that the "credit" is a faithful inviolable promise. And were they to act like traders who risk much money for a small profit which they hope to realize, they would know that what they sacrifice is small, and that for which they hope large. And if they could distinguish between what they have chosen and what they have, forfeited they would perceive that their seizure of something immediate, involving as it does the forfeiture of permanent profit and hurling them into torment, is sheer irreparable loss.

Ignomny of the Mu'tazilite. This latter book was an incisive for Ibn al-Khayyāt to write his *Kitab al-Intisār*, referred to above, an apology of the Mu't'azilite doctrines. This famous work throws considerable light on the dogmas and doctrines of the leading Mu'tazilites living in the second and the third centuries of the Hijra, in as much as Ibn a1-Khayyāt and Ibn Rawandi (to whom frequent references have been made in the *Kitāb al-Intisār)* lived towards the latter half of the third century and were in a personal touch with the followers of the different religious sects of the period.

Although the Mu'tazilite movement is a most rationalistic one in its ideas, yet it cannot be said to be a liberal one in view of the severe persecutions meted out to all those who happened to disagree with it. But it is an undeniable truth, be it said to the credit of the Mu'tazilites that they have been the first to introduce reason into the domain of the religious thinking in Islam. The history of Muslim scholasticism owes its very birth to this mighty movement. Had not Ash'ari been a Mu'tazilite himself, he could not have thought of founding the science of *Kalām,* of which the Muslims are so very justly proud today. By advocating the cause of pure and undiluted monotheism, the Mu'tazilites very ably and successfully fought against the Persian dualism which was manifesting itself in those old times in more ways than one.

CHAPTER III

The Way Wherein the Devil Deludes the Believers in "Shrines"

These are people who assert that every spiritual being of the upper region has a shrine, *i.e.*, one of the heavenly bodies for its shrine, whose relation to the spiritual being belonging to it is that of our bodies to our spirits, so that he (the spiritual being) is its ruler and controller. To the number of shrines belong all the celestial bodies, planets and fixed stars, and these have no access to the spiritual itself. So he approaches his shrine with all sorts of devotion and sacrifice[1]. Others among them say that every celestial shrine has one of the lower individuals in its likeness and of its substance; so they make figures and carve images and build them houses.

Yahya b. Bishr al-Nihawandî states that some maintain that the seven stars (Saturn, Jupiter, Mars, the Sun, Venus, Mercury, and the Moon) are the controllers of this world, and that they proceed by order of "the supreme company" (Surah' xxxvii. 8, xxxviii. 69). They set up images of these in their likeness, and offered each of them the appropriate animal. To Saturn they assigned a huge body of lead, blind, to which a fine bull was offered, being brought' to a chamber excavated, under the image, with a balustrade of iron over the cavity. The bull would be beaten till it entered the chamber walking on the balustrade, through which its forelegs and hindlegs would sink; then fire would be kindled underneath and the animal be burned. The sacrificers would say: Holy art thou; O blind God, whose nature is to do evil, not to do good; we offer unto thee what resembles thee, and do thou accept it, and save us from thy mischief and the mischief of thy foul spirits. To Jupiter they offer a baby boy because they purchase a slave-girl to be violated by the sacristans of the seven images, and when she conceives they leave her till she is delivered,

---

[1] The translation is literal, but the meaning is obscure.

and they bring her carrying the child when he is eight days old; pricking him with bodkins and needles so that he cries in his mother's arms, and they say to the image: O good lord, who knowest no evil; we offer unto thee one that knows no evil, and so is of nature like thine; so accept our offering and bestow on us thy good and the good of thy good spirits. To Mars they offer a man who is ruddy, spotted, with a head in which the white appears through the red; they bring him and put him in a vast tank, fettering him to stakes at the bottom of the tank, which they fill with oil till the man stands therein up to his neck. They mix with the oil drugs such as strengthen, the nerves, but rot the flesh; when a year has passed during which he has been fed on such food as rots the flesh and the skin, they seize his head and wrench the nerves from his skin, and wind them round his head; they then bring him to the image which is in the form of Mars, and say: O evil God; author of troubles and disasters, we offer unto thee what resembles thee; do thou accept cur offering and save us from thy mischief and the mischief of thy evil spirits. They suppose that life remains in the head seven days, and will tell them what good and evil will befall them that year.

To the Sun they offer the woman whose child they have slain for Jupiter, and they carry round a figure of the Sun, saying: Worthy art thou of praise and hymns, O luminous Goddess. We offer unto thee what resembles thee; and do thou accept our offering, and bestow on us thy good and protect us from thy evil.

To Venus they offer a grizzled, dissolute old woman, whom they set before her, crying out all around: O dissolute goddess, we bring thee an offering, white like thyself, dissolute like thyself, humorous like thyself, accept her from us. They then bring firewood, which they place round the old woman, and to which they set fire till she is burned. They then fling the ashes in the face of the image.

To Mercury they offer a lad who is brown, able to count and write, and otherwise educated. They catch him by some wile, and do the like with all their victims. They beguile them, and give them *banj,* and draughts of drugs which destroy their intellects and render them dumb. They present the youth to the image of Mercury, and say: O ingenious God, we bring thee an ingenious individual, being guided by thy nature. Do thou accept from us. The lad is then sawn in two, and then quartered, and set on four pieces of wood round the image;

and these are then kindled so that as they burn the quarters are burned with them. The ashes are then flung in the idol's face.

To the Moon they offer a ruddy man with a large face, saying: O messenger of the gods, and lightest of celestial bodies!

The way wherein he deludes the Idolators

The cause of every affliction wherewith the Devil has confused mankind is inclination to sense and aversion from what reason demands; and since sense finds satisfaction in likeness, the accursed Devil has persuaded many people to worship images; and stopped in their case once for all the operation of the intellect. Some he has satisfied that these only are gods; but, finding in others a little sagacity and knowing that they would not assent to this, he has persuaded them that the worship of these idols will bring them nearer the Creator so that they say *We only worship them that they bring us nearer to God* (Surah xxxix. 4)

The commencement of his deluding the Idolators

The following tradition goes back to Hishām b. Muhammad b. al-Sā'ib al-Kalbi.[2] I was told, he said, by my father that idolatry commenced when Adam after his death had been put by the children of his son Seth in a cave in the Indian mountain whereon he had been made to descend. This mountain is called Naudh, and it is the most fertile mountain on earth. Hishām proceeds: My father informed me after Abû Sālih after Ibn 'Abbās that the children of Seth used to come to the body of Adam in the cave, do it honour, and invoke mercy upon it. Then one of the children of Cain said: Ye children of Cain, see, the children of Seth have a shrine round which they rotate and which they glorify, whereas ye have nothing. So he carved a statue for them, he being the first to do this. My father further informed me that Wadd, Suwa, Yaghûth, Ya'ûq, and Nasr[3] were virtuous men, who all died in one month. Their relatives were distressed concerning them, and one of the children of Cain said: My friends, would you that I should make for you five images in their likeness? Only I cannot put spirits into them. —They said, Yes.—So he carved five images for them in the likeness of these persons and the relatives

---

[2] *Kitāb al-Asnām*, ed. Zeki Pasha, p. 50.

[3] Names of pre-Islamic deities mentioned in the Qur'ān.

would come one to the image of his brother, another to that of his uncle, another to that of his cousin, pay it honour and circle round it; until the first generation had passed away. These images were made in the time of Jared b. Mahalalel b. Kenan b. Knosh b. Seth b. Ādam. Then there came another generation which paid them greater honour than the former. After them came a third generation, who said: Our ancestors can only have paid honour to these images because they hoped for their intercession with God. So they worshipped them, and magnified them, and their infidelity waxed great. God Almighty sent unto them the blessed Idrîs, who called them *to repentance,* but they disbelieved him, and God *exalted him to a high place* (Surah xix. 58). According to the statement of al-Kalbî after Abû Sālih after Ibn 'Abbās their conduct increased in atrocity till Noah grew up, and was given a prophetic mission by God. He was 480 years old at the time, and for 120 years called them to the worship of God Almighty. But they disbelieved and disobeyed him. God then commanded him to build the ark, which he put together, finishing it when he was 600 years old. The people were drowned, and after that he lived 350 years longer. Between Adam and Noah there were 1200 years.[4] The flood tossed these images from land to land, ultimately flinging them on the soil of Jeddah. When the water sank they remained on the shore till the wind covered them over with sand.

Kalbî proceeds[5] Now 'Amr b. Luhayy was a Kāhin, surnamed Abû Thumamah, and one of the Jinn was his familiar spirit. This being said to him: Haste thee and get thee away from Tihāmah with luck and safety, come to the shore of Jeddah, where thou shalt find images ready; bring them down to Tihāmah fearlessly, then call on the Arabs to worship them and they will assent. So he went to the river of Jeddah and unearthed them, carried them to Tihāmah, presented himself at the pilgrimage and called upon all the Arabs to worship them. 'Auf b. Udhrah b. Zaid al-Lāt assented, and to him 'Amr gave Wadd, which he carried off to his home, Wadi al-Qura in Dumat al-Jandal; he named his son 'Abd Wadd, being the first person to bear that name. 'Auf made his son 'Amir priest of Wadd and his descendants continued to worship[6] Wadd till God brought Islam.

---

[4] In the *Kitāb al-Asnām* 2200.

[5] *Kitāb al-Asnām*, p. 54.

[6] In *Kitāb al-Asnām* "to be priests of."

Kalbî adds: I was told by Malik b. Hârithah that he had seen Wadd; my father, he says, used to send me to him with milk, saying give thy god a drink; I would drink it myself. Then, he says, I saw Khâlid b. al-Walid smash it to pieces. The Prophet after the Tabuk campaign had sent him to destroy it, but the Banu 'Abd Wadd and the Banu 'Amir interfered; so Khâlid fought with them and slew them, and knocked the image down and broke it up. On that day he slew one of the Banu 'Abd Wadd named Qâtan b. Shûraih. His mother when he had been slain came forward and said

> That thing, Love,[7] we see, persists not;
>
> Fate destroys and wealth resists not;
>
> Nor doth fate the chamois spare
>
> Spite of mother's tender care.

Then she said:

> O gatherer of entrails and of liver on this earth
>
> Would that thy mother ne'er had born and ne'er
>
> been given birth!

Then she threw herself upon him, sighed, and died.

Kalbî proceeds: I said to Malik b. Hârithah: Describe Wadd to me so that I might seem to be looking thereon.— He said: The statue of a man, as tall as any man that ever breathed. He wore two garments, one an under and the other an upper garment. He had a sword suspended from his neck and a bow over his shoulder, and in front of him a spear with a banner, and a quiver with arrows.

Kalbî proceeds: 'Amr b. Lûhayy also obtained the assent of Mudar b. Nizâr, and gave the idol Suwa' to a man of Hudhail named al-Hârith b. Tamîm b. Sa'd b. Hudhail b. Mudrikah b. Alyâs b. Mudar. It was in a region called Ruhat in the valley of Nakhlah and was worshipped by the Mudarite neighbours. One of the Arabs said:

> Thou seest them stationed round their prince, as
>
> Hudhail takes station round Suwa';
>
> Offerings from the treasures of every shepherd are
>
> all day flung down at his side.

---

[7] The name Wadd means Love, for which a synonym is used here.

Madhhij also assented, and he presented Yaghuth to An'am b. 'Amr the Mudarite. The idol was set up on a cairn in Yemen, where Madhhij and their allies worshipped it.

Hamdān also assented and he presented Ya'ûq to Malik b. Marthad b. Jusham. It was set up in a village called Khaywān, and was worshipped by Hamdān and their Yemenite allies.

Himyar also assented and he presented Nasr to a man of Dhu Ru'ain named Ma'di Kariba. It was set up in a place of the land of Saba named Balkha,' and was worshipped by Himyar and their neighbours. They continued to worship it till they were converted to Judaism by Dhu Nuwās.

These idols continued to be worshipped till God sent Muhammad, who ordered them to be destroyed.

Ibn Hishām[8] says: We were also told by Kalbî after Abû Sālih after Ibn 'Abbās that the Prophet said: I was given a view of Hell, and saw 'Amr b. Luhayy, a short man, reddish blue, dragging his entrails in the fire. I asked who it was. I was told: This is 'Amr b. Luhayy; the first to institute the *bahirah, was'ilah, sa'ibah,* and *hām;* he altered the religion of Ishmael and called on the Arabs to worship idols. I was told[9] by my father and others that when Ishmael came to dwell in Makkah, and children were born to him, who presently became so numerous that they filled Makkah and drove out the Amalekites who were there, Makkah became too small for them. Hostilities and wars broke out between them, and one party was driven out and spread about the country in search of a livelihood. What suggested to them the worship of images and stones was that every emigrant from Makkah would carry with him one of the stones of the sanctuary by way of veneration for it and to retain something of Makkah; wherever they took up their abode they would set up their stone and circle round it as they had done round the Ka'bah; this they did for luck, and retention of the sanctuary and love thereof. They kept up however the practice of revering the Ka'bah and Makkah, and making the greater and the lesser pilgrimage thither, following the footsteps of Abraham and Ishmael. Presently they took to worshipping whatever they fancied, forgot their old cult, and

---

[8] *Surah,* ed. Wûstenfeld, p. 51. *K. al-Asnam,* p. 58.

[9] *K. al-Asnam,* p. 6.

substituted another religion for that of Abraham and Ishmael, worshipped idols, and relapsed into the ways of the nations which had preceded them, restoring the cult of Noah's contemporaries.

Still there were among them relics from the time of Abraham and Ishmael to which they adhered, such as reverence for the House, circling round it, performing the greater and the lesser   pilgrimage, standing at 'Arafah and Muzdalifah, sacrificing camels, and crying out at the commencement of the pilgrimages. Nizar's cry on these occasions was *labbaika, O Allāh; labbaika, labbaika, thou hast no associate save such as hast; thou art his master and master of what he owns.*

The first person who altered the religion of Ishmail[10] and instituted the *sa'ibah* and the *wasilah* was 'Amr b. Rabî'ah, this Rabî'ah being identical with Luhayya b. Hārithah father of Khuzā'ah. The mother of 'Amr b. Luhayy was Fuhairah daughter of Amir b. al-Hārith; al-Hārith being the person in charge of the Ka'bah. When 'Amr b. Luhayy reached maturity he disputed al-Hārith's claim to this office; fought against the tribe Jurhum b. Ishmael, defeated them, drove them from the Ka'bah and banished them from Makkah. He himself undertook to be doorkeeper of the House after them. Presently, he fell seriously ill, and was told that in Balqa' in Syria there was a mineral spring, whither he might go to be cured. He went thither, bathed, and was cured. Finding the inhabitants worshipping images he asked what they were. They said: We ask them for rain and invoke their help against enemies. He requested the people to give him some, which they did; he brought them to Makkah and set them up round the Ka'bah, and the Arabs took to idolatry.

The oldest of these was Manāt,[11] which was set up on the coast near Mushallal by Qudaid between Makkah and Madinah. It was revered by all the Arabs, by the Aus and the Khazraj and all the population of Madinah and Makkah and their neighbours. They sacrificed to it and brought gifts.

Hishām continues:[12] We were told by a Qurashite after Abû 'Ubaidah b. 'Abdallah b. Abi 'Ubaidah b. Muhammad b. 'Ammar b. Yasir as follows; The Aus, the Khazraj, and their followers among

---

[10] *K. al-Asnām*, p. 8.

[11] *K. al-Asnām*, p. 13.

[12] *K. al-Asnām*, p. 14.

the people of Yathrib and elsewhere used to perform the pilgrimage and all the ceremonies except shaving their heads. Only, when they went away they would go to this image, shave their heads before it, and stay by it; they would regard their pilgrimage as incomplete otherwise. Manāt was the idol of Hudhail and Khuzā'ah. God however sent Muhammad, who destroyed it in the year wherein Makkah was taken.

Next[13] they took to themselves al-Lāt in Ta'îf; this idol was later than Manāt, being a square stone. Its priests were of the tribe Thaqif. They had erected an edifice over it, and it was revered by the Quraish and all the Arabs, who gave children such names as Zaid al-Lāt and Tāim al-Lāt. It stood where now stands the left minaret of the mosque at Ta'if. They continued these practices till Thaqif became Muslim, when the Prophet sent al-Mughirah b. Shu'bah, who destroyed it and burned it with fire.

Next they took to themselves al-'Uzza, which is more recent than al-Lāt. The man who introduced it was Zālim b. As'ad; it stood in Nakhlah Shamiyah[14] above Dhāt 'Irq;[15] they built a house, over it and they used to hear a sound proceeding from it.

Hishām proceeds:[16] I was informed by my father after Abû Sālih after Ibn 'Abbās that al- 'Uzza was a female demon who came to three *samurah* trees in the vale of Nakhlah. When the Prophet took Makkah he sent Khālid with orders to go to the vale of Nakhlah, where he would find three *samurahs,* and hew down the first. He did so, and when he came to the Prophet, the latter asked him whether he had seen anything. He said he had not. The Prophet then bade him hew down the second. He went and did so, and when he came back to the Prophet, the latter again asked him whether he had seen anything, and he said he had not. The Prophet then bade him cut down the third, and when he came to it, there was a female Jinni,[17] pulling out her hair and putting her hands on her shoulder, gnashing her teeth. Behind her was Dubayyah the Sulamite, who was her priest. Khālid said

---

13 *K. al-Asnām,* p. 16.

14 According to Yāqut, two wadis belonging to Hudhail two nights journey from Makkah.

15 According to Hamdānî the boundary between Tihāmah, Najd and Hijāz.

16 Ibid., p. 25.

17 In *K. al-Asnam* "Ethiopian."

I praise thee not, but blame thee,

For God, I see, doth shame thee.

Then he smote her and split her head, whereupon she turned into ashes. Then he cut down the tree and slew the priest Dubayyah. He then went and told the Prophet, who said: That was al-'Uzza, and no more shall the Arabs have al-'Uzza.

Hishām proceeds'.[18] Now the Quraish had images both inside and around the Ka'bah, that which they most revered being Hubal. According to my informants he was of red agate, in the form of a man, with his right hand broken; he was found by the Quraish in that condition, and they made him a hand of gold. The first person who set him up was Khuzaimah b. Mudrikah b. Alyās b. Mudar. He was inside the Ka'bah and in front of him were seven arrows: on one of them was written genuine and on the other *suppositicious*. When they were in doubt about the paternity of a child, they offered the idol a gift and then tossed the arrows. If *genuine* came out they affiliated him; if *suppositicious,* they rejected him. When they disputed about anything or intended a journey or any operation; they came to the idol and obtained an augury from the arrows in his presence. He was the deity to whom Abû Sufyān said on the day of Uhud *Magnify,* O *Hual, i.e.,* magnify thy religion. The Prophet said to his companions: Will ye not' reply to them? They asked what they should say. He bade them say: Allāh is higher and more glorious.

They also had Isaf and Na'ilah Hishām says:[19] Kalb'î[20] narrated after Abû Sālih after Ibn 'Abbās that Isaf was a Jurhumite, Isaf b. Ya'la, whereas Na'ilah was the daughter of a Jurhumite named Zaid; he fell in love with her in Yemen; the two came on pilgrimage and entered the House; finding the people inattentive and the House empty, they misconducted themselves in the House, and were transformed *into stone*; the people finding them in this condition removed them from the House, and set them where they stood, where they were worshipped by Khuzā'ah and Quraish, and later Arab pilgrims. Hishām said:[21] When they had been transformed into

---

[18] p. 27.

[19] Ibid., p. 9.

[20] The writer's father.

[21] Ibid., p. 29.

stones they were placed near the House that people might take warning from their fate. Only when they had been there long, and idols were worshipped, they were worshipped also. One of the two was close to the Ka'bah, and the other where Zamzam is. Then the Quraish removed the one that was close to the Ka'bah and put it by the other, and they used to slaughter and sacrifice to them.

One of the images was Dhu'l-Khulasah.[22] It was of white flint, with the form of a crown engraved upon it; it was at Tabalah between Makkah and Madînah,[23] seven nights' distance from Makkah. The tribes Khath'am and Bahilah revered it and offered it gifts. The Prophet requested Jarîr to deliver him from it, and despatched him thither. He marched at the head of the tribe Ahmas, and was opposed by Khath'am and Bahilah; he overcame them and destroyed the edifice of Dhu'l-Khulasah, kindling fire therein. Dhu'l-Khulasah in our time serves as the threshold of the door of the mosque of Tabalah.

Daus had an image called Dhu'l-Kaffain (man of two hands). When the tribe accepted Islam, the Prophet sent Tufail b, 'Amr to burn it.

The Banu'l-Hārith b. Yashkur had an image called Dhu'l-Shard. Quda'an, Lakhm;. Judham, Amilah, and Ghatafan had an image on the outskirts of Syria called al-Uqaisir.

Muzainah had an image called Nuhm; found in the name 'Abd Nuhm.

'Anazah had an image called Su'air.

Tay had an image called Fals.

The inhabitants[24] of every *wadi* in Makkah had an image in their dwelling which they worshipped; and when any of them intended a journey the last thing he did in his house was to rub himself thereon; and when he returned from his journey the first thing he did on entering his house was to rub himself thereon. Some took an edifice *for an idol,* and those who had neither edifice nor image would set up such stone as they approved, and circle round it; they called these *ansab.* When a man was travelling and alighted somewhere, he would take four stones, see which was the finest and make that his lord; the

---

[22] Ibid., p. 34.

[23] The correct reading is Yemen.

[24] Ibid. p. 32.

other three he would make a tripod for his pot. When he went away he would leave it. When he alighted in another place he did the like. When the Prophet got control of Makkah, he entered the sanctuary, where the images were standing round the Ka'bah; he proceeded to thrust the end of his bow into their eyes and faces, saying: The truth is come and falsehood is over. Truly falsehood must perish. Then he ordered them to be thrown on their faces, after which they were removed from the sanctuary and burned. It is recorded that Ibn 'Abbās said: In the time of Yezdajird idols were still worshipped and some people apostatised from Islam.

I was told by Ismā'îl b. Ahmad a tradition which goes back to Mahdi b. Maimun, who said he had heard the following from Abû Raja al-'Utaridi. When the Prophet died and we heard thereof we joined Musailimah the Liar, and we joined Hell. We used in the time of paganism to worship a stone, and when we found a finer stone we would throw the first away and take the other. If we could find no stone we would take a handful of dust, fetch some sheep and milk them over it, and then circle round it. Another tradition reports that the same 'Utaridi said: We used to take sand, put it together, 'and pour milk over it; and worship it. And we used to take a white stone and worship it for a time and then drop it. A tradition which goes back to al-Hajjāj b. Abi Zainab is as follows: I heard Abû 'Uthmān al-Hindî say: In pagan days we used to worship a stone, and we heard a herald proclaim: O ye people of the dwellings, your lord has perished, so seek another. We went forth on every mount, wild or tame and whilst we were thus searching, we heard a herald proclaim: We have found your lord or his like. So we proceeded, and there was a stone, and we slaughtered camels upon it.

The following tradition comes from 'Amr b. 'Anbasah: I was, he said, one of those who worshipped stones, and when the tribe alighted, having no gods, one of them would go out and bring four stones, and place three for his pot, and make of the finest a god to be worshipped. Then he might find one still finer before the tribe started off, when he would leave the first and take the other. The following tradition goes back to a Makkah shaikh: Sufyān b. 'Uyainah was asked how the Arabs came to worship stones and images. He said: The origin of their stone-worship is their saying. The House is of stone, and wherever we set up a stone it will be in lieu of The House. Abû Ma'shar said: Many of the Indians used to believe in a

Supreme Lord, and confess that God had angels; only they used to suppose Him to be a figure of the finest sort; and that the angels were fair bodies but that God and the angels were hidden away in heaven. Therefore, they took to themselves images in what they supposed to be the form of God Almighty, and in that of the angels; worshipped them and made offerings to them, in virtue of what they supposed to be the resemblance. To some of them it was said: The angels, the stars, and the spheres, are the bodies nearest to God, so revere them and make offerings to them. Then they made images.

Many of the ancients built Houses for idols: cne was a House on the top of a mountain in Isfahan, which contained idols, expelled by Gushtasp when he became a Mazdian; he turned it into a fire-temple. A second and a third were in India; a fourth in the city of Balkh, built by Manushihr. When Islam appeared, it was destroyed by the people of Balkh. A fifth was a House in San'a built by al-Dahhāk in the name of Venus; this was destroyed by 'Uthmān. b. 'Affān. A sixth was built by King Qabus in the city of Ferghanah in the name of the Sun; this was destroyed by Mu'tasim.

Yahya b. Bashir b. 'Umair al-Nihawandi states that the Indian Code was made by a Brahmin; he ordained images and erected the finest temple for them at Multān,[25] an Indian city. Therein he set their greatest image which is in form like the greatest Matter.[26] This city was taken in the days of al-Hajjāj and they wanted to wrench away the image. But there was said to them: If you will leave it, we will assign you a third of the money collected for it. So 'Abd al-Malik b. Marwān ordered it to be left, as the Indians made pilgrimages to it from two thousand leagues, and each pilgrim had to bring with him such money as he could afford, from a hundred to ten thousand dirhems, which were respectively the minimum and the maximum permitted. If a man did not bring this with him, his pilgrimage was invalid. He would throw the money into a vast chest that was there, and they would circle round the image. After they had gone the money would be divided, a third going to the Muslims, a third to the repair of the city, and a third to the priests and for the requirements of the temple.

Observation of the author. See how Satan has amused himself

---

[25] The text has been emended. The image is described at length by Ibn Rustah, pp. 135, 599.

[26] The word is likely to be corrupt, Ibn Rustah gives it four faces.

with these people and taken away their intellects, so that they carved with their hands what they worshipped. How well does the Divine Being find fault with their images, when He says: *Have they feet to walk with or hands to handle with or eyes to see with or ears to hear with* (Surah vii. 194). He is pointing to the worshippers, "You walk, handle, see, and hear, whereas the idols are unable to do any of these things, being lifeless matter, whereas you are alive; how then can the perfect worship the defective? Had they reflected they must have known that God makes things, being Himself unmade; combines, but is not combined; things are maintained by Him and not He by them. Surely it befits a man to worship Him who made him, not what he himself has made. As for their fancy that the images would intercede for them, that is a fancy unsupported by any quibble.

The way wherein he deludes the fire-worshippers

The Devil has deluded many people and persuaded them to worship Fire; Fire, they say, is an element with which the world cannot dispense; hence the worship of the Sun found approval.

The historian Tabarî records how, when Cain killed Abel, and fled from his father Adam to Yemen, the Devil came to him and said: Abel's sacrifice was accepted and consumed by fire only because he served and worshipped Fire : so do thou set up a fire which shall be for thee and thy progeny. He (Cain) built the first Fire-temple, and was its first worshipper.

Jāhiz says: Zoroaster, the founder of Mazdism, came from Balkh, and pretended that revelation came to him on the mountain Silan, and called upon the inhabitants of those cold regions who only knew of cold. He threatened them with increase of cold; and he confessed that he had been sent to the mountains only. He prescribed to his followers ceremonial washing with urine and intercourse with their mothers; worship of fire and other ugly things. According to Zoroaster (says Jāhiz) God had existed alone, and when his solitude had lasted long, he meditated, and from his meditation sprang the Devil. When the Devil presented himself before him, he wished to slay him, but the Devil resisted; and when he saw his resistance, he bade him farewell for a period.

The author observes: The fire-worshippers have built many

temples; the first designer of a fire-temple was Feridun, who appropriated a temple to it in Tarsus, and another in Bukhara; Bahman did the like in Sijistan; Abû Qubadh did the like in the neighbourhood of Bukhara; afterwards a number of fire-temples were erected. Zoroaster had made a fire which he asserted had come from heaven, which consumed their sacrifice. His method was to build a temple and set a mirror in the midst of it, and then to wrap the sacrifice in wood and throw sulphur thereon. When the sun was in the middle of the sky it faced a window which he had inserted in the temple, so that the sun's rays entering fell upon the mirror, which reflected them on the wood which took fire. And he told them not to extinguish that fire.

The author proceeds: Further the Devil persuaded some people to worship the moon and others the stars. Ibn Qutaibah says: Some people in pagan times worshipped Sirius, and were devoted to it; Abû Kabshah, whom the pagans made an ancestor of the Prophet, was its first worshipper. He said that this star goes right across the sky, whereas no other star does the like; so he worshipped it, differing from the Quraish. So when God sent the Prophet, and he called people to serve God and abandon the idols, they said. This is the son of Abû Kabshah, meaning that he resembled Abû Kabshah in disagreeing with them, just as the Israelites called Marv Sister of Aaron, meaning resembling Aaron in saintliness. There are two stars of this name, one the above *(Canis Major),* the other *Canis Minor,* which faces it; between the two is the Galaxy. Canis Minor belongs to the stretched out arm in the constellation of the Lion, whereas Canis Major is in Gemini.

The Devil persuaded others to worship the angels, saying they were God's daughters (God be exalted above such notions!). Others he persuaded to worship horses and oxen. The Samiri belonged to a community who worshipped oxen, and that was why he made the Calf. Commentators tell us that Pharaoh worshipped a buck. Among all these there was no one who exercised his thought or made use of his reason to ponder over what he was doing. We ask God to save us in this world and the next.

The way wherein he deluded the Arab pagans

We have already recorded how he misled them to worship images; and his most serious confusion of them in that matter was their imitating their fathers without considering any evidence. As God says: *And when there was said to them Follow what God has revealed, they say: Nay, we will follow what our fathers were in. What, even if their fathers understood nothing and had no guidance!* (Surah ii. 165), *i.e.,* will you still follow them?

Satan also confused a party of them who adopted the doctrines of the materialists, denied the Creator and rejected the Resurrection. These are the people of whom God says *There is only our present life; we die and we live; nothing but time destroys us* (Surah xiv. 23). Also others, who confessed to the Creator, but denied the Prophets and the Resurrection. Also others who said that the angels were God's daughters. He inclined others to Judaism, and others to Mazdism. Such a person was Zurarah b. Jadis among the Banu Tamim) whose father was a chamberlain.

Among persons who confessed to the Creator, to the commencement and the return, and reward and punishment; was 'Abd al-Mûttalib b. Hâshim, and Zaid b. 'Amr b. Nûfail, and Quss b. Sa'idâh, and Amir b. al-Zârib. When 'Abd al-Muttâlib saw a wrongdoer not overtaken by punishment he used to say: By Allâh assuredly beyond this dwelling there is a dwelling wherein the well-doer and the ill-doer will be rewarded. Among these was Zûhair b. Abi Sulma, author of the verse

Put off; yet recorded in writing and hoarded

For day of Accounting, or straightway rewarded

who afterwards became a Muslim. Among these was al-Qalammas b. Umayyah al-Kinani, who used to harangue in the court of the Ka'bah, and the Arabs would not depart from their festivals without a homily from him. One day he said: Ye Arabs, obey me, and we will go right.—They asked what he meant. He said: Ye have separate deities, and I know that God does not approve of all this, and that God is the Lord of these deities, and desires to be worshipped alone. Thereupon the Arabs left him, not listening to his counsels. Among them there were people who asserted that a man over whose grave his mount was tied and left till it perished would be raised mounted thereon, whereas one for whom that had not been done would be raised as a pedestrian. One of the persons who asserted this was 'Amr b. Zaid the Kalbite.

Most of these continued in polytheism, and only a few adhered to monotheism and rejected the idols; of these few were Quss b. Sa'idah and Zaid. The pagans kept on introducing innovations, in numbers, such as " intercalation," which meant sanctifying a profane month and profaning one that was sacred. For the Arabs had adhered to the article of the Abrahamic creed which was the sanctification of four months. When, however, they wanted to profane Muharram for the purpose of war, they would postpone the sanctification till Safar, and so on, so that the year got into confusion. When they went on pilgrimage they would shout: Obedience to Thee, Thou hast no partner except such partner as Thou hast, Thou controllest him and what he controls. Another of their innovations was giving the inheritance to the male to the exclusion of the female; another that when one of them died, his nearest relative had the right to marry his wife. Another was *bahirah, i.e.*, if a camel bore five times successively, the fifth time a female, they would slit its ear, and it was unlawful for the women. Another the *sa'ibah, i.e.*, a camel allowed to go free, being neither ridden nor milked. Another the *wasilah, i.e.*, an ewe, which bore seven times, and whether the seventh was male or female, they would say' it has joined *(wasalat)* its brother," and would not be slaughtered, and was to be used by men only to the exclusion of women; but when it died' both men and women shared therein. Another the *ham, i.e.*, a male which had sired ten times; after which they would say " he has protected *(hama)* his loins," and it would be let loose for their idols, and not employed in carrying. They went on to say that God Almighty had prescribed all this: and this is the import of His words (Surah v. 102) *God has ordained neither bahirah nor sa'ibah nor wasilah nor ham; only the unbelievers father lies upon God.* And again God refutes them in respect of their rendering these creatures sacrosanct or profane saying (Surah vi. 140) *exclusively for our males and forbidden to our wives* 'by His question (vi. 144) *Did He render the two males unlawful or the two females?* The meaning is: If He has rendered the two males unlawful, then all males are unlawful; and if He have rendered the two females, so, then all females are so. And if he have rendered that which the wombs of the females contain unlawful, which may be either male or female, then every embryo is unlawful.

Further the Devil persuaded them to kill their children, so that one of them would kill his daughter and feed his dog. And among. the delusions which the Devil put into their minds was their saying (vi. 149) *Had God so willed, we should not have been polytheists,* *i.e.,* "had He not approved of our polytheism, He would have intervened to prevent it." They fastened on God's will, and neglected the command; God's will embraces all things that come to pass, but His command does not embrace all that He wills. No one has a right to fasten on the will after the command has come down. Many indeed are the foolish doctrines which they invented, which it would be waste of time to record, and which do not require the trouble of refutation.

The way wherein he deludes the deniers of prophecy

The Devil has confused the minds of the Brahmins, Indians, and others, persuading them to deny prophecy, in order that he might block the path which would bring them to God. The Indians differ among themselves, some being materialists, others dualists, some followers of the systems of the Brahmins, while some of them believe in the prophethood of Adam and Abraham. Abû Muhammad al-Naubakhtî records in his *Book of Opinions and Cults* that certain Indian Brahmins acknowledge the Creator, the Apostles, Paradise and Hell-fire, stating that their Apostle was an angel who came to them in human form, without any Book, but having four hands and twelve heads, those of a man, a lion, a horse, an elephant, a pig, and other animals. He bade them revere fire, and forbade slaughter of all kinds, save what was for the fire, and further forbade lying and wine-drinking; on the other hand he permitted sexual promiscuity, and bade them worship kine. If an apostate came back, they would shave his head, beard, eyebrows and eyelashes, after which he would go and prostrate himself before the kine, uttering certain gibberish which it would be waste of time to record.

The Devil put into the minds of the Brahmins six fallacies

The first was rejection of the idea that some among them might have access to information which was hidden from others. So they would say: (xxiii. 24) *This is only a human being like yourselves,* meaning "and how can he have had access to what is hidden from you?" The reply to this fallacy is that if they were to consult their intellects, these would have admitted the possibility of the choice of some individual to possess certain qualities whereby he excelled his fellows, and which would render him fit to receive revelation: since not everyone is suited for this. It is a matter of common knowledge that God Almighty has compounded the constitutions differently, and has brought into existence drugs which counteract bodily mischief that occurs; if then He has supplied herbs and stones with virtues for the cure of bodies created to perish here and to endure in the next world, there is no improbability about His privileging some individual of his creatures with surpassing wisdom and to be His missionary, in order to cure such as are corrupted in the world by immorality and misconduct. It is well-known that our opponents do not deny that certain persons may be privileged with wisdom enabling them to allay the outbursts of evil natures by exhortation: how then can they object to the Creator bestowing on certain individuals messages, talents, and counsels wherewith to cure the world, improve men's characters, and maintain their government? The Almighty has referred to this in His saying (x. 2) *Is it a wonder to men that We have inspired one of them saying Warn mankind?*

Second fallacy. They say: Why did He not send an angel, since angels are nearer to Him, and are less likely to be the object of doubts? Human beings like to lord it over their fellows, and this fact engenders doubt.—The answer to this is in three ways. One is that it is in the power of angels to overturn mountains and rocks, so that they could not produce a miracle which would attest their veracity: for a miracle is a violation of custom, and this is the custom of the angels. A clear miracle is one that is wrought by the hand of a weak human being, proving his veracity. A second, that men incline more to their own kind, whence it is proper that there should be sent to them one of their own kind, that they might not feel aversion, but understand him; further, enabling one of the same kind to perform what the others were unable to perform is a proof of his veracity. A third, that it is not in human power to see an angel; only God Almighty strengthens the prophets with the power of perceiving the angels which He accords them. On this account God Almighty says (vi. 9) *And had We made him an angel We should have made him human; i.e.*, so that they might look on him and associate freely with him and understand him; then He adds *and We should have obscured for them what they obscure, i.e.*, We should have confused for them what they confuse for themselves, so that they would doubt, not knowing whether he was an angel or a human being.

Third fallacy. they say: We see that the things claimed by the Prophets such as knowledge of mysteries, miracles, and revelations communicated to them, are of a sort displayed also by wizards and sorcerers, so that no evidence remains whereby we can distinguish between the sound and the unsound. Our reply to this is that God Almighty has set forth the evidences, and then spread about the fallacies, charging the intellect to distinguish; and a sorcerer cannot revive a corpse nor produce a snake from a staff; and the wizard sometimes proves right, but other times wrong, unlike prophecy which admits no error.

Fourth fallacy. they say: The Prophets must produce either what agrees with the reason or what disagrees with it. If they produce what disagrees with it, it will not be accepted; if they produce what agrees with it, then the reason unaided can do the like.—The answer is: It is certain that many men are unable to deal with worldly matters, and in consequence require someone to supplement them, such as a physician or a Sultan; still more must this be the case with what concerns God and the future world.

Fifth fallacy. They assert that the Codes have produced matters which the reason disapproves: so how can they be sound? Such a matter is the infliction of pain on living beings.—The answer is that the reason dislikes the infliction of pain by animals on one another; but since the Creator has decreed that such infliction should take place, the reason cannot object. This may be explained as follows: The reason knows the wisdom of the Creator; and that it admits of no flaw nor deficiency; this knowledge therefore, enforces on the reason assent to what is hidden from it. If any branch (legislative detail) is obscure to us, we are not at liberty to charge the root (principle of jurisprudence) with futility. Further, the wisdom of this institution is apparent. We are aware that the animate is superior to the inanimate, and that the rational is superior to the irrational, by virtue of the understanding, sagacity, and faculties of speculation and cognizance which have been given to it; there is nothing surprising in the strong taking hold of the weak, or that of which the importance is great doing so to that of which the importance is small; the dumb animal was only created for the benefit of the noble animal, and were the former not slaughtered it would increase to such an extent that pasturage would become scarce, and such animals would die, giving annoyance to the noble animal by their carrion, their existence having been unprofitable. As for the pain inflicted in slaughtering, it is concealed, and some say not felt at all, since what is sensitive to pain is the membrane covering the brain, which contains the sensory organs; and for this reason if that membrane suffers any disaster such as epilepsy or lethargy, the man feels no pain. If the veins of the neck are severed rapidly, the bodily pain does not reach the place of sensation; hence the Prophet said *When anyone of you slaughters an animal, let him sharpen his knife, and make things easy for his victim.*

Sixth fallacy. They say: Probably the givers of the Codes got hold of some properties of stones or wood.—The reply to this is that whosoever utters it ought to be ashamed of doing so. There is not a plant, nor a stone whose properties have not been made manifest, and their secrets revealed. If one of them had got hold of something and manifested its property, those who were acquainted with such properties would have objected, saying "This is not your operation, it is merely a property of such and such an object."[27] Further the miracles are not of one species; but vary from the issuing of a camel from a rock to a staff turning into a snake, or a stone giving forth fountains, or the Qur'ān, revealed not much less than six hundred years ago, perceived by the ears, and pondered by the thoughts, challenging the world to rival it, of which however not one Surah has been approached by anyone. Where then do "properties" and sorcery

---

[27] The object dealt with is that the supposed miracles were natural operations, but of a sort only known to the Prophet who wrought them. The answer is that all the secrets of nature are matters of common knowledge!

and charlatanry come in?

Abû'l-Wâfa' Ali b. Aqil says: The hearts of the heretics were vexed at the spread of the word of truth and the establishment of the Codes among mankind and their obedience to their ordinances; this was the case with such as Ibn al-Rawandî[28] and those like him Abû'l-'Ala;[29] then in addition to that they found that their own doctrines had no vogue nor influence on the contrary the mosques were crowded, and the call to prayer filled men's ears with reverence for the Prophet and confession to the truth of his message, and expenditure of goods and lives on the pilgrimage involving the facing of danger, the endurance of journeys, and separation from wife and children. So some of them began to throw doubts on the transmitters of tradition, vitiate the chains of authorities, and invent biographies and reports; and some recorded thing's resembling the miracles about the properties of stones, violations of natural order found in certain countries, and revelations of mysteries said to have been made by many wizards and astrologers. Such things they strenuously affirmed, as that Satih[30] told that a certain thing that was concealed from him was a grain of wheat in the penis of an ass, and that al-Aswad in his sermons could foretell something that was to occur. And here in our time there are conjurers who talk to the *jinni* who is inside the madman and to whom the *jinni* reveals what has been and what shall be, with other rubbish of the same sort. Now one who sees such things through want of intelligence and inability to see the purpose of the heretics may say: Was not the procedure connected with the prophethoods similar to this? Is not the saying of the wizard "a grain of wheat in the penis of an ass" when the thing had been concealed with the utmost secrecy greater than (Surah iii. 43) "I will announce unto you what ye eat and what ye store in your houses?" So can any more make an impression on the mind, when this horoscope warns against riding on a particular day? And has anyone except the Prophet failed to notice this?

---

[28] See Nyberg's edition of the *Intisar.* Cairo 1925.

[29] Al-Ma'arri.

[30] Pre-Islamic wizard.

Now their object in all this is clear, and their intention obvious. They say (in effect) Come, let us rove over the *countries,* the individuals, the stars and the properties of things, and in all their number we are sure to come across by accident one of these miracles. Everyone will believe in them and in consequence deny that what the Prophets wrought was violation of natural order. Then some Sûfi pretended that someone threw' a vessel into the Tigris which became filled with gold, so such marvels came to count as ordinary "honours" paid by nature to the Sûfis; ordinary forecasts in the case of astrologers, ordinary properties in the case of naturalists; ordinary spells in the case of wizards and diviners. So what force remains to the words of 'Isa "I will announce unto you what ye eat and what ye store in your houses?" And what violation is there, therein of order, seeing that the order of nature is merely the continuance of what exists and frequently occurs?—Now if a wise and pious man point out what is wrong in this, the Sûfi asks: Do you deny the "honours" of the saints? The believers in properties ask: Do you deny the existence of the magnet which attracts iron or the ostrich which swallow's fire? And you are unwilling to deny what has not happened on account of what has happened. Woe to him who speaks the truth with them! The Bātinis are on one side and the astrologers on another and the holders of offices neither bind nor loose save by their word. Praise be to Him who guards this community and exalts its word so that all other communities are under its control. This is how God means to preserve the prophetic office and suppress the dealers in absurdities.

Among the Indians are Brahmins, people whom the Devil has persuaded to curry divine favour by burning themselves. A trench is dug for a man, and people gather together, and the man comes all anointed with *khaluq* and perfume, lyres are played, and drums and cymbals beaten, and they say: Blessed is.this soul which is flying to paradise; and the man says: May this sacrifice be accepted! May my reward be paradise! Then he throws himself into the trench and is burned. If he runs away they ostracize him and outlaw him till he returns. For some of them stones are heated, and the man attaches himself to the stone till it penetrates his body and his entrails come out and he dies. Some of them stand close to a fire till the fat of the body liquefies and they fall; some cut off portions of the shin or thigh and fling them into the fire, while the people are proclaiming their sanctity and admiring them and praying for such rank till the man dies. Some stand in cowdung up to the shin, and set it on fire, wherein they are burned; some adore water, declaring that it is the life of everything, and prostrate themselves before it. For some a trench is dug near water, then the man falls into the trench, until he is ablaze, when he plunges into the water, afterwards returning to the trench till he dies. If he dies when he is between the two his family lament, saying that he has forfeited paradise, whereas if he die in one of the two they testify that paradise is his. Some of them torture themselves with hunger and thirst, till the man is unable first to walk, then to sit down, then loses the power of speech, then his senses, then the power of motion, after which he becomes numb. Some wander about the land till they die; some drown themselves in a river; some have no connection with women, and wear no clothes but a loincloth. They have a high mountain, beneath which is a tree, by which there is a man holding in his hand a book out of which he reads the words: Blessed is he who ascends this mountain, rips open his belly and takes out his entrails with his hand. Some of them take large stones and smash their bodies therewith till they die, the people saying: Blessed art thou. They have two rivers; and on their feast-day some of their devotees go out; and there are men there who take the clothes which the devotees are wearing, rip them open and cut them into halves; one of which they throw into one river and the other into the other; asserting that the two will find their way to paradise. Some go out into the open country accompanied by a number of persons who bless him and congratulate him on his intention; when he is in the uninhabited country, he sits down, and birds of prey gather from every quarter, when the man strips himself of his clothes, and stretches himself out, while the people are looking on, and the birds pounce upon him and devour him. When the birds have scattered; the company approach and take the man's bones which they burn and from which they hope to obtain a blessing; these are only selections from a lengthy series of operations mentioned by Abû Muhammad al-Naubakhtî which it would be waste of time to transcribe. The strange thing is that the Indians are people from whom philosophy and philosophical subtleties are derived, and subtle operations learned. Praise be to Him who hath blinded their hearts so that the Devil thus leads them by the nose. He further states that among them there are people who assert that paradise is of thirty two stages and that the residence of the people of paradise in the lowest stage is 433-620 years; and each stage is the double of that which is lower. Similarly, Hell is thirty-two stages, of which sixteen are forms of torture with cold, whereas the other sixteen are forms of torture by burning.

CHAPTER IV

The Way Wherein the Devil Deludes the Dissidents

The first and most outrageous of the Dissidents was Dhu'l-Khuwaisirah. We have been told by Ibn al-Hasîn by a tradition going back to Abû Sa'id al-Khudrî as follows: 'Alî sent the Prophet from Yemen some gold dust which had not been separated from the soil in a piece of tanned skin; this was divided by the Prophet between four persons. Zaid al-Khail, al-Aqra b. Habis, 'Uyainiah b, Hisn, and 'Alqamah b. 'Ulathah (or 'Amir b. Tufail; the doubt was 'Umârah's, who is one of the chain of reporters. Some of the Companions, the Helpers, and others were annoyed at this. 'The Prophet said : what, ye do not trust me, when I am trusted by Him who is in heaven'! Morning and evening messages come to me from heaven.—Then there came to him a man with deepest eyes, prominent cheeks, projecting forehead, thick beard with his garment tucked up and his head shaven, and said: Fear God, O Apostle of God! —The latter raised his head towards him and said : Ah me, am I not the person on whom it is most incumbent to fear God?—The man retreated, and Khâlid asked whether he should not behead him.— The Prophet said: Perhaps he is praying.— Khâlid said: Many an utterer of prayer says with his tongue, what is not in his heart. The Prophet said: I have no orders to enquire into people's hearts or to split their bellies.—Then he looked at the man, whose eyes showed traces of tears, and said: Assuredly there shall come forth from this man's progeny men who will read the Qur'ān, which however will not go beyond their larynx, and will stray away from religion as an arrows from its mark.

The man mentioned was called Dhu'l-Khuwaisirah the Tamîmîte, and according to one account he said to the Prophet: Deal justly!— The Prophet said: Fie upon you! Who will deal justly if not I? He was the first Dissident who seceded in Islam; and his misfortune was that he was satisfied with his own opinion. Had he paused, he would have known that there is no opinion superior to that of the Prophet. They were followers of this man who fought against 'Alî. For when the war between Mu'awiyah and 'Alî was protracted the adherents of the former raised aloft copies of the Qur'ān and invited 'Alî's followers to abide by their contents. He said: Ye shall send one of·yourselves and we shall send one of ourselves and enjoin them to act according to what is in God's Book.—The people said, We agree, and sent 'Amr b. al-'As. 'Ali's followers told him to send Abû Mûsa. al-Ash'ari; but 'Alî said that he did not approve of appointing Abû Mûsā, and that Ibn 'Abbās was there. They said, however, that they did not want a partisan of 'Ali, so he sent Abû Mûsā, and put off the decision to Ramadān. Then said 'Urwah b. Udhainah: Do ye appoint men to arbitrate in God's affair? There is no judgment but God's! Then 'Alî returned from Siffîn and entered Kûfah, but the Dissidents did not enter it with him, as they went to Harûra, where twelve thousand of them alighted, crying: There is no judgment but God's! This was their first appearance, and their herald proclaimed Shabîb b. Raba'î the Tamîmite battle-commander, and 'Abdallah b. al-Kawwa of the tribe Yashkur leader of prayer. The Dissidents were indeed devout, only their belief that they knew better than 'Ali was a sore disease.

We were told by Isma'îl b. Ahmad in a tradition going back to Simak Abû Zamil that 'Abdallah b. 'Abbās said: When the Dissidents seceded, they entered a dwelling, being in number six thousand, and agreed to go out against 'Ali. Men kept on coming and telling 'Alî that these people were coming out against him, but he said, leave them alone, for I shall not fight them till they fight me, as they ultimately will do. On a certain day I went to him before the midday prayer and said to him: Prince of Believers, put off prayer till later, so that I may visit these people and talk to them.— He said: I fear for you.—I said, Not at all—Now I was a good natured man who never annoyed anyone, and when 'Ali had given me leave, I put on the finest of Yemen robes, started walking and paid them a visit at midday. The people I visited were the most devout I had ever seen; their foreheads were raw from prostrating themselves and their hands as coarse as camel's knees. They wore tunics of cheap material, fucked up, and their faces were wan from sleeplessness. I saluted them, and they said. Welcome to Ibn 'Abbās'! What has brought you?—I said: I have come to you on behalf of the Emigrants and the Helpers, and the son-in-law of the Prophet; to them was the Qur'ān revealed, and they know its interpretation better than you.—One section of them said: Do not wrangle, with Quraish, for God says (xliii. 48) *Nay but they are a wrangling folk.* Two or three of them said: We shall talk with him.—I said: Tell me what you resent in the doings of 'Alî and the Emigrants and the Helpers, the persons to whom the Qur'ān was revealed, not one of whom is among you, and they know its interpretation better than you do.—They said: Three things.—I said: State them.— They said: One is that he made men arbiters in the affair of God, whereas God says (vi. 57) *The judgment is not save God's,* so what have men to do with judgment after what God has said?—I said: This is one, what next?—They said: As for the second, he fought and slew, but neither made captives nor plundered. If they are believers, how is it lawful to fight with and slay them, but not to take them captive?—I said: And what is the third?—They said: He erased from himself the title Prince of Believers; if he is not prince of believers, then he is prince of unbelievers.—I said: Have you anything else?—They said: This is quite sufficient.—I said: As for your talk of the judgment of men in the affair of God, I will read you out of God's Book what will refute that. If it refutes it, will you come back?—They said Yes.— I said: God has transferred some of His judgment to men in the case of a quarter of a dirhem, the price of a hare (and he recited the text v. 96, beginning O *ye that believe, kill not game whilst ye are in the pilgrim state* where the price is to be assessed by two just men, and in the case of a conjugal dispute iv. 39. *And if ye fear a breach between them twain, then despatch an arbiter from his people and an arbiter from hers.* Now I adjure you by God, do ye know the judgment of men for the reconciliation of parties and the sparing of blood to be better or their judgment in the case of a hare or conjugal rights? Which do you regard as the better?— They said: Nay this.—I said: Then have I evaded this?— They said Yes.—I said: As for your saying that he fought, but neither took captives nor plunder, would you take your mother 'A'ishah captive?— If you say She is not our mother, then you have departed from Islam. And if you say We will take her captive and regard as right in her case what we regard as right in the case of other women, then you also have departed from Islam. So you are between two errors; for God says (xxxiii. 6) *The Prophet is nearer to the Believers than their souls and his wives are their mothers.* Have I evaded this? — They said; Yes.—'Then I said: As for your saying that he erased from himself the title prince of Believers, I will bring you an authority which will satisfy you. On the Day of Hudaibiyah the Prophet made peace with the two pagans Abû Sufyân b. Harb and Suhail b. 'Amr, and bade 'Ali write for them a deed. 'Ali wrote *This is whereon Muhammad the Apostle of God made terms,* but the pagans said By Allâh, we do not know that you are God's Apostle; if we knew that, we should not fight you,—Then the Prophet said: O God, Thou knowest that I am God's Apostle; erase it. O 'Alî; and write *This is whereon Muhammad son of 'Abdallah made terms.* Now assuredly the Apostle of God was better than 'Alî and yet he erased the title.

He went on to say that two thousand of them returned whereas the rest seceded and fought against 'Alî.

We were told by Abû Mansûr al-Bazzâr in a tradition going back to Jundub[1] the Azdite who said: When we went off against the Dissidents with 'Alî b. Abî Tâlib, and arrived at their camp, their recitation of the Qur'ân was like the buzzing of bees.

According to another tradition[2] when 'Ali appointed the arbiter there came to him the Dissidents Zur'ah b. al-Burj the Tayite and Hurqus b. Zuhair the Sa'dite. Entering his presence, they said *"There is no judgement save God's."* 'Ali repeated this, and Hurqus said to him: Repent of your sin, repudiate your decision, and lead us out against the enemy whom we shall fight till we meet our Lord; but if thou wilt not give up making men judges concerning the Book of God, I will fight thee, seeking thereby the face of God.—The Dissidents then assembled in the house of 'Abdallah b, Wahb al-Rasibi, who after giving praise to God said: People who believe in the Rahmân and claim association with the judgement of the Qur'ân ought not to give this world, which it is wretchedness to prefer, preference over the enjoining of right and forbidding of wrong and acknowledgement of the truth; so come out with us. —'Alî wrote to them: These two men whom they approved as arbiters have disobeyed the Book of God and followed their fancies, and we adhere to our first course.—They wrote to him: Thine anger was not for thy Lord but for thyself, and if thou wilt testify to thine own unbelief, and

---

[1] Died in the Caliphate of Mu'awiyah (41-60).

[2] Tabari i, 3360.

proceed to repent, we shall consider the relations between us. Else we discard thee altogether.—The Dissidents were met on their road by 'Abdallah b. Khabbab.[3] whom they asked whether he had heard from his father any tradition of the Prophet which he could repeat to them.—He said Yes, I heard him repeating how he had heard the Prophet speak of a civil war, wherein the sitter was better than the stander, the stander than the walker and the walker than the runner. If thou shalt live to witness it, then be the servant of God who is slain.—They said to him: Didst thou hear this from thy father, narrating it as said by the Prophet? He said, Yes.—Then they brought him to the bank of the river and beheaded him, and his blood trickled like a shoelace. They also ripped open his slave girl who was enceinte.

They then alighted under some date-trees that were loaded with fruit, at Nahrawan; a fresh date fell and was picked up by one of them who threw it into his mouth. One of them said to him: Thou hast taken it out of season and without paying a price. Then the man cast it out of his mouth. One of them drew his sword, brandished it, and hit a pig with it by way of testing it. The pig belonged to a member of a protected cult. They said to him: This is doing mischief in the earth. So the man went to see the owner of the pig and paid him what satisfied him. 'Ali sent to them, 'saying: Deliver to us the slayer of Abdallah b. Khabbab.—We are all his slayers, they replied.—He summoned them for three days, and they only repeated the same.—Then 'Alî said: Up and at them!—His followers immediately began slaying them, and during the fight the Dissidents said to each other : Make ready to meet the Lord! This evening to Paradise!—After these another party of Dissidents revolted against 'Alî, who sent troops to fight them. Then 'Abd al-Rahmān b. Muljam met his comrades, who talked of the people of Nahrawan and implored God's mercy on them. They said: By Allāh, nothing will content us with remaining in this world after our brethren who feared no reproach in God's concerns. How would it be for us to sell our lives to God, seek for some other sovereign than these misleaders and demand vengeance of them for our brethren, while delivering mankind from them?

We were told by Muhammad b. Abi Tāhir al-Bazzār in a tradition

---

[3] Tabari i, 3373.

going back to certain teachers of Muhammad b. Sa'd as follows: Three of the Dissidents, they said, responded to the call. 'Abd al-Rahmān b. Muljam, al-Burak b. 'Abdallah, and 'Amr b. Bakr al-Tamîmî. Meeting together in Makkah they made a covenant and a pact that they would slay these three, Ali, Mu'awiyah, and Amr b. al-As, so as to deliver mankind from them. Ibn Muljam undertook 'Ali; al-Burak Mu'awiyah, and 'Amr his namesake. And they bound themselves not to interfere with each other's operations, Ibn Muljam proceeded to Kûfah, and when the night on which he proposed to perpetrate the murder arrived, and 'Alî came out to the morning prayer Ibn Muljam struck him on the brow reaching the crown of the head, and penetrating to the brain. 'Ali bade them see that the man did not escape and he was seized. Um Kulthum said: Enemy of God, thou hast slain the Prince of Believers!—He said: It is only thy father that I have slain. She said: By Allāh, I hope that no harm will happen to the Prince of Believers.—He said: In that case why art thou weeping?—Then he said By Allāh I have been poisoning it (his sword) for a month, and if it have disappointed me, may God cast it away and break it in pieces! When 'Ali died, Ibn Muljam was taken out to be executed, and 'Abdallah b. Ja'far amputated his hands and feet, but the man showed no sign of pain neither did he utter a word. Then his eyes were seared with a heated nail, and again he showed sign of pain, but began to recite (xcvi. I) *Read in the name of thy Lord who created man from a clot* till he finished the Sûrah, while his eyes were oozing blood. Preparations were made to amputate his tongue, and then he showed grief. Asked why, he replied: I hate the thought that I should remain in the world one moment without making mention of God.—He was of a brown colour, with traces of prostration on his forehead. God's curse be upon him!

Now when al-Hāsan wished to come to terms with Mu'awiyah, there came out against him the Dissident al-Jarrāh b. Sinān. He said: You have become a pagan like your father, and thrust him at the edge of the thigh. The Dissidents continued to rebel against the princes, and had various systems. The adherents of Nafi' b. al-Azraq said: We are pagans so long as we remain in the land of the pagans; only when we leave it are we Muslims. Pagans are all who differ from our system, all who commit capital offences, and all who stay away from our battles are unbelievers. These people made lawful the slaughter of women and children of the Muslims and declared them to be pagans. Najdah b. 'Amir al-Thāqafi was one of the Dissidents and he opposed Nafi' b. al-Azraq declaring the lives and goods of the Muslims sacrosanct. He asserted that such of his co-religionists as committed sins would be punished, only not in Hell-fire; that would only be for those who disagreed with his system.

Ibrāhim[4] held that the Dissidents were Unbelievers, only intermarriage with and inheritance from them was lawful, as people were at the commencement of Islam. Some of them held that if a man consumed as much as two *fuls* worth of an orphan's property he incurred Hell-fire thereby. But he would not incur it by killing him, amputating his hands or ripping him open. This was because God had threatened it in the former case.

There are lengthy stories about them and they held strange systems about which I see no occasion to dilate. My purpose is only to glance at the wiles of the devil and the mode wherein he deluded these fools who wrought such mischief and believed that 'Ali and his adherents from among' the Refugees and the Helpers were in error while they themselves were in the right, thought it lawful to slaughter infants but unlawful to eat a date for which they had not paid. True they toiled over their devotions and kept vigil, and Ibn Muljam was distressed at failing to make mention of God. Yet he thought it right to murder 'Alî, and they drew their swords against the Muslims. There is nothing stranger than their satisfaction with their own knowledge and their belief that they knew better than 'Alî! Now Dhû'l-Khûwaisirah said to the Prophet: Deal justly, for thou hast not so dealt. To such atrocities even the devil would not find his way!

We were informed by Ibn al-Hāsîn in a tradition which goes back to Muhammad b. Ibrāhîm that the latter heard the Prophet say: Men shall come forth among you in comparison with whose prayer, fasting, and works you will despise your own; they will read the Qur'ān, but it will not go beyond their larynx. They will go wide of religion as an arrow goes wide of the mark. This tradition is to be found in both *Sahih?*[5]

---

[4] Al-Ibadi.

[5] Bukhari el. Krehl 60§6. Wensinck gives other references.

We were told by Sa'd Allāh b. 'Ali in a tradition which goes back to Ibn Abi Aûfa[6] that he heard the Prophet say: The Dissidents are the dogs of the people of Hell.

It is a doctrine of the Dissidents that the sovereignty belongs of right to no-one unless there are combined in him knowledge and asceticism; when they are combined in an individual he is sovereign even though he be a Nabataean. This suggested to the Mu'tazils their reference of good and evil to the intellect and their doctrine that justice is what the intellect requires. Then there arose the Qadaris in the time of the Companions. Ma'bad al-Juhanî; Ghailān al-Dimishqî, and al-Ja'd b. Dirhām adopted the doctrine of freewill, and the lead of Ma'bad was followed by Wāsil b. 'Atā, who was joined by 'Amr b. 'Ubaid. At that time there arose the system of the Murjites, holding that impiety would do no harm by the side of faith, just as piety would not profit by the side of unbelief. Then such Mu'tazils as Abû'l-Hudhail al-'Allāf, al-Nazzām, Ma'mar, and Jāhiz rɔad the books of the philosophers, and extracted thence material which they mingled with the prescriptions of the Code, such as "substance, accident, time, space and existence," and the first question which they brought to light was their doctrine of the creation of the Qur'ān; and at that time this chapter was called the Chapter of Metaphysics. This question was followed by the questions of the Attributes, such as Knowledge, Power, Life, Hearing, Seeing; some said that these were ideas superadded to the essence, whereas the Mu'tazils denied this, holding that God was Knowing in virtue of his essence, Powerful in virtue of it. Abû'l-Hāsan al-Ash'ārî had at first followed the system of al-Juba'i, but then abandoned it for that of those who maintain *the independent existence of the Attributes.* Then some of the adherent of the latter doctrine began to believe in anthropomorphism, and to suppose that "descending" applied to the Deity meant change of place.

Account of the way wherein he deludes the rejectors

Just as the devil deluded these Dissidents so that they fought against 'Alî, so he persuaded others to go to excess in their love of him. They went beyond all bounds, some maintaining that he is God,

---

[6] Ob. 87.

some that he is better than the Prophets; some were persuaded by him to revile Abû Bakr and 'Umar, indeed even to charge both with infidelity: with other contemptible doctrines which we are unwilling to waste time in recording. We will only allude to some of them. We were informed by 'Abd al-Rahmān b. Muhammad in a tradition which goes back to Abû 'Uthmān al-Mazini,[7] and I heard 'Abd al-Wāhid b.'Alî b. Burhān al-Asadi repeat the same that Ishaq b. Muhammad al-Nakha'i the Red,[8] used to say 'Alî is God. (God is exalted above such ideas!)

In Madā'in there are a number of fanatics known as the Ishāqiyyah, called after this person. Al-Khatib says: There came into my hands a book by Abu Muhammad al-Hasan b. Yahya[9] al-Naubakhti wherein he refutes the fanatics. This Naubakhti was a Shî'i theologian of the Imāmiyyah sect. He mentions the different views of the fanatics, finally saying: Now among those who displayed stark madness in the fanatical cult of 'Ali in our time was Ishāq b. Muhammad known as the Red; he asserted that 'Ali is God Almighty, and that he manifests himself at each time, as al-Hāsan at one time and again as al-Hûsain; and that he it was who sent Muhammad on his mission.

A number of the Rejectors believed Abû Bakr and 'Umar to be infidels; some held that they apostatized after the Prophet's death; some of them repudiated all but 'Alî.[10] We have been told that the Shî'ah demanded of Zaid b. 'Alî that he should repudiate all who opposed the sovereignty of 'Alî but that he refused to do so. Whence they rejected him and were called the Rejectors. Some of them declared the sovereignty to be inherent in Mûsā b. Ja'far, then in his son Alî, then in 'Alî's son Muhammad, then in Muhammad's son Ali, then in al-Hasan b. Muhammad al-'Askari, and then in his son Muhammad, who is the twelfth Imām, who is awaited; they hold that he did not die and that he will return at the end of time and will fill the world with justice. Abû Mansûr al-'Ijli held that Muhammad b. 'Ali al-Bāqir was to be awaited, and that he himself was his deputy. He asserted that he had been raised to heaven and that the Lord had

---

[7] Famous philologist, ob. 248.

[8] Author of a *Kitàb-al-Siràt*.

[9] Mistake for Mûsā.

[10] *i.e.*, of the Pious Caliphs.

stroked him on the head with His hand; and that he was "the piece that was to fall from the sky" (xix. 92).

A section of the Rejectors called Janāhiyyah, followers of 'Abdallah b. Mu'awiyah b. 'Abdallah b. Ja'far "of the two wings" held that the Spirit of God had circulated through the lions of the Prophets till it had come to this 'Abdallah, and that he had not died. A sect called Ghurabiyyah maintained at 'Ali was associated in the prophetic office; and one called al-Mufawwidah (Delegators) held that God having created Muhammad delegated to him the creation of the world. A sect called Dhimamiyyah (Blamers) blamed Gabriel, holding that he, having been told to descend on 'Ali, had descended on Muhammad. Some of them maintained that Abû Bakr had robbed Fātimah of her inheritance. We have heard a tradition that one day when al-Saffāh was preaching a member of 'Ali's family rose up, and said, I am a descendant of 'Alî Prince of Believers' help me against one who has wronged me.—The Caliph asked him who had wronged him.—He said: I am a descendant of 'Alî and the person who wronged me is Abû Bakr, when he took away Fadak from Fātimah. The Caliph asked: And did he persist in robbring you?—The man said, Yes.—The Caliph asked: Who arose after him?—He said 'Umar.—And did he persist in robbing you?—Yes.—And who arose after him?—'Uthmān.—And did he persist in robbing you?—Yes.—And who arose after him?—At this question the man turned in one direction and another trying to find a means of escape.[11]

Ibn 'Aqil observes: The inventor of the Rejectors' doctrine must clearly have intended to strike at the root of religion and prophethood; for the matter produced by the Prophet is something at a distance from us, and we have to rely for it on the transmission of those who preceded us, and the accuracy of their investigations. When anyone in whose piety and intelligence we have confidence has investigated a matter for us, it is as though we had investigated it ourselves. So if anyone says that the first thing they did after the Prophet's death was to rob his family of the Caliphate and his daughter of her inheritance, this must have been due to their want of belief in the deceased; for sound belief, especially in the case of Prophets, would

---

[11] Saffāh's point was that as 'Alî had acquiesced in the robbery, there was nothing more to be said.

involve the observation of their enactments after their death especially in what concerns their families and their offspring. So when the Rejectors say that the people regarded such conduct as lawful after the Prophet's death, our hopes with regard to the Code are disappointed. For between us and it there is only transmission from them and confidence in them. If then this (the robbery) be all that they (the Prophet's family) got after his death, we are disappointed in our expectation that what is transmitted is trustworthy, and we can have no further confidence in that whereon we relied, viz., that we were following persons of intelligence. We have no guarantee that these people having seen reasons compelling them to follow him may not have respected them during his lifetime, but abandoned his Code after his death, only a few of his family remaining in his religion. Thus beliefs will be shaken, and the mind will have no courage to accept the traditions concerning the basis of belief, *i.e.,* the miracles. And this will be most disastrous for the Code.

Now the fanatical love of 'Alî cherished by the Rejectors led them to fabricate a number of traditions concerning his "virtues," most of which rather do him discredit and injury. I have mentioned a number of them in my book of *Fabrications.* One is that the sun set, and 'Alî missed the afternoon prayer, whereupon the sun came back for his benefit. Now this is to be rejected from the point of view of transmission, as no trustworthy authority records it; and from the point of view of the sense absurd.[12] The time having gone by, even supposing that a fresh rising brought the sun back, the time will not have been brought back. Similarly they fabricated a tradition to the effect that Fâtimah washed herself, then died, having given instructions that. That washing should suffice. From the point of view of transmission this is a fiction, and from that of the sense stupid. For the washing is due to the impurity caused by death, so how can it be valid before death?

They have besides various romances for which they furnish no support; legal principles which they have invented, and romances which contradict what is accepted by consensus. I have copied certain of their questions from the writing of Ibn 'Âqil, who states that he copied them from the treatise of al-Murtada concerning the

---

[12] The text here is confused, but the sense, given seems to be what the author intended.

opinions peculiar to the Imāmiyyah. One is that prostration is not permissible on what is not the earth or vegetation growing thence; not therefore on wool, hide or fur. That the use of pebbles as a detergent is sufficient in the case of excrement but not in the case of urine. That to satisfy requirements the head must be rubbed with such moisture as remains in the hand, and that the hand must not be wetted afresh for the purpose; if the hand is dry, the whole process of washing must recommence. Another view peculiar to them is that an adulterer may never marry the married woman with whom he has committed the offence, even though her husband divorce her. They forbid marriage with women belonging to the tolerated religions. They hold that if divorce be made dependent on a condition it is not to be carried out even if that condition be fulfilled. That divorce to be legal must be in the presence of two approved witnesses. That if a man miss the later evening prayer by falling asleep till past midnight, he must when he wakes make compensatory performance, but fast next morning by way of atonement for his omission. That if a woman shave her hair, she must make the same atonement as for unintentional homicide. That one rends his garment for the death of a son or a wife must make the same atonement as for perjury. That if a man unknowingly marry a woman who has a husband already, he must pay five *dirhāms* in alms. That one who has twice suffered chastisement for wine-drinking must suffer death for a third offence. That the beer-drinker is to be chastised like the wine-drinker. That a thief's hand should be amputated from the roots of the fingers, the palm being left him; but if he steal a second time, his left foot shall be amputated. If he steal a third time he shall remain in prison till he dies. They regard the fish *jirri* as unlawful food,[13] as also what is slaughtered by "the People of the Book." They make it a condition of slaughtering that the Qiblah must be faced.

These are a few out of many questions which it would take long to recount wherein they go against the consensus of authorities, and which they were persuaded by the devil to settle without support from either tradition or analogy, but only from their own fancies. Indeed the atrocities of the Rejectors are innumerable. They have forfeited prayer by failing to wash their feet when they purify, and the community by seeking for an infallible Imām, and are afflicted with

---

[13] Jahiz, *Hayawani*. 111, l.4 alludes to this. The fish is not identified by the lexica.

the practice of reviling the Companions. In the two *Sahih* there is a tradition that the Prophet said *Revile not my Companions. For though one of you were to spend a mass of gold as great as Uhud he would not attain their measure nor the half thereof.* We have been informed also by Muhammad b. 'Abd al-Malik and Yahya b. 'Alî in a tradition which goes back to 'Abd al-Rahmãn b. Sãlim b. 'Abdallah b. "Uwaim b. Sa'idah that the Prophet said *God has chosen me and chosen companions for me, and made of them ministers, helpers and sons-in-law for me; on anyone who reviles them there is the curse of God, and the angels and all mankind. God will not accept from such an one on the day of the Resurrection any discharge of duty or act of supererogation* (this is in my opinion the sense of the terms employed).

We have been informed by Abû'l-Barakat b:' 'Ali al-Bazzãr in a tradition going back to Suwaid b. Ghafalah[14] that he said: I passed by some Shi'ites who were attacking and beletting Abû Bakr and 'Umar, and then went to 'Alî b. Abi Tãlib and said to him: Prince of Believers, I have been passing by some of your followers who were speaking unworthily of Abû Bakr and 'Umar if they did not suppose that you harbour the same sentiments about the two which they manifest, they would not venture to do this.— Alî replied: God forbid! God forbid that I should harbour any sentiment about them other than that which the Prophet entrusted to me; which is: *May God curse him who harbours any sentiment about them that is not handsome and kindly! They are the Prophet's brothers, companions, and ministers. God's mercy on them!* Then he rose up with tears in his eyes, and holding my hand proceeded to the mosque, where he mounted the pulpit, and sat down firmly upon it, holding his beard and looking at it, it being white; then, when the people were assembled, he stood up, recited the Creed and preached a short and eloquent sermon; then he said: How is it that certain persons use about the two princes of the Quraish and fathers of the Muslims language from which I not only dissociate myself absolutely, but which I shall punish? By Him who split the grain and created the soul none love those two save pious Believers, and none hate them save wretched miscreants. They accompanied the Prophet loyally and sincerely, ordering and forbidding, displaying anger and inflicting

---

[14] Ob. 30 or 31.

punishment, in nothing that they did going beyond the Prophet's opinion, who too held the same opinions as they, and loved no-one as he loved them. The Prophet passed away well-contented with them; and they passed away enjoying the Muslims' approval. Abû Bakr was given by the Prophet leadership of prayer, which he exercised for nine days during the Prophet's lifetime, and when God took the Prophet away, choosing for him what was with Himself, the Muslims assigned to him the same office, then gave him charge of the alms, and presently made him their sovereign, of their free will and with no compulsion. I was the first of the family of 'Abd al-Muttalib to prescribe this for him, against his wish, as he would have preferred that someone else should have undertaken it in lieu of himself. He was indeed the best of those whom the Prophet had left behind, the most merciful and kindly, the most temperate, the oldest and the earliest to accept Islam. He was compared by the Prophet to Michael for his kindliness, to Ibrāhîm for his dignity and readiness to forgive. He followed the conduct of the Prophet and passed away while doing so, God's mercy on him! Then the government was undertaken by 'Umar after him, I being one of those who approved. He maintained it in the style of the Prophet and his successor, following their footsteps as a foal follows those of his dam. He was assuredly kindly and sympathetic with the weak, helping the injured against their injurers. No censure ever affected him in God's cause, who caused his tongue to utter justice, and made truth his business. So much so that we used to fancy an angel was speaking with his tongue. God made Islam powerful through his acceptance of it, and made his migration a mainstay of Islam, throwing fear into the hearts of the hypocrites; and producing affection in the hearts of the believers. The Prophet compared him to Gabriel for his sternness and severity against the enemies; who can find for you anyone comparable to these two? God's mercy be on them, and may He grant you to walk in their path! If anyone loves me, let him love them, and whosoever loves them not hates me and I repudiate him. Had I previously given you instructions concerning them, I should have inflicted severe punishment for this; but assuredly if after this day anyone is reported to me as having talked in this way, he shall suffer the same penalty as those who fabricate. Most assuredly the best of this community after its Prophet are Abû Bakr and 'Umar. God knows who is the next best. I say these words and ask God's forgiveness for myself and you.

We were informed by Sa'd Allāh b. "Alî in a tradition going back to Abû Sulaiman al-Hamdânî[15] that 'Ali said: There shall come forth in the latter days a party nicknamed. The Rejectors who shall lay claim to our party (the Shî'ah), to which they will not belong; the sign thereof is that they revile Abû Bakr and 'Umar. Slaughter them relentlessly wheresoever ye find them, as they are polytheists!

Account of the way wherein he deludes the Bātiniyyah

These, are people who shelter themselves in Islam, being inclined to "Rejection;" their beliefs and their acts are in contradiction to Islam. The substance of their doctrine is to render the Creator ineffective, to nullify prophethood and religious rites, and to deny the Resurrection. They do not at the first openly avow this, but assert that God is true, that Muhammad is God's Apostle, and that religion is sound; however they hold the other view secretly, not openly. The devil has amused himself with them, going to all lengths, and persuaded them of various opinions. They have eight names.

First *Batiniyyah* (Esoterists). They are so designated because they maintain that the literal expressions of the Qur'ān and the Traditions have hidden meanings whose relation to the literal expressions is that of the kernel to the shell. By their form they suggest to the ignorant certain plain forms, whereas to the intellectual they are hints and indications of hidden realities. So the person whose mind is reluctant to dive for the hidden mysteries in the depths and is satisfied with the literal expressions is under the yokes which are the ordinances of the Code; whereas if one has ascended to the knowledge of the esoteric, these ordinances fall off him and he is relieved of their burden. According to them these are the persons meant in the text (vii. 156). *And he shall put off from them their bond and the yokes which were upon them.* Their purpose is to remove from the beliefs what their letter enjoins in order that they may annul the Code by arbitrarily pronouncing it to be false.

Second name *Isma'iliyyah*. They take this name from one of their leaders Muhammad b. Ismā'il b. Ja'far, to whom they hold that

---

[15] The *Lisan al-Mizan* is unable to identify him.

the sovereignty came round; he being the seventh. They argue that the heavens are seven, the earths seven, and the weekdays seven; which indicates that the round of sovereigns is complete in seven. Hence in the case of al-Mansûr they enumerate al-'Abbās, his son 'Abdallah, his son 'Ali, his son Muhammad, then Ibrāhîm, then al-Saffah, then al-Mansûr. Abû Ja'far al-Taba'rî[16] records in his Chronicle that 'Alî b. Muhammad said on the authority of his father that one of the Rawandiyyah, a leper called al-Ablaq talked extreme Shi'ism, and invited the Rawandiyyah to adopt it. He asserted that the Spirit which had been in 'Isa b. Maryam had come to 'Alî b. Abi Tālib, and then to the other Imams one after another down to Ibrāhîm b. Muhammad. They abrogated the laws of morality; cne of them would invite a number to his house, give them food and drink and then offer them his wife. Asad b. 'Abdallah hearing' of this executed and impaled them. Their practice however continued up to this (Tabarî's) time, they worshipped Abû Ja'far (al-Mansûr), climbed high into the air and flung themselves into it as though they would fly, but died before they reached the ground. A number of them came out in arms against the people and started shouting at Abû Ja'far *Thou art thou.*

The third name is *Sab'iyyah* (Seveners), for which there are two reasons. One, their belief that the cycle of sovereignty is in sevens as we have explained, and that arrival at the seventh is the termination of a cycle, and that is meant by the Resurrection, there being no end to the succession of cycles. The second, their holding that the government of the lower world depends on the seven stars, Saturn, Jupiter, Mars, Venus, the Sun, Mercury, the Moon.

The fourth name is *Babakiyyah,* and belongs to a section of them who are adherents of a man, named Babak al-;Churrami, who was one of the Bātiniyyah. He was a bastard, and came forward in a mountainous region of Adharbaijan in the year 201; he was followed by a large number of persons, whom he rushed; he gave permission for illicit things, and if he learned that any man had a beautiful daughter or sister he demanded her; if the man sent her, well and good: otherwise he would put the man to death, and seize her. He kept this up for twenty years; during which he put to death eighty (according to others fifty-five) thousand, five hundred men. He made war on the government and routed several armies, till al-Mu'tasim sent Afshin

---

[16] Ed. Leiden iii. 418.

to fight him; Afshin brought Babak and his brother captive in the year 223. When they were introduced Babak's brother said to him, Babak, you have perpetrated what no-one else has, so now display endurance such as no-one has displayed. He replied: You shall see what my endurance will be like.—Al-Mu'tasim ordered his hands and feet to be amputated. When this was done he smeared his face with the blood. Al-Mu'tasim said: You, so brave a man, how comes it that you are smearing your face with the blood ? Is it for fear of death?—He said: No; but when my extremities were amputated I suffered loss of blood, and was afraid it might be supposed that the paleness of my face was due to fear of death. So I covered my face with blood so that this should not be seen.—After that he was beheaded, and fire was set to the corpse, and the like was done to his brother. Neither of them uttered a cry or a lament, or displayed any pain. God's curse on both of them!

Some of the Babakiyyah still exist, and it is stated that on a certain night of the year the men and women assemble, extinguish the lights, when the ' men proceed to rape the women; they hold that the chase is lawful and that they are exercising the right which it gives.

The fifth name is *Muhammirah* (the Reds), so-called because they dyed their garments red in the days of Babak, and wore such.

The sixth name is *Qarmatians,* about the origin of which the historians take two different views. One of these is that a man from the region of Khuzistan came to the arable land of Kufah, made profession of asceticism, and urged the claims to the sovereignty of a member of the Prophet's house. He lodged with a man named Karmitah so nicknamed because of the redness of his eyes; the word meaning "sharpeyed " in Nabataean. The man was arrested by the governor of the district and imprisoned; but he left the key of the room under his head, when he went to sleep, and a slave girl who had pity on the man took the key, unlocked the room, let the man out, and returned the key to its place. When the man was sought and could not be found people's delusion about him increased. He went off to Syria, where he took the name of his host, Karmitah, which he presently abridged to Qarmat. His functions were inherited by his family and his descendants.

The second opinion is that the name was given to these people after a man named Hamdan Qarmat, who was one of their first missionaries; a number of people were converted and were called Qarāmitah or Qarmatiyyah. The man himself was of Kufah, and inclined to asceticism; meeting on a road one of the Bātini missionaries, who was driving some cattle in the direction of a village he asked this driver, whom he did not know, whither he was going. The man mentioned Hamdan's village. Hamdan said to him: You had better mount one of the herd or you will be tired. —The man replied: I have not been ordered to do so.—Apparently then (said Hamdan) you only act under orders.—The man said, Yes. —Then by whose order (asked Hamdan) do you act?—He said: By the orders of my master and yours, the master of this world and the next.—You mean (said Hamdan) God, the Lord of the worlds.—You are right, he replied.—Then what (asked Hamdan) is your purpose in the village whither you are making?—I have been ordered (he replied) to call its inhabitants from ignorance to knowledge, from error to guidance, from misery to happiness; to rescue them from the abysses of degradation and poverty, and put them in possession of what will render them independent of toil.—Hamdan said to him: Rescue me (may God rescue you!) and shed on me such light as will vivify me; how much I need the like thereof!—I have no orders (the man replied) to divulge the hidden mystery to anyone till I have confidence in him and can covenant with him.—State your covenant (said Hamdan) for it will be binding on me.—It is (said the man) that you shall give me and the sovereign an oath by God that you will not divulge the secret of the sovereign which I will communicate to you or my secret either. —Hamdan took the oath, and the missionary proceeded to instruct Hamdan in the various departments of his nescience, till he had led him quite astray and obtained his assent. Hamdan then himself became a missionary and indeed one of the founders of the heresy; and his followers were called Qarmatiyyah or Qaramitah. His functions were inherited by his family and his descendants, one of the most energetic among them being a certain Abû Sa'îd, who came forward in the year 286, became mighty, slaughtered innumerable victims, destroyed mosques, burned Qur'āns, assaulted the pilgrims, and made laws for his family and his companions, to whom he told various absurdities. When he went to battle he would say that he had been promised victory at this hour. When he died, a dome was built over his tomb, at the top of which they placed a bird made of gypsum; when this bird flies, they said, Abû Sa'îd will come forth out of his tomb. By the tomb they placed a horse, a suit of clothes and arms. The devil had persuaded these people that if there was a horse by the tomb of a dead man, he would be raised up riding; whereas if there were no horse, he would be raised walking. The followers of Abû Sa'îd used when they mentioned him to invoke God's favour upon him, but not when they mentioned the Prophet; saying: What, shall we eat the food of Abû Sa'îd and invoke God's favour on Abû'l-Qâsim?

Abû Sa'îd was succeeded by his son Abû Tâhir, who acted like his father, attacked the Ka'bah, seized the treasures which it contained, prised out the Black Stone and took it to his own town, making people suppose that it was God Almighty.

Seventh name *Khurramiyyah. Khurram* is a Persian word signifying something pleasant and agreeable, such as gives satisfaction. The purpose of this appellation was to give people power to pursue pleasures and gratify passions in anyway whatever, setting aside injunctions and removing the burdens of the Code from mankind. This had been a designation of the Mazdakites, who were Magian libertines followers of Mazdak in the days of Qubadh, and annulled restrictions on marriage, as well as all other moral restraints. Their name was given to the sect with which we are dealing because it resembled them in the consequences of the system though it differed in the premises.

Eighth name *Ta'limiyyah* (Instructionists) given them because their first principle was rejection of opinion and injuring the employment of the intellect, bidding people take instruction from the infallible Imâm, knowledge being obtainable only by such instruction.

Account of the cause which led people to involve themselves in this heresy

You are to know that the people wanted to slink out of religion, and consulted various Mazdians. Mazdakites, Dualists, and heretical philosophers, asking them to evolve some method which would ease them from the control of the religious, who had made *them keep* silence about their own beliefs, such as denial of the Creator, rejection of the Apostles, and disbelief in the Resurrection; and their view that the Prophets were charlatans and impostors. They found that the doctrine of Muhammad had spread far and wide in the regions, and that they were unable to resist it. So they said: Our best plan is to adopt the belief of one of their sects, the subtlest, the most befogged, and the readiest to accept absurdities and to believe falsehoods—these are the Rejectors; we will fortify ourselves by assuming their name, and endear ourselves to them by deploring the injuries and humiliation which have befallen the family of the Prophet, so that it will be possible for us to revile the ancients who transmitted the Code to them. Once these become contemptible in their eyes, they will pay no attention to what they transmitted, and it will be possible for us gradually to seduce them from the religion. Should any remain among them who cling to the literal expressions of the Qur'ān and the traditions, we shall make them understand that those expressions hide certain mysteries; that the person who is deceived by the literal expressions is a fool, whereas sagacity consists in believing their hidden sense. We shall then communicate our own beliefs to them, asserting that they are what is meant by the literal expressions which they possess; if we augment our numbers with these, it will be easy for us gradually to gain over the rest of the sects. They then said: Our plan will be to choose a man who will help our system, whom we shall declare to be one of the Prophet's house, whom everyone ought to follow, and whom it is their duty to obey, inasmuch as he is the representative of the Prophet, preserved by God from all error or failing. Next, this summons must not be issued in the near neighbourhood of the Representative whom we have designated as infallible; for near neighbourhood pierces the veil, whereas if long distance intervene one who responds to the invitation cannot investigate the character of the Imām or ascertain the truth about him. Their design in all this is power and mastery over men's possessions; further to avenge themselves for the shedding of their blood and the despoiling of their goods in former times. This is the end at which they aim and the principle on which they started.

They have expedients for seducing people, and distinguish between those whom they can hope to mislead and those whose case is hopeless. If they are hopeful about anyone, they study his character; if he have a tendency towards asceticism they call on him to be loyal, veracious, and continent: if he have a tendency towards debauchery, they assure him that devotion is stupidity and chastity folly; sagacity, they tell him, consists in seeking pleasure out of this transitory world. To each person they affirm what is agreeable to the system which he holds; they then suggest doubts about his beliefs. The people who respond to them are either fools or descendants of the Sasanian kings and Mazdians the empire of whose ancestors was terminated by that of Islam, or people anxious for power but unbefriended by fortune to whom they promise the realization of their hopes: or someone, who would like to raise himself above the vulgar level and cherishes the idea of initiation into realities: or a Rejector whose religion involves reviling the Companions: or some heretical philosopher, dualist, or person bewildered about eligion; or some individual whom love of pleasure has enslaved, and who finds the prescriptions of the law irksome.

Specimens of their doctrines

Abû Hamid al-Tûsi[17] says: the Bātiniyyah are people who profess Islam, and are inclined to Rejection; but both their beliefs and their practices conflict with Islam. One of their doctrines is the existence of two gods, from eternity, their existence having no commencement in time, only one of the two is the cause of the existence of the second. The prior of the two ought not to be described as existent or non-existent, being neither, also being neither known nor unknown, neither possessing attributes nor lacking them. From the prior there arose the latter, who is the first created being, then there arose the universal soul. According to them, the Prophet is an expression for an individual on whom a pure and saintly faculty has emanated from the prior through the medium of the latter; Gabriel, they hold, is an expression, for the intelligence which descends on him (the Prophet), not for an individual. They are agreed that there must be in every age an Imām who is infallible; maintaining the truth, to whom resort should he made for the interpretation of the literal expressions, equal to the Prophet in infallibility. They reject the " return " (in the sense of the Resurrection), holding that return means the return of a thing to its origin, and that the soul will return to its origin. As for the prescriptions of the law, it is reported of them that they waive them altogether, and permit all forbidden things; only when this is stated concerning them, they deny it, avowing that there must be such prescriptions for a human being, only he is released from them when he becomes acquainted with the hidden meaning of the literal expressions. Being unable to divert people from the Qur'ān and the

---

[17] Better known as Al-Ghazzali.

Sunnah, they diverted them from their meanings to fictions of their own devising: had they openly rejected them, they would have been executed. So they say the meaning of *uncleanness* is premature divulging of the mystery to a neophyte: of *ablution* renewal of the covenant to a person who has done this: of *adultery* communicating the seed of esoteric knowledge to one who has not previously entered into the covenant: of *fasting* abstaining from revealing the mystery. The *Ka'bah* is the Prophet: the *Door* is 'Alî: the *Deluge* is the deluge of knowledge wherein the adherent to fallacy is drowned: the *Ship* is an amulet which protects him who responds to their call. The *Fire of Ibrahim* is an expression for the wrath of Nimrod, nor for any actual fire; the *Sacrifice of Isaac* means taking the covenant: the *Rod of Moses* means his argument; *Yajuj and Majuj* (Gog and Magog) are the literalists.

Other authors assert that according to them when God created the spirits, He showed Himself among them, so that they had no doubt that He was one of themselves, but presently they recognized Him, the first who did so being Salman al-Fārisi, al-Miqdad[18] and Abu Dharr; the first of those who failed to do so and is called Iblîs, was 'Umar b. al-Khattāb, with other—absurdities which precious time should not be wasted in enumerating.

Now people of this sort are not attached to some fallacy, so that they can be argued with; they merely invent out of their own fancies what they please. If discussion with one of them should come about, he should be asked: Do you know these things which you assert necessarily or by study, or by transmission from the infallible Imām?— If he reply Necessarily, How then (we ask) is it that persons of sound intellect disagree with you? 'Further if a man might so glibly claim necessity for anything that he fancied, it should be possible to silence him by claiming necessity for what contradicts his claim.— If you say By study—study (we answer) is with you valueless; for that is controlled by the reason, and with you reason is untrustworthy.—If you say From an infallible Imām we answer: What is it that induces you to accept his words without a miracle, and abandon the words of the Prophet in spite of miracles? Further how can you be sure but that what has been heard from the infalliable Imām may not have some hidden sense other than the literal?

---

[18] Ob. 33. Associated with 'Alî and these are four persons love of whom was enjoined by the Prophet.

Next they may be asked: Should these hidden senses and explanations be concealed or revealed?—If they say Revealed, then we ask: Why did Muhammad conceal them?—If they say Concealed, we ask:' How then can it be lawful for you to divulge what the Apostle had to conceal?

Ibn 'Aqil says: Islam has come to grief between two sects, the Esoterists (Bātiniyyah) and the Literalists. The Esoterists abrogate the literal sense of the Code by the interpretations which they claim to give, for which they have no evidence: so much so that there is nothing left in the Code to which they do not assign a hidden meaning, causing the obligatory to be non-obligatory, and the forbidden to be non-forbidden. The Literalists, on the other hand, take hold of everything according to the literal expression even where there must necessarily be an explanation that is not the literal sense. The truth is between these two positions, which is that we should accept the literal sense where there is no evidence to divert us from it, and reject every hidden meaning where the Code furnishes no evidence for its existence.

Were I to meet the head of the sect called Bātiniyyah, I should not tread with him the path of knowledge, but that of rebuke and scorn for his intellect and those of his followers. I should say to him: Hopes have certain paths that they can tread and destinations which they can reach; and it is folly to place hope where despair should be placed. Now of all the sects which have covered the earth the most plausible is that Islamic system, which you profess, which you are anxious to ruin. It has obtained such hold that the desire to weaken it, let alone to destroy it, is folly. Each year it has an assembly at 'Arafah, each week in the cathedrals, each day in the mosques. When then can you aspire to render turbid this swelling ocean, to eclipse this brilliant phenomenon? Over the quarters of the globe each day thousands of us hear the call to prayer with the words *I attest that there is no god but God and that Muhammad is the Apostle of God.* The utmost that you can attain is a private conversation, or the commander of a fortress, who, if he utter a word is slain like a dog and is flung away.[19] When can a sensible man hope that your system will prevail over this catholic system which covers the countries? I know of no one more foolish than you. *This will be my line* till he comes to discussion with rational proofs.

---

[19] This passage appears to be defective.

In the year 474 the fuel of the later Bātiniyyah burst into flame, and the Sultan Jalāl al-daulah[20] executed a number of them when he had obtained knowledge of their system: the number of persons executed exceeded three hundred. Their property was examined, and it was found that one of them had seventy rooms filled with embroidered rugs, about which he wrote a letter to the Caliph, who ordered that any person supposed to hold this doctrine should be arrested, and no-one ventured to intercede on behalf of any of them for fear of being supposed to have an inclination towards it. This led the populace all the more to persecute anyone whom they wished, and it came to pass that any man who harboured a grudge against another would charge him with being an adherent of the doctrine, would, arrest him and pillage his goods.

The first that was known of the doings of the Bātiniyyah in the days of Malik Shāh Jalāl al-daulah was that they met for the prayer of the Feast at Sawah; the police official learned about them, arrested and imprisoned them, and then released them. Then they assassinated a Muedhdhin of Sawah, whom they endeavoured to proselytize; when he refused; they, fearing that he might delate them, put him to death treacherously. The matter came to the ears of Nizām al-Mulk who ordered the arrest and execution of the man suspected of the murder. He was a carpenter. Their first murder of consequence was that of Nizām al-Mulk; they used to say: You slew one of our carpenters and we have slain in retaliation Nizām al-Mulk. Their movement acquired serious proportions in Isfahān, and when Malik Shāh died things reached such a pitch that they would kidnap a man, murder him, and fling him into a well, and people began to despair about anyone who had not returned home when afternoon approached. They examined various places, and found a woman lying on matting and never moving; they removed her and found underneath the matting forty corpses. They killed the woman and burned the house and the whole quarter. A blind man used to sit at the gate of the street in which this house was. He would ask a passerby to lead him a few steps to the street; when the passenger had got within it, the people of the house would pull him and get him in their power. The Muslims of Isfahān made a keen search after them and slew a great number of them.

---

[20] Malik Shāh, whose title was Jalāl al-din is meant.

The first fort of which the Bātiniyyah got possession was one in a Dailemite district called Rudhbar;[21] it had belonged to Malik Shāh's friend Dumah, who when he had been put in charge of it had been suspected of adherence to these people's doctrine. In the year 483 in the time of Malik Shāh this man sold the fort to them for 1200 dinars. Its first chieftain was al-Hāsan b. Sabah; originally of Marv, and secretary to the Chief 'Abd al-Razzāq b. Bahram. This was in his youth; then he went to Egypt where he learned their doctrine from these people's missionaries, to return as a leading missionary and principal. This fort came into his hands, and his method of propagating his system was only to invite some simpleton who could not know his right hand from his left, or was unacquainted with affairs. He would feed the man on walnuts, honey, and coriander, so that his brain would expand. Then he would recount to him the wrongs and injuries which the family of the Prophet had sustained till that got fixed in his mind. Then he would say to him. If the Azraqites and Dissidents sacrificed their lives in fighting against the Umayyads, why should you grudge your life in defence of your Imām? By this language he would leave the man fodder for the sword.

Malik Shāh had sent to this Ibn al-Sabāh summoning him to obedience, threatening him if he resisted, and ordering him to cease sending his followers to murder savants and princes; in answer to this message he said in the messenger's presence: The answer is what you shall see. He then said to a number of men who were standing in front of him: I wish to send you to your master on a certain business, and who will volunteer?—Everyone of them was anxious to go. The Sultan's messenger supposed that he was entrusting them with a message. Then Ibn al-Sabah pointed to a youth among them, and said to him: Kill yourself.—The lad drew a knife, cut his throat with it and fell down dead. Then he told another to throw himself from the fort; he did so and was smashed to pieces.— Then Ibn al-Sabāh turned to the Sultan's messenger and said: Tell him that I have with me twenty-thousand of these people whose obedience to me goes to this length. This is my answer.—The messenger returned to the Sultan Malik Shāh and told him what he had seen. The Sultan marvelled thereat, and ceased parleying with them.

They got a number of forts into their hands; and proceeded to murder numerous princes and viziers.

---

[21] The reference is to Alamut. See Le Strange's *Mustawfi*, p. 66.

In our History we have told strange stories about these people, and see no occasion to dilate on them here.

Many an atheist with hatred of Islam in his heart has come out, worked hard, exerted himself and made plausible pretensions with which to confront his followers. The hidden purpose in belief was to wriggle out of the net of Islam, and in action to enjoy pleasures and to make lawful forbidden things. Some of them have obtained the pleasures at which they aimed, only after murdering people and doing grievous harm like Babak the Khurramite and the Qarmatians, and the leader of the Zamj who rebelled and seduced the black slaves, promising them the kingdom. Others while persisting in their misleading lost both this world and the next, like Ibn al-Rawandî and al-Ma'arrî. We were informed by Muhammad b. Abi Tāhir on the authority of Abû'l-Qāsim 'Alî b. al-Muhassin al-Tanûkhi after his father that Ibn al-Rawandî attached himself to the Rejectors and the Heretics, and when people remonstrated with him said he only wanted to know their doctrines. Presently he removed the mask and argued openly.

Whoever studies the case of Ibn al-Rawandî finds him a leader of heretics. He composed a book which he called *The Brainer* wherein he claimed that he had "brained" this (the Muslim) Code. Praise be to Him who brained him; he was taken when he was still young. He attacked the Qur'ān, declaring that it was inconsistent and wanting in correctness, knowing all the time that the most eloquent of the Arabs were amazed when they heard it—still more those whose speech was incorrect. As for Abû' l-'Ala, his poems make no secret of their heresy; he went to all lengths in his hatred of the Prophets, but all through floundered about in his attempts to mislead, being afraid of execution, till he died in his destitution. There has been no period without successors to these two parties, only, thank God, the fuel of the more audacious has been extinguished. There only remain such Bātinis as hide themselves, and such pretenders to philosophy as conceal their opinions. These indeed are the most misleading, the most contemptible, and the most squalid. We have explained the doings of a number of both these parties in our History, and see no occasion to deal with them at length.

CHAPTER V

The Way Wherein the Devil Deludes the Jews and the Christians

He has indeed deluded them in numerous matters of which we will mention a selection which will serve as a guide to the rest. Among them is their assimilating the Creator to the creature; were such assimilation correct, He would be liable to what they are liable; to our colleague'[1]. Abû 'Abdallah b. Hamid records how the Jews maintain that the God who is to be worshipped is a man of light upon a throne of light, having on His head a crown of light, and having the same members as a human being. Another is their assertion that 'Uzair is the son of God; had they understood that filiation belongs to division, and that God is not divisible, since He is not composite, they would not have asserted such filiation. Further, a son is of the same category as his father, and 'Uzair must have been maintained by food, whereas God is the maintainer of things, not maintained by them. Now what suggested this to them together with their ignorance of reality, was that they saw him come back after death and recite the *Torah* from memory; and they talked about this with erroneous fancies. And what shows that these people were far from intelligent is that, having seen the effect of the divine power in the dividing of the sea, then, coming across idols, they demanded the like, saying, (Surah vii. 134) *Make unto us gods even as they have gods.* And when Moses rebuked them for this, still the idea remained in their minds, and that which was hidden came to lignt when they worshipped the calf, a course to which they were impelled by two things; one, their ignorance of the Creator, and the second their wanting something which would appeal to the sense, so dominant was sensation with them, and so far removed were they from reason. Had they not been so ignorant of the object of worship, they would not have dared to use improper expressions concerning Him, saying, (Surah iii. 177) *Verily God is*

---

[1] *i.e.,* Hanbalite.

poor and we are rich and (v. 69) *The hand of God is fettered.* God is high above all that!

They were aware that the system of Adam permitted marriage with sisters and other prohibited degrees, and working on the Sabbath day: then this was abrogated by the Code of Moses. They say: If God enjoin anything, that is wisdom; and it may not be altered.—I reply: At certain times alteration may be wisdom; the change in the human being from health to disease and from disease to death is wisdom, all of it. He has forbidden you to work on the Sabbath day, and permitted you to work on the Sunday: and this belongs to the category of what you disapprove. Further God commanded Ibrāhîm to sacrifice his son, and then forbade him to do so.

Another delusion which he inflicted on them is their saying, (ii. 74) *The fire shall not touch us save for a certain number of days,* these being the days wherein they worshipped the calf. Indeed their atrocities are numerous, and then the devil induced them to practise pure contumacy, so that they rejected the description of our Prophet which was in their books and altered it. They had been ordered to believe in him; but they were content to be damned. Their learned men were contumacious, and the ignorant among them followed their lead. It is indeed a marvel that they should have altered and mutilated what had been prescribed to them, and made what they wanted their religion. What place has service with one who neglects the command and acts according to his lust? Further they contradicted Moses and found fault with him, declaring that he had a personal defect and charging him with the murder of Aaron; just as they charged David with seizing Uriah's wife.

The following was told us by Muhammad 'Abd al-Bāqî al-Bazzāz, with a chain of authorities going back to Abû Hurairaі,. He said: The Prophet went to the school of the Jews, and said: Bring out to me the most learned among you. There came out 'Abdallah b. Suriyah, and they had a private interview. The Prophet adjured him by his religion and God's bounty in feeding them with manna and quails, and causing the cloud to overshadow them, to answer the question: Do you know that I am God's Apostle? — He replied: Yea, by God! And indeed the people know what I know, and that your description and characteristics are clear in the *Torah;* only they are envious of you.—The Prophet said: Then what binders you yourself?—He said: I am unwilling to go against my people; possibly they may follow you and accept Islām, in which case I shall do the like.

I was told the following by Hibat Allah b. Muhammad b. Abd al-Wāhid with a chain of authorites going back to Salāmah b. Salāmah b. Waqsh. He said: We had a Jewish neighbour among the Banu 'Abd al-Ashhal, who one day before the Prophet's mission came out to us from his house, and stood in the assembly of that tribe. I (said Salāmah) was at that time the youngest person there, and was lying on a garment in the court of my family. He spoke of the gathering, the resurrection, the reckoning, the scales, paradise and hell, to polytheists and idolators, who did not believe in any gathering after death. They said to him: What? Do you believe that will really happen, that people after death will be gathered to a world wherein are paradise and hell, and will be recompensed there for their deeds?—He said: Yea, by Him by whom men swear one of you would wish that he had one flash of that fire in the largest oven in the house, and that after being heated he should be put into that oven and have it closed upon him, and that he might be rescued from that fire tomorrow.— They said to him: Pray what is the sign thereof?—He said: A Prophet who shall be sent from somewhere in these regions, and he pointed with his hand towards Makkah and Yemen.—They said: And when shall we see him?—He said, looking at me, who was the youngest of them: If this lad lives his full term, he will overtake him. Salāmah said: Now by Allāh not a day and a night had passed before God sent His Prophet; the man being still alive and among us. We believed in him; but the man disbelieved, out of malice and jealousy. We said to him: Plague on you, are not you the person who told us about him?—He said: I am, only this is not the man.

Account of the way wherein he deludes the Christians

This is of many kinds, one of them being that the devil makes them fancy that the blessed Creator is a substance. The Jacobites, followers of Jacob; the Malekites, followers of the imperial religion, and the Nestorians, followers of Nestorius, maintain that God is a single substance, self-maintained, being one in substantiality, three in personality; one of the persons according to them is the Father, another the Son, and another the Holy Ghost. Some of them say that the Persons are properties; others that they are qualities; others that they are individuals. These persons forget that if God were a substance. He would be liable to those things to which substances are liable, limitation in space, motion and rest, and colours. Then the devil suggested to some of them that Christ is God; Abû Muhammad al-Naubakhti says: The Maiekites and Jacobites maintain that the person born by Mary is God. To some of them Satan suggested that Christ is the son of God; some of them hold that Christ is two substances, one of them ancient and the other modern. In spite of their saying this concerning Christ they admit that he needed food; neither differing on that point nor on the fact that he was crucified, and was unable to protect himself. They say that this was done only with the humanity; why then did not the divinity in him protect the humanity?

Further he deluded them with regard to our Prophet, so that they rejected him after he had been mentioned in the Gospel. Some of the "People of the Book" admit that he was a Prophet, only sent exclusively to the Arabs. This is one of the devil's delusions, wherein he has got them off their guard. For if it be certain that he was a Prophet, then a Prophet cannot lie; and the Prophet said "I am sent unto all mankind;" and he wrote letters to Caesar, Khosroes, and the rest of the foreign kings.

Account of the way wherein he deludes both Jews and Christians

An example is their saying God will not punish us for the sake of our ancestors, since of us are the saints and the Prophets. God tells us about this saying of theirs, (Surah v. 21) *We are the sons of God and His beloved, i.e.,* to us belong His sons 'Uzair and Isa. The dispelling of this illusion is that every individual is answerable for God's claims upon him, which no relative can avert; and if love of an individual could be transferred to another in virtue of relationship, hatred also would be transferable. Our Prophet said to his daughter Fātimah, *I cannot avail thee at all against God.* The advantage of the loved one is by reason of his piety, and whoso lacks this, lacks the divine love. Further God's love of a creature is no passion like that of one human being for another; were it indeed like that, then such transference would be admissible.

Account of the way wherein he deludes the Sabians

This name Sabians comes from a verb which means to go out from one thing into another, and is used of stars coming out, and of people bringing others out. The Sabians then are people who "go out" from one religion into another, and scholars have ten views of their systems. (1) That they are intermediate between Jews and Mazdians. This is recorded by Salim after Sa'îd b. Jubair and Laith after Mujāhid. (2) That they are intermediate between Jews and Mazdians. Recorded by Ibn Abi Najih-after Mujāhid. (3) That they are intermediate between Jews and Christians. Recorded by al-Qasim b, Abi Barrah after Mujāhid. (4) That they are a Christian sect, only more moderate than the others in their doctrine. Recorded by Abû Sālih after Ibn 'Abbās (5) That they are polytheists with no sacred book. Also recorded by al-Qāsim after Mujāhid. (6) That they resemble the Mazdians. Asserted by al-Hasan. (7) That they are a sect of the People of the Book, reading the Psalms. Asserted by Abû'l-'Aliyah. (8) That they are people who turn in prayer to the Qiblah, worship the angels and read the Psalms. Asserted by Qatādah and Muqātil. (9) That they are a sect of the People of the Book. Asserted by al-Suddî. (10) That they used to say *There is no God but Allāh,* but have no ritual nor book nor Prophet; only the formula which has been quoted. Asserted by Ibn Zaid.

These are the opinions of the commentators on the Qur'ān, but as for the theologians, they assert that the Sabians follow different systems. Some of them believe in the existence of a hyle which is eternal, and that the demiurge has from eternity been forming the world therefrom. Most of them however assert that the world is uncreate; they call the stars angels, though some of them call them gods, and prostrate themselves before them, and build them sanctuaries; they claim that the Sacred House (the Ka'bah) is one of these sanctuaries, being that of Saturn. Some of them hold that God can have no attributes save such as are negative, not positive, so that you may say he is not created, not mortal, not ignorant, not impotent, in order (they say) that there may be no anthropomorphism. They have certain religious practices, *e.g.,* they assert that they are bound to perform three daily prayers, the first, of eight inclinations, with three prostrations for each inclination, the time for it ending with sunrise; the second and third are each of five inclinations. They also are bound to fast for a month beginning the eighth of March, and for seven days beginning with the ninth from the end of December, and seven days beginning with the eighth of February; they terminate their fasts with almsgiving and sacrifices. They taboo camel's flesh with other follies which it would be waste of time to record. They hold that the good spirits ascend to the fixed stars, and the light; and that the bad spirits descend to the lowest of the earths, and the darkness. Some of them hold that this world is imperishable, and that reward and punishment are in transmigration.

Doctrines of this sort do not require trouble to be taken over their refutation; since they are postulates, without proof. The devil has also persuaded some of them to take the view that perfection lies in procuring relation between them and the upper spiritual beings by the use of purifications, regulations, and invocations. They occupy themselves with astrology and fumigation, and declare that there must necessarily be some intermediary between God and His creation to furnish knowledge and to guide to what is profitable; only such intermediary must be spiritual not corporeal. We, they say, procure for ourselves a holy relation between Him and ourselves, which serves as a means of approaching him. These people do not reject the resurrection of the body.

Account of the way wherein he deludes the Mazdians

Yahya b. Bishr b. "Umair al-Nihawandî says: The first king of the Mazdians was Kumart, who introduced his religion. Then there were among them a succession of persons who claimed prophethood, till Zoroaster became famous for it. They used to say that God is a spiritual individual, simultaneously with whose appearance things appeared, being spiritual and perfect; he said "It will not be possible for any other than Me to create the like of this which I have created," and from this thought of His there was begotten Darkness, since this thought involved a denial of anyone else's power. Then began Darkness to strive with Him for victory.

Among the things ordained by Zoroaster were the worship of fire and prayer towards the sun, their explanation of the latter practice being that the sun is queen of the world, and brings day and removes night; gives life to plants and animals, and restores heat to their bodies. They would not bury their dead in the earth out of reverence for it, saying that it is the source of living things, so we must not defile it; nor would they wash themselves with water, out of reverence for that element, which, they say, contains the life of everything, without first using the urine of oxen or the like, nor would they spit therein. They did not approve of the slaughter or sacrifice of animals, and would wash their faces with the urine of oxen, which they regarded as lucky, the luckier the older it was. They approved of intercourse with mothers, holding that the son was the fittest person to gratify the mother's desire, and that if a husband died, his son had the best right to the wife. If there were no son, a man was to be hired at the expense of the deceased. They permitted marriage with a hundred or even a thousand wives, *et si mulier menstruans volebat se lavare, dabat denarium magorum principi, qui ducebat eam ad domum ignis, jubebat eam procumbere in manus et pedes, et purgabat eam indice digito.*

This system was proclaimed by Mazdak in the days of Qubad, who permitted promiscuous intercourse; and himself married the wives of Qubad, that he might be imitated by the populace, who did the like with their womenfolk. When the turn came to the mother of Anushirwan, he said: Bring her out to me, for if you refuse me my desire, your faith will be imperfect. The king thought of bringing her out; but Anushirwan began to weep before Mazdak and kiss his feet, in the presence of his father Qubad, begging Mazdak to grant him his mother. Qubad said to Mazdak: Do you not maintain that the Believer must not be restrained from his desire? He said: It is so.—Why, then; said the king, do you restrain Anushirwan from his desire?— I grant her to him, he said. Further he permitted the eating of carrion. When Anushirwan came to the throne, he exterminated the followers of Mazdak.

Among the doctrines of the Mazdians is that the earth is infinite downwards, that the heaven is one of the skins of the demons, and that the thunder is the motion proceeding from the snoring of the fiends imprisoned in the spheres after being captured in a war, from whose bones are the mountains, and from whose urine and blood are the seas. A man of note arose among the Mazdians at the time of the transference of the empire from the Umayyads to the 'Abbasids' who misled many people, and about whom there are many stories which it would take too long to recount. He was the last person of distinction whom the Mazdians produced. Some savants assert that the Mazdians had books which they studied and that they invented a religion, but that their books were removed.

One of the most extraordinary delusions wrought upon them by the devil is this: noticing that there is good and evil in actions, he persuaded them that the doer of good does not do evil, whence they assume two gods, one of them being light and wise, doing only good, the other a demon, darkness, who only does evil: a similar doctrine to that of the dualists which we have recorded.

We have already mentioned their fallacies and the reply to them. Some of them say: The Creator is eternal and from him comes only good; the demon is created, and from him comes only evil. We may say to them: If you maintain that Light created the demon, then He created the source of evil.

Some of them state that the Creator is Light, but that he thought an evil thought, saying "I fear that there may come into existence in my realm someone who will oppose me;" this thought of His was evil, and from it there arose the devil, who was content to have evil ascribed to him, after it had been established that he was a partner in the realm. Naubakhti records that according to some of them the Creator doubted about something and from that doubt the devil arose. Some of them, he adds, hold that God and the fiend are two eternal bodies, between whom there was a space. The world was immune from trouble, the fiend being away from it; presently the devil planned to pierce the heaven with his hosts, when the Almighty fled from their doings and sanctified Himself from their language, but was pursued by the devil, who besieged Him and fought against Him for three thousand years, during which he was unable to get at the Almighty, and the Almighty was unable to repulse him; the Almighty then made peace with him on condition that the devil and his hosts should be in the world for seven thousand years. The Almighty thought the best course was to put up with the devil's mischief till the term fixed came to an end, until which time mankind will endure trials. After that they will return to bliss. The devil stipulated that he should be allowed to institute evil things in this world. When the two, he goes on to say, had agreed on the terms, they had them attested by two just persons, to whom they handed their swords, bidding them slay whichever of the two violated his engagement.— There is a lot more rubbish which it would be waste of time to record, and which we have therefore neglected. And indeed this balderdash is only worth mentioning in order to show the lengths to which the devil's delusions go.

It is marvellous that after making the Creator good, they should make an evil thought issue from Him; according to their doctrine, a sovereign, the devil, can issue from a thought. We may ask them: Is it possible that the fiend may keep his promise?—If they say No, then we may say that it is not in accordance with wisdom to keep him alive. If they say Yes, then they admit that good faith (a commendable thing) can proceed from one who is evil. Further how is it that the fiend obeyed the "two just persons," when he disobeyed his Lold? And how can God be assailed? Were it not interesting to study the havoc played by the devil with men's reason, there would be no use nor sense in recording these absurdities.

Account of the way wherein he deludes the astrologers and astronomers.

Abû Muhammad al-Naubakhtî says: Some maintain that the sphere is eternal, uncreate: whereas Galen records that according to some Saturn only is eternal. Some hold that the sphere is a fifth nature, having neither cold nor heat, neither moisture nor dryness; neither light nor heavy. Some supposed the sphere to be a fiery substance, which had released itself from the earth by the force of its revolution. Some say the stars are of a body resembling stone. Some that they are of cloud which is extinguished every day and lights up again at night, like coal which blazes up and goes out. Some say the body of the moon is composed of fire arid air; some that the sphere is of water, wind, and fire, and resembles a globe, moving with two motions, from east to west and from west to east; Saturn, they say, revolves round the sphere in about thirty years, Jupiter in about twelve years, Mars in about two years, the Sun, Venus, and Mercury in one year, and the moon in thirty days. Some say that the spheres of the stars are seven; the nearest to us is the sphere of the moon, next comes that of Mercury; next that of Venus, next that of the Sun, next that of Mars, next that of Jupiter, next that of Saturn, next the sphere of the fixed stars. There is difference of opinion about the magnitude of the stars, most of the philosophers holding the Sun to be the greatest, its magnitude being 160 times that of the earth. That of each of the fixed stars is about 94 times that of the earth; that of Jupiter about 82 times, that of Mars about one and a half times. The distance round and back from anyone point in the sphere is 100,664 leagues. Some suppose the sphere to be alive, and the heaven an animal, and that each star has a soul in it. The ancient philosophers held that the stars do good and evil, give and withhold in accordance with their natures, which are lucky or unlucky; that they influence men's souls, and are themselves living and active.

Account of the way wherein he deludes those who deny the resurrection

He has deluded many persons into denying the resurrection and regarding restoration after decay as chimerical. He suggested to them two fallacies; first he pointed out to them the weakness of the material, and secondly the mixing up of the portions that were dispersed in the depths of the earth. They said: one animal eats another, so how is resurrection possible? Their fallacies have been noticed by the Qur'ān and God says about the first (xxiii. 37) *Doth he promise you that when ye are dead and have become dust and bones ye shall be brought out? "Tis a far cry to that which ye are promised!* And with reference to the second He says (xxxii. 9) *What, when we have wandered over the earth, are we to be in a new creation?* This indeed was the view of most of the pagans; one of them says

> The Prophet tells us that we shall revive;
>
> But how are carcases and skulls to live?

Another

> To live, to die, and then to rise again—
>
> This is, dear lady, but a fiction vain.

The reply to the first of these fallacies is that the weakness of the material, *i.e.*, dust, for the new creation is shown to be no argument against it by the origin and process of the embryo; further the original man, Adam, was formed from dust; and indeed God Almighty invariably creates admirable objects from contemptible material, man from *semen virile*, the peacock from a mouldy egg, the green giraffe from a foulsmelling snake; attention should be directed to the power and might of the maker, not to the weakness of the material. And such attention will furnish the reply to the second fallacy. Further He has shown us by way of a specimen how what is scattered can be reassembled; if gold filings be scattered over a quantity of dust, and a small amount of mercury be thrown over them, the gold which is scattered will reassemble; how much more— then can be accomplished by the divine power, one of whose operations is the creation of everything out of nothing? Besides, if we were able to turn the dust into that into which the bodies turn,[2] this would not affect the man's soul: for the man exists by his soul, not by his body; he becomes thin or stout, changes from smallness to bigness yet is throughout the same.

One of the strongest evidences of the resurrection is that God displayed by the hand of His Prophets something even more marvellous than the resurrection; such as the change of a staff into a living snake, and the production of a she-camel from a rock. And by the hand of Jesus he displayed actual cases of resurrection.

This we have further explained in our refutation of the philosophers. The devil has further confused persons who witnessed the Creator's power, but into whose minds there came the two fallacies which we have mentioned, in consequence of which they hesitated about the resurrection, and one of them said (xviii. 34) *And if I be returned to my Lord, I shall find one better than it for a change* and al-As b. Wā'il said (xix. 80) *I shall be given wealth and offspring.* They said these things in consequence of their doubts, the devil having confused them on the subject. What they meant was "If there be a resurrection, we shall be all right, since He who has bestowed wealth upon us in this world will not deprive us of it in the next." This, I must observe, is an error, for the gift may be a form of temptation or punishment; a man may guard his son, but allow his slave to indulge his passions.

Account of the way wherein he deludes the believers in Transmigration

He has deluded some people into believing in transmigration, and that the spirits of the good when they depart enter into good bodies and are at rest, whereas the bad spirits enter into evil bodies, and endure tortures therein. This doctrine came forward in the time of the Pharaoh of Moses. Abū'l-Qāsim al-Balkhî states that the believers

---

[2] This seems to be the sense, but the words are likely to be corrupt.

in this doctrine, seeing the pain suffered by infants and animals both wild and tame, regarded it as impossible that such pain could be for the torture of other beings or for retribution, or for no other reason than that these creatures were held in bondage: hence they concluded that it must have been earned by sins which had been previously committed by them in another state. Yāhya b. Bishr b. 'Umair al-Nihawandî states that according to the Indians there are four natures: a composite hyle, soul, reason, and loose hyle; the composite is the lesser lord, and the soul is the lesser hyle, the reason the greater lord; and the hyle also is greater. When the souls quit the world, they come to the lesser lord, *i.e.*, the composite hyle; if they are virtuous and pure, he receives them into his nature and purifies them till he brings them out to the lesser hyle, *i.e.*, the soul, so that they may proceed to the greater lord, who will draw them out into the greater composite hyle. If a soul be perfectly virtuous, it will remain with him in the simple world; if it be imperfectly virtuous, he will send it back to the greater lord, who will send it back to the lesser hyle, which will send it back to the lesser lord, who will bring it forth mingled with sun's rays till it become a common vegetable, which will be eaten by a man and turn into a man to be born anew into the world, and this will he his course in every death that he dies. As for the vicious; when their souls come to the lesser hyle they are inverted and become herbs eaten by cattle, so that the spirit enters into a beast and is transformed into another on the death of that beast; it remains transformed, shifting through various diseases, and once in a thousand years returns to humanity. If it prove virtuous in human form it joins the virtuous. Observe, I say, these stages which the devil arranged for them according to 'his fancy with no support!

I was informed by Muhammad b. Abi Tāhir al-Bazzār after 'Alî b. al-Muhassin after Abûl-Hasan 'Alî b. Nazif the metaphysician as follows:[3]

There used, he said, to attend lectures with us in Baghdād an Imāmi Shaikh, Abû Bakr b. al-Fallās. He told us how he had visited a man whom he had known as a Shi'ite, but who afterwards adopted the doctrine of transmigration, I found him with a black cat in front of him, which he was stroking and scratching between the eyes. I noticed

---

[3] This story comes from the *Table-talk of a Mesopotamian judge*, Part viii, §.25.

that its eyes were dropping tears as is usual with cats. The man was weeping copiously. I asked him why he wept.—He said: Do you not see that this cat sheds tears whenever I stroke her? Doubtless she is my mother, and she only weeps out of grief when she sees me.—He began to talk to her in the style of one who supposed that she understood. The cat began to mew just a little, and I said to him: She understands, does she, what you are saying to her?—He said, Yes, Then I said: Do you understand her mewing?— He said No.—I said: Then you are the transformed, and she is the human being.

Account of the way wherein he deludes our community in their beliefs and religious practices

The devil found his way into the beliefs of this community by two avenues; one of them imitation of parents and ancestry, and the other diving out of their depth. Thus he brought the adherents of this section into various forms of confusion.

As for the first avenue: he persuaded the imitators evidences admit of doubt, and the truth at times is hidden, whereas imitation is safe. Many people have been led astray along this avenue, and whole multitudes have thereby been ruined. Jews and Christians have imitated their fathers and their savants. The same was the case with the pagan Arabs. Now the reason which they allege for approving imitation deserves censure: for if evidences admit of doubt and the truth is hidden, imitation should be avoided lest it lead into error. God reproaches those who stand still in imitation of their fathers and ancestry in the text (xliii. 22) *Nay, but they say: Verily we found our fathers following a system and we are on their footsteps imitating. Say: What and if I bring you better guidance than that wherein ye found your fathers? i.e.,* will ye still follow them? And indeed God says (xxxvii. 98) *Verily they found their fathers astray, and they rush in their footsteps.*

The imitator has no certainty about that which he imitates, and such imitation frustrates the utility of the reason. For the reason was given for the purpose of reflexion and consideration. It would be disgraceful that anyone who had been given a candle to light him should extinguish it and walk in darkness. Now the majority of the adherents of the systems revere some individual in their hearts and follow his saying without reflecting on what he says. And this is the essence of error, since attention should be directed to the saying not to the speaker, as 'Alî said to al-Hārith b. Hut, who had said to him " Is it to be supposed that we shall think Talhah and Zubair to have been in the wrong?" He replied "Hārith, you are under a delusion: the right is not to be known by persons: know what is right and then you will know what persons are in the right." Ahmad b. Hanbal used to say: "A man must be straitened in his knowledge if he imitates the belief of some other man." For this reason Ahmad b. Hanbal accepted the view of Zaid about the grandfather, and rejected that of Abû Bakr al-Siddîq.

If it be said: "Ordinary folk cannot know the evidence, how then can they do otherwise than imitate?" the reply is that the evidence for belief is obvious as we have hinted in our account of the materialists, and the like thereof is not hidden from any intelligent person; only, as for the details of legislation, since their applications are numerous and difficult for the laity to know, so that they are likely to be mistaken about them, the best thing one of them can do is to follow someone who has made a profound study of them; where he has to display independence is in the choice of someone to follow.

As for the second avenue: the devil; having got control of the foolish and plunged them in imitation; driving them like cattle, presently noticed some among them who had some sagacity and intelligence, and so misled these to the extent of his control over them. Some of them disapproved of those who were praised as imitators, and these the devil bade reflect; he then misled each one of them by a particular method. He showed some of them that to rest satisfied with the literal sense of the Code was incompetence; so he drove them to the system of the philosophers, and would not leave them alone till he had drawn them out of Islam; we have already dealt with these in our refutation of the philosophers. Some of these he persuaded not to believe anything save what was perceived by the senses; to these we may say: Is it by the senses that you know the soundness of your doctrine? If they say yes, then they will be making an audacious assertion, since our senses cannot perceive what they say, since there can be no difference about what the senses perceive. If they say: By something other than the senses, they will be contradicting themselves.

Some of them were made by the devil to dislike imitation and persuaded to plunge into metaphysics, and study the inventions of the philosophers, in order to remove themselves, as they supposed, from the common herd. The conditions of the metaphysicians varied, most of them being brought by their metaphysics to doubt, while some became heretical; the ancient jurists of this community did not keep silence, about metaphysics out of incompetence, but because they saw that this study brought no satisfaction, but rendered the healthy unsound: so they left it alone and forbade the study. So much so that Shafi'i said: It would be better that a man should be afflicted with everything which God has forbidden save only polytheism than that he should study metaphysics. He also said: If you hear a man say "the name is identical with the thing named," then attest that he is a metaphysician and irreligious. My ruling, he said, for the metaphysicians is that they should be beaten with palm-branches, and dragged about the clans and tribes, with the proclamation: This is the punishment of him who abandons the Book and the Sunnah and takes up with metaphysics. Ahmad b. Hanbal said: No metaphysician will ever prosper; the experts in this subject are atheists.

I myself ask: How can metaphysics be other than culpable, seeing that they led the Mu'tazils to assert that God knows the generalities of things but not the details? Jahm b. Safwan maintained that God's knowledge, power, and life were all created. Abû 'Alî al-Juba'i. Abû Hâshim and their followers among the people of Basrah maintained that the non-existent was a thing, an essence, a soul, a substance, whiteness, yellowness, redness; and that the Creator cannot make an essence nor an accident, and is only able to bring an essence from non-existence into existence. The qadi. Abû Ya'la in the book *al-Muqtabas* records that the Mu'tazilite al-'Allâf said to him: The bliss of the people of Paradise and the torment of the people of Hell are things which ability to avert must not be ascribed to God. If this be so, God should be neither desired nor feared, since He has, according to this, no power to do good or evil, to benefit or to injure. So, he goes on to say, the people of Paradise will remain motionless and silent, not uttering a word, nor moving, neither they nor their Lord being able to do anything of the sort. For all events must necessarily have an end which they will reach, after which there is to be nothing. God is exalted high above all this! Abû'l-Qâsim "Abdullah b. Ahmad b. Muhammad al-Balkhi in his book *Maqalat* states that Abû'l-Hudhail (Muhammad b. al-Hudhail al-'Allâf, a native of Basrah client of the tribe 'Abd al-Qais) was alone in the opinion that the motions of the people of Paradise will come to an end and that they will come to permanent quiescence, and that there is a limit to what God can do, if it came into actuality, which however it will not do. He thought it absurd that there should be ascribed to Him power for aught else. He used to say that God's knowledge is God, and God's power is God. Abû Hâshim said: whoso repents of everything else except of having drunk a draught of wine will be punished eternally with the punishment of the unbelievers. Nazzâm said that God is unable to do any evil, whereas the devil can do both good and evil.

Hishâm al-Ghuti[4] said: the epithet 'knowing from all eternity' must not be ascribed to God. Some of the Mu'tazils say that it is permissible that God should lie, only this has not occurred. The Determinists assert that man has no power, but is like dead matter, without choice or power of acting. The Murjites hold that a man who utters the two formulae of the Creed and then commits every sin will not enter Hell at all: contradicting the genuine traditions which deal with the removal of the monotheists out of Hell. Ibn 'Aqil said: It is most probable that the founder of the Murjite system was an atheist; for the prosperity of the world lies in maintaining the threats and the belief in reward. The Murjites, being unable to deny the Creator, owing to people's disapproval and that doctrine conflicting with the reason, annulled the advantage of maintaining the belief in his existence, which is fear and expectation. Thus they demolished the policy of the Code; and they are the sect which does most mischief to Islam.

The author proceeds. Now Abû 'Abdallah Muhammad b. Karram followed and selected the worst of the systems and the weakest of the traditions, and inclined to anthropomorphism, holding that accidents might enter into the person of the Creator; he asserted that God cannot restore bodies and substances, He can only create them. The Salimiyyah assert that God will be revealed on the Day of

---

4 Mu'tazilite doctor, whose views are given by Shahrastāni.

Judgment to everything in its own conception, to man as a man, to a Jinni as a Jinni. They also say that God has a secret, revelation of which would ruin the government of the world.

I personally implore God's protection from studies and sciences which involve such hideous doctrines. The metaphysicians indeed pretend that faith is imperfect without the knowledge of their systems. They are mistaken, since the Prophet commanded men to believe but did not command them to study metaphysics. And under these conditions there passed away the Companions, whom the Lawgiver attested to be the best of mankind. As we have shown, the study of metaphysics was censured in tradition, and we have been informed of cases wherein metaphysicians have withdrawn from their pursuit after seeing the mischief to which it led. I was told by Abû Mansûr al-Qazzâz by a chain of authorities ending with Ahmad b. Sinan that the latter said: Al-Walid b. Aban al-Karabisî was my maternal uncle, and when he was about to die, he said to his sons: Do ye know of anyone more skilled than I am in metaphysics? They said No.' He said: 'Do you mistrust me?— They said No.— He said: If I give you a charge, will you accept it?—They said Yes.—He said: Follow the way of the Traditionalists for I see that they are in the right.

Abû'l-Ma'ali al-Juwaini[5] used to say: I have traversed the world of Islam, and its sciences, sailing the ocean and diving into all that has been forbidden them, all in the search for truth and fleeing from imitation; now I have come back from all to the word of truth. Follow the religion of the licit; if God does not cause his loving kindness to overtake me, so that I shall die in the religion of old wives, and my time terminate on the day of my departure with the word of Sincerity[6] then woe to Ibn al-Juwaini!

He used to say to his friends: Friends, do not occupy yourselves with metaphysics: had I known to what it would lead, I should never have busied myself therewith.

Abû'l-Wafa b. 'Aqil said to one of his friends: I am certain that the Companions of the Prophet died without knowing *substance* and *accident*. If you are satisfied to be like them, be so; but if you think

---

[5] Yusuf b. Abdullah, called Imam al-Haramain, ob. 478.
[6] The reference is to Surah cxii., which is a brief statement of monotheistic doctrine.

that the path of the metaphysicians is better than that of Abû Bakr and 'Umar, then that is a wrong view. For, he added, metaphysics has brought its followers into doubts, and many of them into heresy: further the odour of heresy is about the casual utterances of the metaphysicians.

The source of this is that they are not content with what contents the Codes, and search for realities; and it is not in the power of the reason to attain to the wisdom which God alone possesses. Neither has God revealed to His creatures the realities which He knows; so, he says, having for a lifetime gone to all lengths in the former,[7] I now retrace my steps to the system of the books.

They only say that the old wives' system is safer, because, having gone to the limit in subtlety of investigation, they found no evidence of those justifications and explanations which the reason rejects, and had to stop at the indications of the Code, discarding the theory of motivations, the reason admitting that there is above it a divine wisdom to which it submits; the proof of this is: You say "He wanted to know, He desired to mention," and someone else says "Was he seized with the desire to bestow good, did any motive invite him to shed bounty?" Now it is well-known that a motive is something or other that occurs to the person, certain desires of the soul, and all that this means is that some desire enters the person to procure what he has not got, but which he wants; and when this object is attained, the emotion calms and the motive is weakened. The foolish person who asks these questions is called a " becauser,"[8] and it is well-known that the Eternal has ascribed to Him sufficiency, essential independence requiring no addition, subject to no occurrence. Now if we examine His bounty we find it laden with deficiency and sufferings, and pain endured by animals. When the reason would fain find a bounteous reason for this, investigation proceeds and perceives that the Doer can be either kindly or unkindly, and by rational evidence perceives that He is far removed from avarice which would cause Him to withhold what He is able to procure, and from inability to avert the evil which befalls these creatures;

---

[7] The study of metaphysics.

[8] This seems to be the sense; the word is derived from the preposition which, is used, for the motive.

being then unable to find causes, it does better to submit. The mischief only came in from the supposition that the Creator enforces what is profitable and averts what is harmful to the extent of His ability; had they introduced into their science the notion that He is wise, they would have been compelled to resign themselves to His will on account of His wisdom, and so would have lived in the comfortable home of committing affairs to Him without opposition.

Certain people have stopped short at the literal sense of the texts, interpreting them in terms of sense; some of them asserting that God is a body (God forbid!), which was the view of Hishām b. al-Hakam[9] 'Alî b. Mansûr,[10] and Muhammad b. al-Khalîl and Yûnus b. 'Abd al-Rahmān,[10] differences arose between them, some saying that He is a body like other bodies, whereas others say unlike other bodies. These again differed, some saying that He is light, others that He is like a white ingot, this last being the view of Hishām b. al-Hakam he held that God was seven of His own spans (God forbid!), and that what is beneath the earth is seen by a ray stretching from Him to the object of vision. Abû Muhammad al-Naubakhtî records after Jāhiz after al-Nazzām that Hishām b. al-Hakam formulated in one year five different views of anthropomorphism, finally deciding that the Deity is seven of his own spans; that some said He is in the form of an ingot, others that He is in the form of a clear crystal sphere, which exhibits the same form from whatever point of view you see it. Hishām maintained that He is finite in substance, so that a mountain is larger than He. His substance, he added, is known only to Himself.

This view (I observe) involves His possession of quality which would be inconsistent with monotheism. It is established that the sense of touch can only belong to a member of a class, whom other objects resemble, from which he needs to be separated and distinguished. But God Almighty is not a member of a class or resembled, neither can finiteness be attributed to His essence: not in the sense that He stretches infinitely in all directions, the meaning being only that He is neither a body nor a substance,

---

[9] Shi'î theologian, died in time of Ma'mān.

[10] Shi'i theologian.

involving finiteness.

Al-'Naubakhtî further states that many metaphysicians assert that Muqātil b. Sulaimān[11] Nu'aim b. Hammād,[12] and Dawûd al-Hawarî[13] maintain that God has a form and members.

Now I ask: How, pray, can these ascribe eternity to Him but not to human beings? Why do not they admit the possibility of the same things happening to Him as happen to human beings, disease and destruction? Then there may be said to anyone who maintains that the Deity has bodily form: By what evidence do you prove that bodies are not eternal?—and thereby we shall prove to you that the God whom you believe to be a create body is not eternal. Some of those who believe that God is a body hold that He may be felt and touched; to these we may say: Then, according to you, He may also be embraced ! Some of them say that He is a body which is space, wherein are all bodies. Bayan b. Sam'an asserted that the object of his worship was entirely of light, in the shape of a man, having possession of all his members except his face; he was executed by Khālid b. 'Abdallah.[14] Al-Mughîrah b. Sa'id al-'Ijli[15] asserted that the object of his worship was a man composed of light, on whose head is a crown of light, with members and a heart whence issues wisdom, his members having the form of the letters of the alphabet. This person maintained the sovereignty of Muhammad b. 'Abdallah b. al-Hasan b. al-Husain. Zurarah b. A'yan[16] used to assert that the Creator had not from eternity been knowing, powerful, or living till He created these qualities for Himself (God forbid!). Dawûd al-Hawarî said that He is a body of flesh and blood with limbs and members, hollow from mouth to chest, and solid for the rest.

---

[11] Ob. 150.

[12] Ob. 228.

[13] His view is given in *al-Farq bain al-Firaq*, p. 216.

[14] *Al-Qasri*. 119 A.H. *Tabari* ii. 1620.

[15] Executed at the same time. *Tabari loc-cit.*

[16] Follower of Muhammad b. Ali al-Baqir (59-114).

CHAPTER VI

The Way Wherein the Devil Deludes Savants in Different Departments of Knowledge

You are to know that the devil intrudes on people with his delusion by different paths, one of them manifest, only by encouraging the man's passion he gets the better of him, so that he blinds him to what he knows: another path is obscure, and so is concealed from many of the learned. We shall point out various forms of his delusion, those which we mention serving as a guide to those which we neglect; since to exhaust the methods would take too long. God will keep us from error.

Account of the way wherein he deludes the Readers of the Qur'ān

One is a man's occupying himself with the uncanonical Readings and procuring them, wasting most of his life in collecting them, booking them, and teaching them to people. This will divert him from learning precepts and duties. You will often find the Imam of a mosque undertake to teach the reading of the Qur'ān, when he does not know what vitiates prayer; and often the desire to be first makes him out of sheer ignorance give as a reply to a legal question the first thing which occurs to him, though it be unlawful in the system of law which he follows.[1] Had such people reflected, they would have known that what is wanted is to know the Qur'ān by heart, to get the pronunciation of it correct, then to understand it, then to act according to it, then to proceed to what will reform the soul and purify the character, then to study some important topics of the Code. It is gross stupidity to waste time in what is not of chief importance. Al-Hāsan al-Basri said: The Qur'ān was revealed that men should act

---

[1] The text of the MSS. differs here, and the reading is uncertain.

according to it. Such a case is when one of them reads in his sanctuary according to an uncanonical text rejecting the traditional vulgate. Now the learned are sure that prayer is not valid with uncanonical readings, the purpose of using them being to display out-of-the-way knowledge in order to win people's praise, so that they will flock to him; while he holds that he is studying the Qur'ān. Some of them combine Readings saying *malik, malik, mallak*[2] which is not permissible, since it takes the Qur'ān out of its order. Some combine prostrations, utterances of the creed, and repeat the formula " God is greater," to which practice also there is objection. They also have started lighting numerous fires for their completions of the Reading of the Qur'ān, thus combining waste of substance with imitation of the Mazdians, and providing an occasion for the assembling of women and men at night with mischievous results. The devil persuades them that therein is the glorification of Islam. This is a serious delusion, since a Code is glorified by practising what it enjoins. To this category belongs the case of those who allow themselves to claim that they have studied with persons with whom they had not studied, though they may have received a licence from them. Such a person will say falsely "I was informed by so-and-so," regarding this as a light matter, since he is recording Readings, which he supposes to be a virtuous act, forgetting that this is a falsehood to which the liars' penalty attaches. To it also belongs the case of the competent teacher of Reading who studies with two or three teachers, talks with any visitor while his mind cannot contain all these things, and then declares in writing that he has read with so-and-so according to the Reading of so-and-so.[3] Now some scrupulous persons used to maintain that two or three should come together and study with one. To it further belongs the case of Readers who vie with each other in the amount that they can get through. I have seen shaikhs among them who hold meetings and put forward an individual who on a long day gets through the whole Qur'ān three times. If he fails, he is ensured, and praised if he succeeds. The populace gather for such an occasion, and admire the man as they would a runner. The devil persuades them that heavenly reward is earned by much reading. It is however one of his delusions; since reading ought to be for God, not to win

---

[2] In the first Surah, where there are these differences of vocalization. Apparently the people, referred to combined the different views.

[3] It is not clear whether the author is referring to the teacher or the student.

admiration. Further it 'ought to be slow, since GoJ says (xvii. 107) *That thou mayest read it unto the people slowly* and (lxxiii. 4) *And chant the Qur'ān chanting.* To this category also belongs the case of a number of Readers who have invented musical reading, which had indeed previously been used to a moderate extent. Ahmad b. Hanbal and others disapproved of it, but not al-Shafi'i. We were informed by Muhammad b. Nasir in a Tradition going back to al-Rabi' b. Sulaiman that al-Shafi'i said: There is no objection to listening to camel-drivers' music or Bedouin intonation, nor to reading the Qur'ān with chant and modulation of the voice.

My own opinion is that Shafi'i merely referred to contemporary practice, in which slight modulation was practised, whereas in the present day it is done according to the rules of vocal music and the more closely it approaches singing, the more is it to be disapproved. If the Qur'ān is removed from its original structure, it is forbidden.

To the same category belongs the case of Readers who permit themselves certain sins, such as maligning the'r rivals, or even some greater offence, in the belief that their knowing the Qur'ān by heart will avert punishment from them, and alleging the saying of the Prophet: *If the Qur'ān were placed in a skin it would not burn.* This is one of the devil's delusions, since the punishment of one who knows is greater than that of one who does not know; greater knowledge strengthens the case against him. Then there is another sin in the Reader not respecting what he has committed to memory. God says *What, is one who knows like one who knows not?*[4] And concerning the Prophet's wives He says (xxxiii. 30) *And whoever of'you doeth manifest foulness, her punishment shall be doubled twice.* We were informed by Ahmad b. Ahmad al-Mutawakkili in a Tradition going back to Ma'ruf al-Karkhi that Bakr b. Khunais said: Verily in Gehenna there is a ravine against which Gehenna implores aid seven times in the day; and in that ravine there is a pit against which both Gehenna and the ravine implore aid seven times in the day, and in the pit there is a snake against which Gehenna, the ravine, and the pit, implore aid seven times in the Jay; its operation commences with evil-doers who know the Qur'ān by heart. They will say: O Lord, is it to commence with us before the idolaters? And

---

4 Inaccurate quotation.

there will be said to them: One who knows is not like one who knows not.

Let us confine ourselves to this specimen in what concerns the Readers.

Account of the way wherein the devil deludes the Traditionalists

To this category belongs the case of people who have spent their lives in hearing Tradition, travelling in pursuit of it, collecting numerous avenues,[5] and looking for authoritative chains and unfamiliar texts. They are of two classes. One class aims at preserving the Code by ascertaining which Traditions are sound as opposed to the accused, and they deserve gratitude for their endeavour, only the devil deludes them by distracting them through this from the duty, which is incumbent on every individual, of ascertaining what his obligations are, striving to discharge them, using Tradition as a source of law. If it be said that many of our ancestors did the like, such as Yahya b. Mu'in, Ibn al-Madini, al-Bukhari, and Muslim, the reply is that these persons combined knowledge of important matters of religion and the laws concerning them with their search for Tradition. They were helped herein by the shortness of the chains and the small quantity of Tradition, so that they had time for both these things. In our time, the avenues are lengthy and the works dealing with the subject vast, wherein only the avenues are different. It is scarcely possible for anyone to combine both these things; you will find a Traditionalist write, hear, and collect books for fifty years without knowing their contents; supposing that any accident occurs during prayer he will stand in need of one of the young law-students who come to him to hear Tradition. These give a handle to the assailants of the Traditionalists, who call them book-laden animals, who do not know what they are carrying. If one of them is fortunate enough to look into his Tradition, very likely he will act according to an abrogated Tradition, or will understand his Tradition in the sense wherein the vulgar understand it, and act accordingly, although that was not what the Tradition meant. Thus we have been told that a certain Traditionalist recorded that the Prophet had forbidden a man receiving the water of another man's plantation. Several of he audience said:

---

[5] *i.e.,* different chains of authorities for the same Tradition.

It has been our practice if we had more water than we wanted in our gardens to send it on to our neighbours: we ask God's pardon for having done so. Neither the reader nor the hearer understood or perceived that the reference was to *coitus cum feminis captivis praegnantibus.* Al-Khattabi says: One of our shaikhs used to recite a Tradition that the Prophet had forbidden *(halq)* cutting the hair before prayer, on Friday, and informed me that for forty years he had never cut his hair before prayer. I said to him: The word is *halaq* (circles), the objection being to people gathering for study and discussion; what the Prophet commanded was that a man should occupy his mind with prayer and listen to the sermon. The man said to me: You have indeed relieved me, and he was a pious man. Ibn Sa'id was of high rank among Traditionalists, only having had little intercourse with jurists he could not understand how to answer a legal, question. We were told by Abû Mansûr al-Bazzar in a Tradition going back to the jurist Abû Bakr al-Abhari that he said: I was with Yahya b. Muhammad b. Sa'id when a woman came to him and said: Shaikh, what say you of a well into which a chicken has fallen and died: is its water clean or unclean?—Yâhya said: Tell me, how came the chicken to fall into the well?—She said: It was not covered.—He said: Why did you not cover it so that nothing could fall into it?—Al-Abhari said: I said My friend, if the water has changed, it is unclean, otherwise it is clean.

Ibn Shahim[6] composed many works on Tradition, the smallest of them one volume and the largest a commentary in 1000 volumes; yet he knew nothing about law. Some of them ventured to give legal opinions that were erroneous for fear of being thought ignorant. Some became laughing-stocks in consequence of their opinions. One of them was asked a question about the division of an inheritance, and wrote in reply let it be divided in accordance with tne ordinances of God. We were informed by Muhammad b. Abi Mansûr in a Tradition going back to Ibrahim al-Harbi[7] that he said: I was told that a woman came to 'Ali b. Dawud[8] while he was repeating Traditions, having in

---

[6] 297- 335. His name was 'Umar ? Ahmad. His ink cost him 700 *dirhâms.* List of his works in Dhahabi, Huffâz iii. 196.

[7] 198-235.

[8] Died 262. He was one of Tabari's teachers.

front of him some thousand persons. She said to him: I have sworn to give my wrapper in alms.—He said: How much did you pay for it?—She replied: Twenty-two *dirhāms*.—He said: Then go and fast twenty-two days.—When she had left, he began to lament saying: Alas, we made a mistake. We ordered her to perform the atonement, for a repudiation.

Now, I would observe, consider these two disgraces, that of ignorance and that of venturing to give a legal opinion with such a muddle. And know that the majority of the Traditionalists take what concerns the attributes of the Creator in its literal and material sense, thus adopting anthropomorphist doctrine;[9] because they have not associated with jurists so as to learn how to interpret the ambiguous texts in accordance with the ascertained law. In our time we have seen such a person amass books and hear much, without understanding what he has procured. Some of them do not know the Qur'ān by heart, or know the rules of prayer. These people suppose that they are occupying themselves with what is enjoined on the community as a whole, instead of what is enjoined on the individuals. Now to prefer the unimportant to the important is a delusion of the devil.

The second section consists of persons who have heard much Tradition, only their purpose was not sound. By collecting the "avenues" they did not want to ascertain what was genuine and what not, what they wanted were Traditions of high antiquity, and such as were little known,, and they would go round the countries in order that one of them might say I met so-and-so, and I have chains of authorities which no one else has, and I have Traditions which are known to no one but me. A student of Tradition came to us in Baghdād, and he would take a teacher and set him down in al-Raqqah[10]— a garden on the bank of the Tigris—and read with him; he would then say in his collections "I was informed by so-and-so son of so-and-so in al-Raqqah," leading men to suppose that it was the Raqqah in the direction of Syria, and to think that he had undertaken arduous journeys in search of Tradition. Or he would set him down between the Nahr 'Isa and the Euphrates and say "I was informed by so-and-so Beyond the River," to make people suppose that he had crossed

---

[9] This is attacked by the author in his *Dar'Shubhat al-tasbih*.

[10] See Le Strange; *Baghdād*, p. 261.

the Oxus in search of Tradition. Or he would say "I was informed by so-and-so on my second or my third journey," that people might know the amount of trouble which he had taken in pursuit of Tradition. He won no blessing, as he died while still a student.

All this, I may observe, is far removed from sincerity; their object is leadership and vainglory. And this is why they follow after the rare and strange Traditions. It often happens that one of them gets hold of a note-book containing the Traditions which some fellow-Muslim has heard, and conceals the fact in order to monopolize the transmission; and he may die without ever having transmitted the contents, so that both these persons will lose their reward. Often too it happens that one of them travels to a teacher whose name can begin with either a Q or a K, in order to write that fact in his copy and nothing more.

To the delusion which the devil practises on the Traditionalists belongs their fault-finding with one another, to satisfy private grudges, which they carry out in the style of the "discrediting and crediting"[11] which was practised by the earlier representatives of this discipline, whose object was the protection of the Code. God indeed knows best what people's intentions are; but the proof that the intentions of these people are base lies in the fact that they say nothing about the persons from whom they themselves have received. The ancients did not act thus; 'Alî b. al-Madini[12] used to report from his father, who was untrustworthy, but he would add "and the reports of this shaikh are such as they are." We were informed by Abû Bakr b. Habib al-'Amiri in a Tradition going back to Yusuf b. al-Hussain[13] that he said: I asked Harith al-Muhasibi about backbiting, and he said: Beware of it, for it is the worst of acquisitions. What think you of a thing which will rob you of your merits in order to give satisfaction to your opponents? How will you be able to satisfy one whom you hate in this world when he is your opponent on the Day of Judgement? Either he will take some of your merits or you will take some of his demerits, since there will be no dinars nor dirhems there. Beware of it therefore and learn its source. Backbiting by the vulgar and the

---

[11] Technical terms for attacking and defending the credibility of persons who transmitted Traditions.

[12] His name was 'Alî b. Abdallah, 161-234.

[13] Al-Razi. A notice of him in Nicholson's Kashf al-Mahjub, 536.

134 *Talbis Iblis (Delusion of the Devil) Vol. I*

ignorant springs from the desire to gratify anger, ill-will, envy, and suspicion, qualities that are manifest, not concealed. Backbiting by the learned springs from self-deception, the man thinking that he is displaying sincere care for others, and from interpretation of a report which is untrustworthy, and which, were it trustworthy, would not assist backbiting. The report is the saying attributed to him (the Prophet?) *Do you dislike recording it? Record it stating the objections to it, that people may be on their guard against it.* If this report were preserved and correct, it would not involve the open defamation of a brother Muslim except when you are asked about him. If, *e.g.*, a man comes and asks your advice saying I want to marry my daughter to so-and-so, and you know the man to be an innovator or not to be trusted with a Muslim woman, you should dissuade the parent as courteously as possible. Or if another comes and says to you I want to deposit a sum of money with so-and-so, and the man is not fit to be trusted with a deposit, you should dissuade the proposing depositor as courteously, as possible. Or if a man says to you I want to pray behind so-and-so or make him my authority for some branch of knowledge, you should also dissuade as courteously as possible but not gratify resentment by backbiting.

In the case of Qur'ān-readers and devotees it springs from self-conceit. A man reveals his brother's defect, and then plumes himself on praying for him secretly. He makes free with his Muslim brother's flesh, and then glorifies himself by praying for him.

In the case of high officials such as are called *Ustadh*[14] it springs from the desire to make a show of kindliness. The man will say: Poor fellow, he is afflicted with such and such a failing, how trying! God protect us from such abandonment! The man plumes himself on his display of kindliness towards his brother, and then on praying for him in the presence of his fellows, he will say: I have only revealed that to you in order that you may offer many prayers for him.—We ask God's protection from backbiting whether indirect or direct. Beware of it, for the Qur'ān has declared it to be odious. God says (xliv.12) *Would one of you like to devour the flesh of his dead brother? Nay, ye abhor it.* Many a saying of the Prophet to the same purport is reported.

Among the ways wherein the devil deludes the Traditionalists is

---

[14] For this title see index to the *Eclipse*.

the reporting of spurious Traditions without stating that they are spurious. This is a crime against the Code, and their purpose is to advertise their Traditions and the quantity of their information. The Prophet said: Whosoever reports a Tradition as from me, while holding it to be false, is a liar.—To this category belongs their falsification of authorities, when one of them says "X from Y" or "Said X on the authority of Y" suggesting that he had heard from him a Tradition; in whose chain of authorities a link is missing, whereas he did not hear it; and this is reprehensible, because it is giving the broken chain, the authority of the complete chain. Some of them report on the authority of a "weak" transmitter or a liar, either not naming him or giving him a name that is not his, or calling him by his *kunyah* or after some ancestor in order that he may not be recognized. This is a crime against the Code, because it bases a rule on what is no proper basis for it. As for the case in which the transmitter cited is a trustworthy person, and his relation to an ancestor or merely his *kunyah* is given so that it may not seem that the same person is cited too frequently, or the case in which the transmitter is on a level with the reporter of the Tradition and the latter is ashamed to mention the former, though such procedure is to be disapproved and far removed from correctness, still it is venial on condition that the transmitter is trustworthy—may God guide us!

Account of the way wherein the devil deludes the jurists

In old times the jurists were the students of the Qur'ān and the Tradition, but the practice constantly declined till the later generation said: It suffices us to know the legal texts of the Qur'ān and to rely on the celebrated works on Tradition such as the *Sunan* of Abû Dawud, etc. Presently they neglected this also, and a jurist would allege a verse of which he did not know the meaning, or a Tradition which for all he knew might be genuine or spurious. Many a time too he would rely on an analogy which was opposed to a genuine Tradition, being unaware of this, owing to his having paid little attention to the subject of transmission. Now jurisprudence is extracting from the Book and the Sunnah: and how can a man extract from a thing with which he is not acquainted? It is reprehensible to make a rule depend on a Tradition of which the soundness or unsoundness is not ascertained. Such knowledge was at one time hard to procure and a man needed to travel far and undergo much fatigue in order to obtain it; then books were composed, *Sunan* established, and the sound distinguished from the unsound. Only the later generations have been too completely overcome by idleness to read the literature of Tradition; so much so that I have seen a great jurist say in a work of his concerning words occurring in the collections of sound Tradition "the Prophet cannot have said this," and I have seen him say when arguing about a certain question "our proof is the report of certain persons that the Prophet said something," his reply to the citation of a sound Tradition by his opponent being "that Tradition is unknown." All this is crime against Islam.

To the delusions which the devil inflicts on the jurists belongs their reliance on their acquisition of eristic (the science of disputation), claiming that they are searching for the correct ascertainment, of the evidence for a rule, and the elicitation of minute points of law, and the grounds for doctrines. If their claim were just, they would occupy themselves with all the questions, whereas they confine themselves to great questions, whereon they can dilate, so that the disputant may gain repute with the public in the process of discussion. One of them concerns himself with arranging his disputation and inquiring into contradictions, with the object of gaining glory and defeating rivals. Often he is unacquainted, with the rule dealing with a small question, which however involves general disaster.

Account of the way in which he deludes them into introducing into their disputation the talk of the philosophers, and into relying on their inventions

To this category belongs their preferring analogy to the Tradition which furnishes evidence on the question at issue in order to get greater scope for their discussion. If anyone of them adduces a Tradition as evidence, he falls into disrepute, although propriety would demand that the adduction of Tradition should have the preference. To this category also belongs their making discussion their chief occupation, unmingled with what is calculated to soften the heart, such as reciting the Qur'ān, listening to Tradition, and the biography of the Prophet and his Companions. It is well-known that the heart is not rendered humble by repeated removal of impurity and dirty water; what it needs is reminding and exhortation that it may set itself to earn the next world. Disputed questions may indeed belong to jurisprudence, but they do not furnish every requisite. Those who have not penetrated the mysteries of the ancients and the character of those systems they have adopted cannot tread their path. It should be understood that human nature is predatory and if left alone with its contemporaries it steals from their characteristics and becomes like them; whereas if it study the lives of the ancients it emulates them, and models itself on their character. One of the ancients said: A narrative which softens my heart is more agreeable to me than a hundred judgments of Shuraih.[15]—He only said this because the softening of the heart is what is wanted, and there are causes which produce it.

To the same category belongs their confining themselves to disputation while neglecting to memorize the system and the other studies connected with the Code. You will see a consulting jurist asked about a text of the Qur'ān or a Tradition and ignorant of it. This is imposture: pride has no place for deficiency! Further, discussion was introduced for the purpose of bringing the truth to light; and the aim of our ancestors was to help people by showing what was right. They would proceed from argument to argument and if some matter escaped one of them, the other would call his attention to it, their purpose being to make clear what was right. Hence if one of these old jurists based a judgment by analogy on an established rule for a reason which he surmised, and he was asked what is the evidence that the judgment in the case of the established rule is based on the reason assigned, he would say: This is what appears to me; if something preferable appears to you, then state it, for the opponent cannot compel me to state it.—He is right in saying that he is not bound to do so, only where it is a case of giving sincere advice and bringing the truth to light, he is so bound.[16]

To the same category belongs the case wherein it is made clear to one of them that the truth lies with his opponent, but for all that he does not recant, being oppressed by the thought that his opponent

---

[15] Famous judge, died about 96.

[16] This passage is likely to be corrupt.

is shown to be in the right. Indeed often-times he will try hard to confute that opponent while aware that the right is on his side. This is indeed outrageous, since the whole object of disputation is to arrive at the truth. Shafi'i said: Whenever a person with whom I have disputed has declined to accept a sound argument, I have despised him, whereas if he has accepted it, I have respected him; nor have I ever, when disputing with anyone, cared which was the winning side: if it were my opponent's, I would go over to him.

Further their desire to achieve supremacy by discussion arouses the ambition which is latent in their souls, and if anyone sees in his discourse some weakness which will enable the opponent to vanquish him, he proceeds to commit himself to preposterous propositions, and if he finds the opponent openly claim the advantage over him, and give way to the passion of pride, he will counter that with abuse, so that the disputation turns into a brawl.

To the same category belongs the licence which they allow themselves when the opponent is not present, on the pretence of reporting a discussion: one of them will say "I talked with so-and-so, and he said nothing." With this plea he uses language which will enable him to gratify himself at the expense of the opponent's honour.

Further the devil has deluded them into thinking that Jurisprudence by itself is the science of the Code, with no other, so that if a Traditionalist is mentioned to them, they say: Oh, that man does not understand, forgetting that Tradition is the source. If some saying is cited to them calculated to soften the heart, they say Oh, that is what preachers say.

To the same category belongs their venturing to give legal opinions without having reached the rank which would justify their doing so; frequently improvising they give opinions which contradict the texts; it would be better if they were to take their time over difficult questions. I was told by Isma'il b. Ahmad al-Samarqandi in a Tradition going back to 'Abd al-Rahman b. Abi Laila'[17] that the latter said: I have been contemporary with a hundred and twenty of the Prophet's Companions and when one of them was asked concerning a question he would refer it to another and he to another and this

---

[17] Died about 82.

other to a third till it came back to the first. 'Ata b. al-Sa'ib[18] is reported to have said: I also heard 'Abd al-Rahman b. Abi Laila say: In this mosque I have come across a hundred and twenty Helpers who are Companions of the Prophet, not one of whom would repeat a Tradition but wished that his brother had repeated it instead of him, or would be asked about a question but would wish that his brother would deliver an opinion in his stead.

We have been told that Ibrahim al-Nakha'i[19] being asked about a question said: Could you find not anyone to ask except me?—It is related that Malik b. Anas said: I have never given a legal opinion without having first asked seventy shaikhs whether they approved of my giving it and their assenting. He was asked: And suppose they had forbidden you?—Had they done so, he replied, I would have refrained. A man said to Ahmad b. Hanbal: I have sworn and I do not know how I have sworn. —He said: Would that when you knew how you had sworn I knew how to give you an opinion.

This (I observed) was the style of our ancestors owing to their fear of God and their reverence for Him. One who studies their careers will be enlightened.

One of the ways wherein the devil deludes the jurists is their association with princes and Sultans, their flattering them, and declining to find fault with them though they are able to do so. Often they give them permission to do what, they have no right to permit, in order to acquire some temporal advantage; thereby mischief comes in three directions: first, the prince says "were I not in the right, the jurist would have found fault with me; Surely I must be in the right, since he is maintained by my property.[20] Secondly, the ordinary man says "There is nothing the matter with this prince or his wealth or his acts, since this particular jurist remains with him." Thirdly, the jurist, who ruins his religion thereby.

The devli has deluded them concerning their appearing before the Sultan, so that one of them says: We only appear before him in order to intercede for a Muslim. This delusion is cleared away by the observation that had anyone else gone to the Sultan to intercede,

---

[18] Died about 137.

[19] Died 96. His is the first biography in Ibn Khallikan.

[20] The text has been emended.

this would not have pleased the jurist, who might very well have attacked such an individual for monopolizing the Sultan's attention. The devil further deludes him on the matter of taking the Sultan's money, saying "You have a right to it." Now it is well-known that if that money comes from an illegal source, the man has no right to take any of it, and if it is from a doubtful source, the better course is to abstain from it; if however it comes from a lawful source, it is permissible for the jurist to take such amount as religion allows, not such as can be expended in the maintenance of a luxurious establishment. Now often the populace imitate what they see the jurist do, and regard as lawful what is not so.

The devil also deludes men of learning, who keep away from the Sultan in order to practise devotion; he persuades them to malign those scholars who do present themselves to the Sultan, thereby rendering them victims of two vices, maligning others, and self-praise. In general it may be said that appearance at the courts is a serious danger, for whereas the intention at the commencement may be good, it changes with the bestowal of honours and gifts, or through covetousness; so the man cannot keep himself from flattering the Sultan, and abstaining from finding fault with him. Sufyan al-Thauri said: I am not afraid of their humiliating me; I am only afraid of their doing me honour, so that my heart will incline to them.

The learned men of antiquity used to keep away from princes, owing to their manifest wrongdoing: so the princes used to send for them, needing them to give legal opinions and to undertake governments; so there sprang up a class of men who were very desirous of worldly prosperity, studied the sciences which are of use to princes, and brought their knowledge to them in order to gain worldly advantage. The proof that they had the princes in view in their studies lies in the fact that at one time the princes liked to hear the arguments about the principles of religion, and people produced the science of metaphysical theology; then some of the former showed a taste for legal discussion, and the people took up with eristic; then some of the former showed a liking for homilies; and many a student took up with this pursuit. And when the mass of the populace had a liking for anecdotes, the anecdote-mongers became numerous, and the number of jurists declined.

Among the ways wherein the devil deludes the jurists is this:

one of them may live upon a trust fund belonging to a school built for students, and stay therefor years without studying, being satisfied with what he already knows, or indeed he may have come to the end of his study, so as to have no share in the endowment, which was meant for persons still learning, unless indeed such an individual may be a reciter or teacher, and so continually employed.

To this category there belongs what is reported of some among the younger law-students, viz., that they allow themselves licence in forbidden things, some of them wearing silk and ornaments of gold, at the cost of the school in which they protract their stay, and whose endowment they employ for other iniquities as well; the reasons for their licentiousness vary, some of them having no sound belief in the basis of religion, and studying law to acquire respectability or to get a share in the endowment, or to gain eminence or to dispute; whereas others are sound in belief, but are overcome by passion and concupiscence, having nothing to divert them therefrom, since the mere practice of arguing and disputing encourages conceit and pride, inasmuch as a man can only keep himself straight by ascetic exercise and perusal of the lives of the ancients—practices from which most of them are far removed, all that they do being calculated to encourage natural pride, so that passion is unrestrained. Some of them are deluded by the devil with the thought that they are savants, jurists, and muftis, and that learning exempts its possessors from ill consequences: it does nothing of the kind, for the man's knowledge in such a case convicts him, and doubles his punishment, as we have stated in the case of the Readers. Al-Hasan al-Basri said: He only is a jurist who fears God Almighty, Ibn Aqil said: I saw a jurist of Khorasan wearing silk and gold rings, and said to him: What is this?—He said: Gifts of the Sultan and vexation of the enemies.—I said: On the contrary, the triumph of the enemies over you, if you are a Muslim, since the devil is your enemy, and if he has got you to wear what angers the Code, you have let him triumph over you. Is the prohibition of the Merciful, satisfied with the Sultan's gifts, wretched man? The Sultan has robed you, but you have been stripped of your faith. Better would, it have been that the Sultan should make you strip people of the robe of wickedness and clothe you with the robe of piety. May God cast disgrace upon you inasmuch as you have made light of His commandment! Would that you had said: These are natural vanities! As it is, your condemnation is complete, since your contumacy proves that you are inwardly rotten.

One of his ways of deluding them is that he persuades them to despise preachers and forbid their visits, saying: Who are these people---story-tellers! The devil's purpose is to prevent the jurists from being present where the heart will be humbled and softened. The story-tellers are not to be censured because of this name, since God says (xii. 3) *We shall tell thee the best of stories* and (vii. 175) *And tell thou the stories.* The story-tellers are only to be censured because they are given to dilate without introducing any useful knowledge, and most of them mix things up in their narrations, or insist on absurdities. But when the stories are true, and edifying, the story-teller is worthy of praise. Ahmad b. Hanbal used to say: How much men need a truthful story-teller!

Account of the way wherein he deludes preachers and story-tellers

In old times, the preachers were scholars and jurists; 'Abd Allāh b. 'Umar used to attend the meetings of 'Ubaid b. 'Umair, and 'Umar b. 'Abd al-Aziz used to attend the meetings of a story-teller. Later on the profession became degraded, and was taken up by ignorant men, so that discreet persons kept away from their company, which was sought by the vulgar and women. These persons spent no time in acquiring knowledge, but concentrated on anecdotes and what suited the taste of the ignorant. Various innovations were introduced into this profession.

We have mentioned their failings in the *Book of Story-tellers and Narrators,* but will also give some account of them here. One is that some of them invent Traditions calculated to encourage or to warn, being deluded by the devil and supposing that their purpose is to urge to virtue and deter them from vice. This, however, is an insult to the Code, since such conduct on their part implies that it is defective, needing a supplement. Further they forget the saying of the Prophet *Whoso intentionally lies about me had better secure his place in Hell.* To this category also belongs their looking out for what will tickle people's minds and gratify their hearts, so that they vary their style accordingly, and you will find them reciting delightful erotic songs; the devil deludes them into thinking that the purpose of such is to point to the love of God, whereas the majority of their audience are common people, whose interior is filled with the love of passion; so the story-teller is misled, and by his procedure there is also misled the man who displays more emotion and humility than he actually feels. A larger audience necessitates additional simulation, and the soul will concede more tears and more humility: if one of them is feigning, he has forfeited the next world: and the man who is genuine cannot keep his sincerity free from an admixture of hypocrisy. Some of them make the motions with which the intonation of tunes is accompanied, and the intonations which they produce in our time resemble singing, and so come closer to what is forbidden than to what is merely disapproved. The Reader chants and the story-teller recites erotic verses, clapping his hands and beating with his feet, so that the performance resembles a drunken bout, and it causes mental agitation and exhilaration, with shouting by men and women, and rending of garments by reason of the passions hidden in the mind. Then they go away saying, it was an agreeable meeting, " agreeable" referring to something illicit. Some of those who practise the conduct that has been explained recite dirges over the dead, describing the afflictions which they endure, and telling of travelling and those who have met death in a strange land: causing the women to weep so that the place comes to be like a wailing room: but it would have been more fitting to speak of resignation to the loss of the departed, not what makes people despair. Some of them talk of the subtleties of asceticism and the love of God: and the devil deludes them with the suggestion "you are of those to whom this epithet applies, since you would not have been able to describe it all had you not known what you describe and walked the path." The removal of this delusion is the fact that a description is a case of knowledge, whereas walking is not knowledge. Some of them talk of catastrophes and illegal "intoxication," quoting amatory verses, with the 'object of increasing the applause of the company though the subject be improper. Many one of them utters flowers of speech with no underlying meaning; most of their talk in the present day is of Moses and the mountain, and Zulaikha and Joseph; they scarcely ever mention the divine ordinances, or forbid sin. When, then, is the adulterer or usurer likely to repent, or a woman to recognize her husband's rights and those of her relations? Alas, these people have abandoned the Code, and that is why their wares find so good a market; for truth is heavy, and falsehood light. Some of them urge people to asceticism and vigils, without explaining to the populace the purpose of these proceedings; in consequence one of them may repent and retire to a hermitage, or to the mountain, leaving his family without provision. Some of them talk of hope and desire, with no admixture of what will induce fear and caution, only emboldening people thereby to commit sin, and enforcing this by their own taste for worldly things such as fine horses, and splendid attire; so their words and actions corrupt men's hearts.

The preacher indeed may be sincere and well-meaning, only some of them get imbued with ambition as time goes on; and want to be revered; the sign of this is that if another preacher comes to take such a man's place or assist him with the congregation, the former preacher dislikes it; whereas, were he in earnest, he would have no objection to being helped with the morals of the congregation.

Some story-tellers mix the men and the women at their meetings, and you may see the women uttering many cries, out of emotion, as the story-tellers suppose, who find no fault with these cries, hoping to win all their hearts. In our time, the story-tellers act in away which has no connection with delusion, since it is an evident way of making the stories a source of livelihood, and of getting gifts from tyrannical princes, or obtaining the like from the gatherers of unlawful imposts, and earning money by them in the provinces. Some of them go to the cemeteries where they dilate on affliction and parting with friends, drawing tears from the women, but not exhorting them to take warning.

The devil even deludes the conscientious preacher, saying to him: You are not the person to preach, *that* should be done by one who is wide awake: urging the man to silence and retirement. This is one of the devil's suggestions, who thereby prevents good being done, as he goes on to say: You take delight in what you recount, and find solace therein; hypocrisy may well enter into your discourse, so that the path of isolation is safer. Satan's object thereby is to block the way of good. There is a Tradition on the authority of Thabit that al-Hasan was at a meeting, and said to al-'Ala: Speak. Al-'Ala said: We shall be weakening your authority; he proceeded to recount the troubles connected with speaking and its consequences.—I, said Thabit, was pleased; then al-Hasan spoke, while we were in this state of mind, and said: Satan would like you to accept his doctrine, so that no one would enjoin right or forbid wrong.

Account of the way wherein he deludes philologists and scholars

He has deluded the majority of them, distracting them by the study of grammar and the dictionary from those important matters which are obligatory on the individual, such as knowledge of their religious duties, and from more appropriate studies such as moral science and the reformation of the heart, and more excellent studies, such as the interpretation of the Qur'ān, Tradition, and Law. They give up all their time to studies which are not wanted on their own account but for something else; for when a man understands the word, he ought to proceed to act accordingly, since that is the purpose of the former. You will find one of these people scarcely knowing more than a little of the lore of the Code or of jurisprudence, and paying no attention to the purification of his mind and the reformation of his heart. And withal they are exceedingly proud and have been persuaded by the devil that they are the savants of Islam, because grammar and lexicography are Islamic sciences, and by them the meaning of the glorious Qur'ān is ascertained. This indeed cannot be denied; only the knowledge of the amount of grammar necessary for the correction of the tongue, and of lexicography for the interpretation of the Qur'ān and the Tradition, is easily acquired and indeed incumbent; anything more is superfluous and unnecessary, and it is a mistake to expend time in acquiring this unimportant superfluity while neglecting what is important; and preferring it to what is more profitable and more excellent, such as Jurisprudence and Tradition, is wasteful. If life were long enough for the acquisition of all knowledge, it would be all right; but since life is short, it is proper to give the preference to the more important and the more excellent.

The author proceeds to give examples of fetwas given where the ruling should distinguish two senses of the same word, which would call for different rulings. They are not fit for translation.

Being chiefly occupied with pagan poetry, nature finding no restraint to its instincts from the perusal of Traditions and the biographies of the saints of old, it carries them away to the abyss of

passion, and the floodgates of frivolity are opened. Rarely will you
see one of them troubling himself about piety, or scrupulous about
food: the grammarian is a courtier, and will eat the rulers' forbidden
food, as indeed Abû 'Alî al-Farisi enjoyed the protection of 'Adud al-
dãulah, and others; through want of understanding they fancy that to
be lawful which, is not so, as happened to Abû Ishaq Ibrahim b. al-
Sari al-Zajjaj.[21] I was, he said, tutor to al-Qasim son of 'Ubaidallah,
and I said to him: If you attain to your father's rank and are invested
with the vizierate, what will you do for me?—What *would* you like?
he asked.—I said: I should like you to give me twenty thousand
dinars.—This was the summit of my ambition, and only a few years
elapsed before he was invested with the vizierate while I was still in
his employ. I had become his messmate and felt tempted to remind
him of his promise, but I was afraid of him; on the third day of his
vizierate he said to me: Abû Ishaq, I have not seen you reminding
me of the vow.—I said: I relied on the good faith of the vizier, who
needs no reminding of a vow which he made with regard to a
meritorious servant.—He said: It is Mu'tadid; were it not for him it
would not be difficult for me to pay you this sum straight off; only I
am afraid that he would talk to me about it, so kindly take it in
instalments. I said Certainly.—Then he said: You are to sit and receive
people's petitions on important matters, and be quick with them,
never failing to ask me for something about which you are addressed,
whether it be right or wrong, until the sum of the vow has come into
your hands.— I did this, and used every day to present papers to
him, which he would sign, sometimes asking me how much had
been promised me for getting it through, when I would tell him, and
he would say You have been cheated; this is worth so much, so
make the man pay more. —I would then go back to the people, and
haggle with them till they had raised their offers to the amount which
he had fixed. So in a short time I had amassed the 20,000 dinars
and more.—After a month he asked me whether I had amassed the
amount which he had vowed; I said No, and I went on presenting the
papers, and once a month or so he would ask me the same question,
and I would say no for fear of the income coming to an end. This
went on till I had amassed the double of the amount, and one day
when he asked me I was ashamed of continuing to lie, and replied:
By the good luck of the vizier that sum has been amassed.—-He

---

[21] See *Irshad al-Azib*, i. 48.

said: You have relieved me, by Allāh, for I have been in anxiety till you got it.—He then took his inkhorn and wrote an order on his treasurer for three thousand dinars as a bonus. I took this and then ceased presenting documents to him, not knowing what view he would take of my conduct. The next day I went to him and sat in my usual place, when he signed to me to bring what I had got, meaning to demand the petitions as usual. I said: I have taken no paper from anyone, since the vow has been fulfilled, and I did not know what view the vizier would take.—He said: Good heavens, do you suppose I would deprive you of a business that has become your practice, about which people know and which has won for you their respect and made them come to your door morning and evening? The cause of the stoppage will not be known and people will suppose that it is due to a weakening of your influence with me, or a change in your position. So present the petitions as usual, and take your fees without reckoning.—I kissed his hand, and next morning brought him the petitions, and kept on bringing him something every day till he died, having an established position with him.

I would observe that here we may see the effort of ignorance of the law. Had this great grammarian and philologist known that this procedure of his was illegal, he would not have narrated it with such pride. The presentation of complaints is obligatory, and it is unlawful to take bribes for doing this, or any other of the public business which the vizier committed to him. And this shows the superiority of jurisprudence to other studies.

Account of the way wherein he deludes the poets

He deludes them into thinking that they are men of learning and possessors of sagacity which distinguishes them from their fellows, and that He who favoured them with this sagacity is likely to pardon their failings. Hence you find them "philandering in every valley" of falsehood, slander, satire; vilification and confession of atrocities. The mildest of their methods is to eulogize a man, who fearing that the poet may satirize him, will pay him, out of fear or shame before the company. All this is a sort of blackmail; and you may see many a poet and man of letters wearing silk without scruple, and lying beyond measure in his eulogies; narrating love-feasts and wine-bouts, "I with other men of letters made a party and did thus and thus." Such procedure is far removed from. "learning;" that is "reverence" towards God shown by practising piety.

And most of these poets and men of letters when in straitened circumstances repine, disbelieve, and start finding fault with destiny, as in the following utterance

> Although my ambition may soar to the skies,
>
> My luck, buried deep underground, cannot rise;
>
> Full many a buffet from fate must I bear;
>
> How mischievous, fate, how unkind, how unfair!

These people forget that their own misconduct is what causes their distress; they suppose themselves to be worthy of favours, and to deserve immunity from trial, having paid no attention to their duty of obeying the enactments of the Code. Their sagacity therefore is at fault in this negligence.

Account of the way wherein the devil deludes the most accomplished scholars

Certain ambitious people have acquired all the sciences connected with the Code, Qur'ān, Tradition, Jurisprudence, Philology, etc., and then been privily deluded by the devil making them "think more highly of themselves than they ought to think" in consequence of their attainments and the services they have rendered to their fellows. Some of them he puffs up with the thought of the length of time they have devoted to study, and recommends indulgence to them, saying "How long is this labour to last? Give your limbs some rest from these arduous occupations, and indulge your soul in its desires; if some lapse occurs, your knowledge will avert the punishment," dilating on the superiority of the learned. If the man accepts this, and yields to the delusion, he is lost; if he is helped by God, he should reply: The answer to you is threefold: one is that the superiority of the learned lies in their acting according to their knowledge; it would have no sense unless it were to be practised. If I do not act in accordance with it, I am like one who does not understand its purport, and might be compared to a man who amasses food, but does not eat, so that his hunger is not thereby allayed. A second mode of reply is to confront him with texts which censure him who does not put his knowledge into practice, such as the Prophet's saying *The man who will be punished most severely is a savant whom God has not profited by his knowledge,* and his narrative of a man who shall be thrown into hell-fire and his bowels gush out, and who will say "I used to enjoin right and not do it, and forbid wrong and commit it." And a third is to recount to him the punishment of those who perished having known but not acted by their knowledge, such as the devil and Balaam. And sufficient censure of the person who knows but does not act is to be found in the words of God (lxii. 5) *the like of an ass that carries books.*

The devil has deluded some of those who are sound in both knowledge and practice in another way: he persuades them to be conceited of their knowledge, jealous of rivals, and to play the hypocrite in order to gain supremacy. Sometimes he makes them think that this is something which is their due; sometimes he encourages their desire for it, which they do not abandon though knowing it to be sinful. The remedy for this in the case of those who are helped by God is to think carefully about the guilt of conceit, jealousy, and hypocrisy, and assure the mind that knowledge will not avert the mischief of these acquirements. On the contrary their punishment will be doubled, there being a double reason for it. One who studies the biographies of those ancients who both knew and practised will despise himself and feel no pride. Whoso knows God will be no hypocrite; and whoso observes how fate works as His will demands will feel no jealousy.

The devil approaches these people with a curious fallacy. There is nothing wrong, he says, in your seeking elevation, since you are the representatives of the Code, and your object is merely to glorify religion and suppress innovations. Your giving free rein to your tongues concerning those who are envious of you is indignation on behalf of the Code, since those persons censure its supporters; and what you suppose to be hypocrisy is nothing of the kind, since whosoever among you humbles himself and makes show of weeping will be imitated by people, just as they imitate a physician who practises cautery on himself more than one who merely prescribes it.

This delusion can be thus dispelled. If some other member of their class were to claim superiority over another and take a higher place in the assembly, or were to be slandered by an envious person, this savant would not feel as indignant as he would in his own case even if the victim were a representative of the Code, so that it would be known that his anger was not on his own account but on that of the Code. As for hypocrisy, that is inexcusable in all cases, and is unsuitable as a means of conversion. Ayyub al-Sakhtiyani[22] used to sweat when he repeated a Tradition, but would wipe his face, and say: what a bad cold I have! Further "acts are to be judged by the intentions," and critics have sharp eyes. Now many a man who will not himself slander Muslims will rejoice in his heart when they are slandered in his presence, incurring threefold guilt thereby: first by his rejoicing, since this was what caused the slanderer to commit the offence; secondly by his taking pleasure in the maligning of Muslims; and thirdly by not remonstrating.

The devil has yet further deluded these experts, who stay up all night and labour all day in the composition of learned works, by making them suppose that the object is the propagation of the faith. Their secret object is the propagation of their own fame, increase of reputation, supremacy and the attraction of students from all regions to the writer.

The delusion can be thus dispelled. If one of these students were to desert the writer for someone more learned than he, this would annoy the former; and this is no characteristic of a sincere teacher, for the sincere teacher should be like a physician, who treats patients for God Almighty's sake, and rejoices if a patient be cured by some other physician. We mentioned up above the Tradition of Ibn Abi Laila, which we will repeat here with a different chain of authorities going back to 'Abd al-Rahman his son. He said: I have been contemporary with a hundred and twenty of the Prophet's Companions of the Helpers, and there was not one of them but if asked about any matter would have wished that one of his brethren would have answered for him; and likewise with the reporting of Traditions.

Now the experts at times escape the delusions of the devil which are known among them, and such as he conceals; to such a man the devil says: Never have I met your like! How well you know my coming in and my going out!—If the man accepts this, he is ruined by his conceit; if he declines to accept it, he escapes. Al-Sari al-Saqati said: Were a man to enter a garden containing all the trees

---

[22] 66—131.

created by God, with all the birds created by God perched on them, and every bird to address him in his language, saying "Peace upon thee;' O saint of God," and he were to acquiesce, he would be a prisoner in their hands. God is the guide, there is no God but He!

CHAPTER VII

The Way Wherein the Devil Deludes Governor and Sovereigns

He deludes them in numerous ways of which we shall mention the chief categories. The first is making them suppose that God loves them, and were it not for that, He would not have given such a man His office or made him His deputy over His servants.—This delusion is to be dispelled by the consideration that if they are His deputies in reality, they had better judge in accordance with His Code, and follow His pleasure. In that case He will love them for their obedience. As for the titles king and sovereign, they have been given by God to many whom He hates, as indeed He has bestowed worldly prosperity on many on whom He would not look; to a number of such persons He has given authority over saintly and pious men, whom they have murdered and to whom they have done violence. Such a gift, however, is not for their benefit, but for their disadvantage; this being a case of the text (iii. 172) *We only give them respite that they may increase in guilt.* The second is his telling them that government requires awe, so that they become too proud to seek knowledge and make assessors of the learned, so as to act by their advice and be instructed in religion. Now it is well-known that a man's nature borrows from the qualities of his associates, and when men mix with those whose preference is for worldly prosperity and who are ignorant of the Code, their natures will borrow these people's qualities in addition to what they already possess of the like, and will disapprove of all that opposes such or warns therefrom; and this leades to ruin.—The third is his making them afraid of enemies, and bidding them screen themselves securely so that complainants can have no access to them, and official appointed to remedy injustices can neglect his duties. Abû Maryam al-Asadi[1] has reported the following Tradition of the Prophet: Whenever, he said, a man whom God has put in charge

---

[1] His name was 'Abdallah b. Ziyad.

of Muslim business screens himself from attending to their wants God will screen. Himself from attending to that man's wants, needs, or distress.—The fourth is getting them to put in office unsuitable, ignorant, and ungodly persons. The injuries which these officials inflict on people cause their curses to fall on the sovereign. Further the devil gives them illicit profits out of illegal sales and the infliction of punishment on innocent individuals. They suppose that they can free themselves from responsibility with God for what they have put on the neck of the deputy. They are mistaken. If the minister of alms appoints rogues to distribute them, and they cheat, he has to make their defalcation good.—The fifth is his persuading them to act arbitrarily, amputating hands which the law does not permit to be amputated, and executing persons who ought not to be executed. He makes them fancy that this is politic; the underlying idea being that the sacred Code is imperfect, and requires supplementing, so that we are to supplement it according to our own views.

This is indeed the worst of delusions; for the Code is a divine polity, and it is absurd to suppose that there can occur in God's polity any flaw which it needs human polity to remedy. God says (vi. 38) *We have neglected nothing in the Book* and (xiii. 41) *there is none that can rebut His judgment.* Hence one who claims to be politic claims that there is some flaw in the Code. We have been told how 'Adud al-dāulah was attached to a slave-girl, and finding that she occupied his mind, he ordered that she should be drowned lest she divert his mind from managing his realm. This is sheer madness, since it is unlawful to put a Muslim to death save for a crime. His belief that such an act was lawful was infidelity; but if he believed it to be unlawful, only thought it advantageous, then there is no advantage in what is contrary to the Code.

The sixth is his persuading them to be lavish with money, supposing it to be under their control.—This delusion can be dispelled by the observation that such control is withdrawn from a man who is extravagant with his own property: how much more must this be the case with one who is hired to look after other people's property! Only such amount of the money is his as is in proportion to his work; he has no right to squander. Ibn 'Aqil said: it is recorded that Hammad the Reciter repeated some verses to al-Wālid b. Yazid, who gave him 50,000 *dirhāms* and two slave-girls; this, he observes, is recorded by way of praise, but it is in fact a serious charge; for it means squandering the treasure of the Muslims. The devil further persuades some to withhold from the deserving their due, and this is as bad as squandering.

The seventh is to suggest to them that they may indulge in offences, deluding them with the idea that their protection of the roads and making the country safe will avert punishment from them. The reply to this is to tell them that they have been put in authority for the purpose of guarding the country and making the roads safe, and these are duties incumbent upon them; the offences wherein they indulge are illicit and their discharge of their duty will not avert punishment.

The eighth is to delude most of them with the consideration that such a one has discharged his duty inasmuch as things are superficially right; whereas if he were to scrutinize he would find that there was much disorder. It is recorded of al-Qāsim b. Talhah b. Muhammad that he said: I observed how the vizier 'Alî b. 'Isa set a salaried official over the Melon House,[2] his business being to go round the dealers in grapes; if a man bought a basket of grapes suitable for wine, he was not to interfere with him: but if he bought two or more, he was to throw salt over them, that it might not be possible for the man to make them into wine. Further, he says: I have witnessed sovereigns forbidding astrologers to sit in the streets so that the practice of acting by the stars might not spread. I have also known the army to be without a single beardless boy with tresses until Bachkam the foreigner[3] appeared.

The ninth is to persuade them to procure money and extort it by violent scourging, confiscating all the possessions of the dishonest officials and making them swear *that there* is *nothing more.* We have been told how 'Umar b. 'Abd al-'Aziz received a letter from a retainer to the effect that certain persons had embezzled the money of Allāh, and that he could not make them disgorge except by the infliction of torture; and the Caliph wrote him: *I prefer that they should meet Allāh with their dishonesty to my meeting Him with their blood.*

The tenth is to suggest to them to give alms after plundering, telling them that a dirhām given in alms wipes away the guilt of ten

---

[2] Near where the Tabik Canal joined the Nahr 'Isā was the building known as the "Melon House" (Le Strange, Baghdād, p. 85).

[3] For an account of this person, see Index to the *Eclipse.*

obtained by plundering. This is absurd for the guilt of the robbery endures, whereas the dirhām given in alms will not be accepted if it be obtained by robbery, whilst if it be obtained from a lawful source it will not avert the guilt of robbery, since the gift to a poor man will not invalidate the other man's right.

The eleventh is to encourage them while persisting in their iniquities to visit saintly men and implore their prayers, and make them think that this will lighten their guilt. This good act will not cancel the other bad act; Mani[4] said: A trader passed by a tithe-collector, and an embargo was put on his vessel. The trader went to Malik b. Dinār[5] and informed him about this. Malik arose and went with him to the tithe-collector. When the people saw Malik, they said to him: O Abû Yāhya, why did you not send some to us about your business? He said: My business is that you should release this man's vessel.—They said: We have done so.—Now they had an urn into which they put the dirhāms which collected from the traders. They asked Malik to pray for them. He said: You had better tell the urn to pray for you; How can I pray for you when a thousand others are calling down curses upon you? Do you suppose one man's prayer will be answered, and those of a thousand receive no answer?

The twelfth is in the case of officials who are in the service of a superior, and do wrong when they are commanded to do it, for the devil to delude them with the idea that the guilt falls not on them but on their superior. This is false, since such a person aids in wrongdoing and whosoever assists transgression is himself a transgressor. For the Prophet cursed ten persons in the matter of wine, and cursed the taker of usury, the man who lets him take it, and those who witness the act. To this category belongs collecting taxes for a superior who, it has known, will squander and embezzle. For this too is a case of giving help in wrongdoing. It is recorded that Ja'far b. Sûlaiman said: I heard Malik b. Dinār say: It is sufficient dishonesty for a man to be the trusted agent of one who is dishonest. It is God who guides us to the truth.

---

4 Probably Mani' b. Majid b. Matar *(Lisan al-Mizan)*.

5 Died 123.

CHAPTER VIII

The Way Wherein the Devil Deludes Devotees and their Devotion

You should, know that the widest doorway whereby the devil enters is ignorance[1]. He can get at the ignorant with impunity; at the learned only with difficulty. The devil has deluded many devotees by reason of their lack of knowledge, since most of them are occupied with their devotion and have acquired no profound knowledge. Rabi' b. Kāthaim[2] said: Study jurisprudence, and then become an anchorite.

His first delusion is the idea that devotion is superior to knowledge; whereas knowledge is more excellent than works of supererogation. He puts into their minds that the object of learning is work, and the only work which they know is what is done with the limbs of the body, being unaware that work is the work of the heart, and that the work of the heart is superior to the work of the limbs. Mûtarrif b. 'Abd-allah[3] said: excellence in knowledge is better than excellence in devoutness: Yûsuf b. Asbat[4] said: one chapter of knowledge learned is better than seventy raids. Al-Mu'āfa b. 'Imran[5] said: The writing out of a single Tradition is to my mind preferable to a whole night spent in prayer.

Now I observe that these people having suffered this delusion, causing them to prefer acts of devotion with their limbs to knowledge, the devil was enabled to delude them in various forms of devotion.

---

[1] Al-Duba'i: died 178.

[2] Died 61.

[3] 137-214 .

[4] Died 195.

[5] Al-Zihri al-Himyari. Among the Shaikhs of Malik b. Anas.

Account of his delusions in the matter of ablution

There are some whom he deludes in the matter of intention, and you will see such a person say "the filth has been removed," after which he will say "prayer is permissible," and then after that he will say "I will remove the filth." Now the source of this delusion is ignorance of the Code; for intention is in the heart not in the utterance, and there is no need to take the trouble of uttering, and further there is no sense in repeating the utterance. There are some whom he deludes by examination of the water used tor ablution, saying to such a person How do you know that it is clean?—making all sorts of improbable suggestions about it. He ought to be satisfied with the decision of the Code that purity is the essence of water, and an essential quality is not to be rejected for a possibility. Some are deluded into using a quantity of water, to which there are four objections; waste of water: frittering away invaluable life over what is neither necessary nor commendable; encroaching on the law, since such a person is not satisfied with the small amount of water which satisfies the law; entering on a course forbidden by the law, by exceeding the three *washings of the hands.* Often-times such a person takes so long over his ablution that he misses the prayer time or its commencement, which is of prime importance, or misses public prayer.

Account of the way wherein he deludes them in the Call to prayer

A case of this is intoning the Call; Mālik b. Anas and other men of learning disapproved of this practice exceedingly, because it removes the Call from being a reverential performance to resemble singing. Another case of it is their mixing the Call to the morning prayer with exhortations, praises, and homilies, inserting it in between. Learned men have disapproved of all additions to the Call. We have seen people mount the minaret at night and exhort or preach. Some read Surahs of the Qur'ān in a loud voice, interfering with people's sleep, and confusing the reading of those who keep vigil. All these practices are reprehensible.

Account of the way wherein he confuses them in prayer

A case of this is his deluding them in the matter of the clothes with which they cover themselves; you will see one of them wash a clean garment a number of times, and wash it after a Muslim has touched it. Some of them wash their garments in the Tigris, thinking that washing them at home is insufficient. Some of them plunge the garment into the well, as do the Jews; the Prophet's Companions did not do these things: indeed they prayed in Persian clothes, when they conquered the country, and made use of the Persian mats and wearing apparel. Some of the misguided sprinkle water over the garment and wash the whole of it, which sometimes makes them late for public worship. Some of them neglect public worship because of a little rain, which they fear may drip on their clothes.

Let not anyone suppose that I object to cleanliness and decency; only excess which is beyond the limits of the Code and involves waste of time is what I forbid.

Another case is his deluding them in the matter of intention in prayer. One of them says: I will make such and such a prayer, and presently repeat this, thinking that he has lessened his intention, whereas intention is not lessened by his dissatisfaction with the wording. One of them says *Allahu Akbar,* then cancels it, and when the Imam makes an inclination, this deluded person says the words and makes inclination simultaneously; I should like to know what has produced the intention at the latter rather than at the former time, unless it be that the devil wishes the man to miss the advantage.[6] There are deluded people who swear "By Allah I will not say *Allahu Akbar* except this time;" and some who swear with the sanction of loss of property and divorce. All these are delusions of the devil. The Code is liberal, easy, and free from these afflictions. Neither the Prophet nor his Companions practised anything of the sort. We have been told that Abû Hazim once entered the mosque when the devil suggested to him that he was about to pray without ablution. He said: You are not as careful of my interests as that!

The illusion is thus to be dispelled. Let it be said to the victim of it: If what you want is to produce the intention, such intention is

---

[6] Of earlier utterance.

already present, since you are about to perform a religious obligation, and that is an intention; and the seat of intention is the heart, not the utterance, so the utterance is unnecessary. Further you have uttered it in a sound state; so why repeat it? Do you suppose that you have lost the memory of what you have said? That indeed would be unsoundness.

A certain shaikh told me a strange story about Ibn 'Aqil. He was met by a man who said: I wash a member of my body and say that I have not washed it; and I utter *Allahu Akbar,* and say that I have not uttered it.—Ibn 'Aqil said to him: Omit to pray as it is not incumbent on you. —Some people said to Ibn 'Aqil: How can you say this? — He said to them; The Prophet said "The Pen[7] is withdrawn from a madman till he recover." A man who utters *Allahu Akbar,* and then says he has not uttered it is not sane, and prayer is not incumbent on the insane.

I would observe that you are to know that the cause of such delusion about intention in prayer is mental disease and ignorance of the Code. It is certain that a man would be thought to be of unsound mind if when he rose up in honour of a learned visitor he were to say "I am going to stand up as a mark of respect to the visit of this scholar on account of his learning," coming forward to greet him, because the man must have had the notion in his mind from the time when he saw the scholar. Similarly a man's rising to pray in order to perform his religious obligation is a notion which takes shape in his mind in a single moment which takes no time; time is only taken by the stringing of these words, which are not obligatory; the delusion is mere ignorance, Further the deluded person forces himself to produce in his mind the ideas of purity, performance, and obligation, all at once in separate utterances which he reads—and this is impossible. Were he to undertake the like in the matter of rising up before the scholar he could not do it. The man who knows this knows intention. Further it is permissible to prefix it with a brief interval to the utterance *Allahu Akbar* provided the man does not cancel it; why then take such trouble to attach it to that utterance, since, if the man make it and does not cancel it, he has practically attached it to that utterance? Musawwir is reported to have said: Ma'n b. 'Abd al-Rahmān showed me a document which he swore was in the script,

---

[7] *i.e.,* that of the recording angel.

of his father, containing the words: 'Abdallah said: "By him than whom there is no other God I have never seen anyone more vehement against the prolix than the Prophet, nor anyone after him more afraid on their account than Abû Bakr; and I think 'Umar was more afraid on their account than anyone in the world."

There are some deluded persons who after making sincere intention and uttering *Allahu Akbar* are careless about the rest of the prayer as though that utterance were the sole purpose of the ceremony. This delusion may be dispelled by the thought that the purpose of that utterance is to enter into worship. How then may worship be neglected when it is the dwelling, the man contenting himself with taking care to guard the door?

Certain deluded persons are satisfied with uttering the formula *Allahu Akbar* behind the Imam when the inclination is not quite complete, and then start afresh and utter the formula of "taking refuge" after which the Imam makes the inclination. This too is a delusion; for the fresh start and the formula of taking refuge are enactments of the Sunnah, whereas that which he neglects, viz., the recitation of the Fatihah, is according to a number of learned men obligatory; when an enactment of the Sunnah should not be preferred to it.

I may observe that in my youth I used to pray behind our master the jurist al-Dinawari, who once saw me do this; he said to me: My boy, the jurists differ as to the obligation of reciting the Fatihah behind an Imam, but they do not differ about the starting formula being a Sunnah; so pay attention to what is obligatory and omit the Sunnahs.

The devil has further deluded various people who have neglected many Sunnahs owing to fancies which have occurred to them. Some would keep back from the front row, such a man saying that his intention was proximity of heart; someone would not let one hand down on the other in prayer, saying "I am unwilling to make a display of humility which is not in my heart." These two proceedings have been told us of certain saints. It must have been due to want of knowledge; in the *Sahih* of Muslim there is a Tradition that according to Abu Hurairah the Prophet said: If men only knew the value of the Call to prayer and the front row, and found no other way to get into it, they would draw lots for it. And among the Traditions of Abû Hurairah found only in Muslim there is this: The best row is the front, and the worst is the back. As for putting one hand on the other, this is a Sûnnah. Abû Dawûd in his *Sunan* records that Ibn Zûbair said: Placing hand upon hand is of the Sunnah. Also that Ibn Mas'ud used to pray putting his left hand on his right, but the Prophet seeing him do this placed the right hand on the left.

I will state my objection to the man who says he meant nearness of heart and will not put one hand on the other, however great a man he may be. It is the Code which objects, not we; someone said to Ahmad b. Hanbal that Ibn al-Mubarak[8] said so-and-so: Ahmad replied that Ibn al-Mûbarak had not descended from heaven. Someone quoted to him Ibrāhim b. Adham,[9] and he said: You have brought me evidences of the Way; what you should produce is the Original.[10] This ought not to be neglected for the saying of someone for whom there is personal respect. For the Code is greater, and mistaken interpretation may become current.—It is, however, possible that he had not heard the Tradition.

The devil has further deluded certain persons in the pronunciation of the letters in their prayers. You may see a man saying the word *al-hamd* (praise) twice; such repetition is a transgression of the proper practice in prayer. Sometimes he deludes people in the doubling of a consonant, or in the pronunciation of the word *maghdub* (in the phrase "against whom there is anger"); I have known people to pronounce it *maghsub* owing to the stress which they put on the *dad;* what is wanted is the correct pronunciation of the letter, nothing more. The devil gets them away from correctness by an increase of effort, and distracts them from understanding what they recite by over-attention to the letters. All this is his delusion. It is recorded that Sa'id b. 'Abd al-Rāhman reported that Abû'l-'Amya[11] had been told by Sahl b. Abi Umamah[12] as follows. He and his son visited Anas b. Mālik when he was performing an abbreviated prayer like that of a traveller, and said to him: God have mercy on you, do you regard this as the prescribed prayer? Is it the Prophet's prayer or an additional act of

---

[8] 118-81. His name was Abdallah.

[9] Famous ascetic.

[10] By evidence of the way he probably means proofs belonging to a particular discipline

[11] His father.

[12] Abû Umamah's name was Sahl b. Hunaif.

worship?— He said: It is the Prophet's prayer; any mistake I may have made is unintentional. The Prophet used to say: Do not make things difficult for yourselves lest God make them difficult for you. This happened to certain people, of whom the relics are in the cells and the monasteries. *Monkery which they invented, and which We had not prescribed for them* (lvii. 27).—Among the Traditions of 'Uthman b. al-'As found only in Muslim there is the following: I said to the Prophet "Truly the devil comes between me and my prayer and confuses my recitation." The Prophet said: "That is a demon called Khanzab. When you perceive him, ask God's protection from him three times, and spit on your left." I did so, and God removed him from me.

The devil has further deluded a number of ignorant devotees into thinking that devotion consists merely in standing and squatting. They are sedulous in these performances, knowing no better. I have noticed how a number of people say the *salam* when the Imam says it, although they have not finished reciting the obligatory confession of faith; that obligation cannot be borne vicariously by the Imam. He has deluded others into prolonging the prayer and increasing the recitation while neglecting what the Sunnah has prescribed in the prayer, and perpetrating what is disapproved therein. I once visited a devotee who was uttering a non-obligatory prayer in the daytime, and reciting aloud, I said to him : The Sunnahs ought not to be neglected because you stay awake at night, so when sleep overcomes you, sleep, for your soul has certain rights over you. Buraidah is recorded to have said: The Prophet said: If a man recites, aloud in the daytime, fling dung at him.

The devil has deluded a number of devotees into praying much in the night, some of them staying awake the whole night, taking more pleasure in staying up and praying midday than in performing the prescribed devotions; only such a person may fall asleep a little before dawn, and so miss the prescribed prayer. Or he may get up and make ready for it but miss the assembly, or feel lazy in the morning and unable to earn for his family. I saw a devout, shaikh named Hussain al-Qazwini walking for much of the day in the Mosque of al-Mansur. I asked him why he walked, and said it was in order not to fall asleep. I said: This is ignorance of what is demanded by the Code and the reason. As for the Code—the Prophet said "Your soul has certain rights over you" so go to sleep. He used also to say: Go gently, for if anyone treats this religion with violence, it will overcome him.—It is recorded that Anas b. Mālik said: The Prophet entered the Mosque one day and noticed a rope stretched between two pillars. He asked what is this? He was told that it was for Zainab; she was praying, and could take hold of it when she felt lazy or faint. He bade them loosen it ; and he said: Let anyone of you pray when he feels vigorous, and if he feel weak or faint; let him squat. A'ishah is recorded to have said: The Prophet said: If one of you dozes, let him lie down till his sleep passes from him; for if he were to pray while dozing, he might start asking for forgiveness and revile himself.

I may observe that this is a genuine Tradition, recorded by Bukhari and Muslim, whereas the previous one is found only in Muslim.

As for the intelligence: since sleep renovotes the powers which are tired out by wakefulness, if a man keeps it off at the time when he needs it, it affects both his body and his mind; so we ask God to protect us from ignorance, if anyone say: You have reported to us that a number of the ancients used to stay awake all night: the reply is that those persons gradually acquired the capacity to do so, and could be sure of attending public prayer at dawn. Further they used to get help from a siesta and from paucity of food. Hence they could do this without harm. In addition we have no record that the Prophet ever kept awake for a whole night, taking no sleep therein; and his is the practice which should be followed.

The devil has deluded several of those who keep vigil into talking about it in the daytime. Such a man will say: A certain, *muedhdhin* uttered the Call to prayer at such and such an hour, in order that people may know that he was awake at the time. The least objection to this, supposing it to be free from hypocrisy, is that it removes the action from the sphere of secrecy to that of publicity, and so reduces the divine reward.

He has deluded others who isolate themselves in the mosques for prayer and devotion, and are known to do so, so that people gather round them and follow their lead in prayer, and they become famous. This is a temptation of the devil, whereby the soul is enured to devotion, knowing that this will spread abroad and earn eulogy. Zaid b. Thabit is recorded to have stated that the Prophet said: A man's best prayer is one offered in his own house, except the prescribed prayers.

I may observe that this Tradition is to be found in both *Sahih*. 'Amir b. 'Abd Qais[13] used to dislike being seen praying, and would offer no additional prayers in the mosque; yet he prayed a thousand inclinations every day. If anyone visited Ibn. Abi Laila while he was praying, he would lie down.

Some devotees, have been deluded into weeping while people are around them. Such a fit may overtake a man, and he be unable to suppress it. A man who displays it when he can conceal it lays himself open to the charge of hypocrisy. It is recorded on the authority of 'Asim, that when Abû Wa'il prayed at home, he used to sob violently; only he would not do the like in anyone's presence, though the whole world were offered him. Ayyûb al-Sakhtiyani used to rise up when he was overcome by a fit of weeping.

A number of devotees also have been deluded into praying night and day while taking no trouble to reform secret faults, nor about food. Attention to such matters would be their duty rather than supernumerary prayers.

Account of the way wherein he deludes them over the reading of the Qur'ān

A number of people have been deluded into frequent recitation of the Qur'ān which, they gabble without modulation of the voice and without pauses; this practice is not commendable. It is indeed recorded that some of the ancients used to recite the whole Qur'ān every day or at every inclination, but this was exceptional. If people persist in this practice, though it may be permissible, still modulation and pausing are preferred by the learned. The Prophet said: He will acquire no sound knowledge who takes less than three days to read the Qur'ān.

The devil has deluded some Readers to recite the Qur'ān on the minaret of a mosque at night all together with loud voices, to the extent of one or two Parts. These people combine public annoyance by keeping people from sleep with exposing themselves to the charge of hypocrisy. Some recite in the mosque at the time of the Call to

---

13 A Companion of the Prophet.

prayer because that is the time at which the congregation assembles.

The most curious case that I have seen of this sort is that of a man who used to lead morning prayer on Friday, then turn and read the two final Surahs, and then pronounce the prayer said when a man has read the Book through, in order that people should know that he had been doing this. This was not the procedure of the ancients. They used to conceal their devotions; all such acts of al-Rabi' b. Khaitham were performed in secret. Sometimes a visitor would come when he had opened the Sacred Volume; in such a case he would cover it with his garment. Ahmad b. Hanbal used constantly to read the Qur'ān, but no one ever knew when he had perused the whole.

We have now recorded various ways wherein the devil deludes the readers of the Qur'ān; God knows best what is right and He it is Who guides.

Account of the way wherein he deludes them in the matter of fasting

He has persuaded people to fast perpetually, which is permissible provided the fast is broken on the days wherein fasting is unlawful. Only trouble arises therein in two ways. One is that the process is likely to lead to debilitation, so that the man is unable to earn for his family, and perform his conjugal duties; in both the *Sahih* there is a Tradition that the Prophet said: You have duties to your wife. Such supererogatory act often leads to neglect of the obligatory. The second is that the man misses the better way. For there is a genuine Tradition that the Prophet said: The best fast is that of the Prophet David, who used to fast and break his fast on alternate days. There is a Tradition by a chain of authorities going' back to 'Abdallāh b. 'Amr who said: I was met by the Prophet who asked me; Have I not been told that you stay awake all night and that you are the person who says I shall assuredly stay awake during the night, and fast during the day?"—I fancy he replied: Yes, O Prophet of God, I did say that.—The Prophet said: Stay awake and sleep, fast and break your fast. —Fast three days in every month, and that will count as a perpetual fast.—He said: I replied: O Prophet of God, I can do more than that.—The Prophet said: Then fast one day and break your fast two days, He said: I can do better than that.—The Prophet said:

Then fast one day and break your fast one day, which is the most reasonable form of fasting, being that of the Prophet David.—He said: I can do better than that.—There is nothing better than that, said the Prophet. This Tradition is to be found in both *Sahih*. If anyone object that a number of the ancients are reported to have fasted continuously, the answer is that they were able to combine fasting with discharging their duties towards their families; perhaps in most cases they had no family and so need for earning. Some of them too only did this towards the end of their lives. Still the saying of the Prophet "There is no form of fasting better than that" disposes of such stories. Many among the ancients who fasted continuously, only eating coarse food and little of that, lost their eyesight or had their brains dry up. Such procedure is neglect of the soul's just claims and putting on it an intolerable burden. Hence it is not permissible.

A report sometimes gets about that a devotee fasts continually, and learning of this report he either does not break his fast at all or only does so in secret for fear of losing reputation; so this is a latent hypocrisy. If such a man meant to be sincere, and conceal his conduct, he would break his fast in the presence of those who know him to fast, and then return to his fasting without this being known. Some of them record the amount they have fasted, *e.g.*, "Today makes twenty years in which I have not broken fast." He is deluded into supposing that he reports this in order that he may be imitated, whereas God knows the real purpose. Sufyan al-Thauri said: A man performs an act in secret, but Satan does not leave him alone till he talks about it, so transferring it from the register of secret to that of public performances. It is the practice of some to fast on Mondays and Thursdays, and when such a man is invited to a meal he says "Today, Thursday, is my fasting day;" if he were to say "I am fasting," it might be supposed that this was due to some affliction;[14] the form in which he puts it means that he fasts every Thursday. Some of these people look down on other people because they break their fast; some while fasting long do not trouble with what sort of food they breakfast; or while fasting do not abstain from slander, petulance, and inquisitiveness. The devil makes them suppose that their fasting will atone for it all. All this is delusion.

---

[14] This is probably the sense.

Account of the way wherein he deludes them in the matter of pilgrimage

Sometimes a man discharges his obligation by a single pilgrimage, and then repeats the performance without his parents' consent, and this is an error. Or he goes on pilgrimage while in debt or having claims against him, or does so for amusement or on money from a tainted source. Many a pilgrim likes to be met and called *The Hajji,* and the majority of them neglect on their journey the obligations of purity and prayer. They assemble round the Ka'bah with impure hearts and internal uncleanness. The devil shows them the external form of the pilgrimage, deceiving them; for what is intended by the pilgrimage is proximity of heart not of body. This can be realized only by maintenance of piety. Many a man goes to Makkah thinking only of the number of his pilgrimages, and saying "I have stood in this place twenty times." Many a man has resided long in Makkah, and not even started cleansing himself within, his mind being very likely concentrated on the favours which he will get from someone or other. Very likely he will say "I have now been a neighbour (of God) for twenty years." Many a man have I seen on the Makkah road intent on pilgrimage, yet beating his companions to get at the water and jostling them on the way.

The devil has further deluded many of those who make for Makkah into omitting their prayers, and cheating when they sell, supposing that the act of pilgrimage will atone for it all. Some he has deluded into inventing ceremonies which do not belong to the pilgrimage. Thus I have seen many adopting fanciful fashions in their costume, such as baring one shoulder, and remaining whole days in the sunshine so that their skin may peel off, and their heads swell, hoping to gain credit with people thereby. Among the Traditions of Ibn 'Abbas to be found only in Bukhari there is one to the effect that the Prophet saw a man making the circuit of the Ka'bah with a halter, and cut it; or according to another account that he saw one man leading another through whose nose a ring had been passed, and cut the cord with his hand, ordering the guide to lead the other with his hand.—This tradition indicates that religious innovation is forbidden even if the intention be to do a pious act.

He has deluded some into professing reliance on God and so starting without provision for the journey, supposing this to be "reliance." This is a grievous error. A man said to Ahmad b. Hanbal: I wish to start for Makkah in reliance without provision.— Ahmad said to him then start apart from the caravan.— The man said No, with the caravan.—Your reliance, said Ahmad, is then on other people's knapsacks. We ask God to guide us.

Account of the way wherein the devil deludes the raiders

The devil has deluded many people into proceeding to the sacred war with the hypocritical and vainglorious intention of being called *Ghazi,* or at times the object is to be called hero; or the quest of spoil: whereas "Acts are according to their intentions" The following Tradition goes back to Abû Mûsâ. A man came to the Prophet and said: O Apostle of God, tell me, one man fights out of bravery, another out of patriotism, and another for display; which of these is in the path of God? —The Prophet said: When a man fights in order that God's word may be uppermost, he is on the path of God.—This Tradition is to be found in both *Sahih.*

The following is recorded as having been said by Ibn Mâs'ud: Beware how ye say so-and-so died or was slain as a martyr; for a man may fight for the sake of spoil, or to obtain mention, or to exhibit his prowess.—There is also a Tradition connected by a chain of authorities with Abû Hûrairah that the Prophet said: The first people to have sentence pronounced on them on the Day of Resurrection are three: A man who has died in battle, who will be brought and reminded of the benefits which he received and will acknowledge them, and will then be asked what he did in return. He will say: I fought for Thee till I was slain.—He will be told: Thou liest. Thou foughtest in order that it might be said What a brave man!---as indeed was said. An order will then be given that he be dragged on his face and cast into Hell. Next a man who has studied and acquired knowledge and read the Qur'ân, who will be brought and reminded of the benefits which he received and will acknowledge them, and will then be asked what he did in return. He will say I studied and acquired knowledge on Thy account, and read the Qur'ân.—He will be told:

Thou liest; thou didst study in order that it might be said What a learned man!—as indeed was said. And thou didst read the Qur'ān in order to be called a Reader, as indeed thou was t. An order will then be given that he be dragged on his face and cast into Hell. Next a man to whom God has been bountiful, bestowing on him every sort of wealth, who will be brought, reminded of the benefits which he received, which he will acknowledge, and then be asked what he did in return. He will say I left no object whereon Thou wouldst have money spent but spent it thereon for Thy sake.—He will be told: Thou liest. Thou didst do this in order that it might said What a generous man! —as indeed was said. An order will then be given that he be dragged on his face and cast into Hell.—This Tradition is found only in Muslim.

There is a Tradition which goes back to a Companion of the Prophet reported by Abû Hatim al-Razi. I heard, he said, 'Abadah b. Sûlaiman narrate as follows: We were on an expedition with 'Abdallah b. Mubarak in Byzantine territory, when we came across the enemy. When the two armies met, one of the enemy came forward and challenged to single combat. A man on our side came forward, engaged the other for a time, then thrust him and killed him. The same thing happened with another champion and a third. Then our champion challenged to single combat, and the challenge was accepted by a man who engaged our champion for a time and then slew him. The men thronged round him, I being one of them; we found that our champion had veiled his face with his sleeve. I lifted a corner of the sleeve, and lo and behold, he was 'Abdallah b. Mûbarak, who said: You too, then, Abû 'Amr, are among those who disgrace us—So consider, I said, this sincere hero, who feared lest his sincerity should be tainted through his being seen by men and winning their praise, and so hid himself!—Ibràhim b. Adham used to fight, but when booty was procured would take none of it in order that his reward in heaven might be all the greater.

The devil also deludes the religious warrior when he takes booty; often-times he takes what it is unlawful for him to take. Possibly he may be so ignorant as to suppose that the goods of Unbelievers may be taken by anyone, or not to know that embezzlement of spoil is sinful. The following Tradition of Abû Hûrairah is to be found in both *Sahih.* We marched (he said) against Khaibar with the Prophet, and God granted us the capture thereof; we did not take as booty gold or silver, only furniture, food, and clothing. Then we proceeded to the Wadi. The Prophet was accompanied by a slave of his and when we alighted this slave started loosening his saddle, when he was hit by an arrow which caused his death. When we were felicitating the man on his martyrdom, the Prophet said Not so, by Him in whose hand is Muhammad's soul. His garment will burst into flames upon him, since he took it out of the plunder on the day of Khaibar, when it had not been apportioned to him.—-The people, he said, were frightened, and a man brought a shoestrap (or a pair of them), saying I got this on the day of Khaibar. A strap (or a pair of straps) of fire—said the Prophet.

The raider may indeed know of the prohibition, but seeing a great quantity of booty be unable to restrain himself. Or he may think that his having fought in the sacred war will atone for his act. And here we may see the effect of faith and knowledge. It is recorded by a chain of authorities ending with Hûbairah b. al-Ash'ath after Abû 'Ubaidan al-Anbari. When, he said, the Muslims entered Mada'in and collected the spoil, a man came forward with a casket which he gave to the officer incharge of the spoil. Those who were present said: We have never seen any object like this; all that we have got would not equal it or approach it in value. The man was asked whether he had taken anything from it. He said: You may be sure that, were it not for God, I would never have brought it to you.—They saw that the man was of some importance and asked him who he was. He said: I will not tell you in order to be praised by you nor will I encourage you to eulogize me; I will praise God and be satisfied with His reward.—They sent a man to follow him, and when he had joined his comrades, the follower asked about him, and found that he was 'Amir b. 'Abd Qais.

Account of the way wherein he deludes many of those among them who have a reputation for virtue

They are of two classes, the knowing and the ignorant. He approaches the knowing in two ways. The first is ostentation seeking fame and admiration for their conduct. There is a Tradition with a chain of authorities going back to Ahmad b. Abi'l-Hâwari who heard Abû

Sulaiman say that he had heard Abû Ja'far al-Mansûr sob in his sermon on a Friday. Anger, he said, overtook me, and I intended to rise up when he descended from the pulpit and admonish him with reference to what I knew of his conduct. Only, he said, I did not like to stand up and admonish a Caliph while the people were sitting looking at me, so that I would be guilty of ostentation and be executed without being in the right. So I sat quiet.

The second way is anger on one's own account. This may be at the start, but often comes on in the course of enjoining right owing to the contumely which the censor endures, leading to personal hostility. So 'Umar b.'Abd al Aziz said to a man: Were I not angry, I should punish you. He meant: You have made me angry, so that I was afraid the punishment would be out of wrath for God mingled with wrath for myself.

When the person who enjoins right is ignorant, Satan plays with him, and his injunction does more harm than good. For he may well forbid some act which is agreed to be legitimate, or censure some performance whose doer is acting according to the theory of some school. Such a man may break open a door or climb over a wall and beat and abuse the wrongdoers; if they retort with language which annoys him, he becomes angry on his own account. He is likely to reveal what the Code bids him conceal. Ahmad b. Hanbal was asked about people who had in their possession forbidden articles covered up, *e.g.*, a harp or some intoxicant; he said, if such a thing be, do not smash it; but according to another Tradition he said Do smash it. This is to be interpreted as meaning that the article is covered with some thin material through which its outline can be seen, whereas the former Tradition deals with the case in which it is not visible. He was asked about a man who heard the sound of drum or lyre, not knowing what it was; he answered You are under no obligation with regard to what is out of your ken, so do not enquire about it. It may happen that such a censor may refer the culprits to someone who will deal unjustly with them. Ahmad b. Hanbal said: If you are sure that the Sultan, will inflict the legal punishments, then refer the matter to him.

Among the delusions which the devil practises on the censor is causing him, when he censures, to sit in an assembly, describe what he has been doing and boast of it, and further revile the culprits in the style of an angry man, and curse them; yet they may have repented, and may be better men than he, being penitent, whereas he is proud. His talk may involve exposure of the Muslims, by giving information to the ignorant, whereas it is his duty to hide the failings of Muslims so far as it is possible to do so. I have heard how a certain ignorant censor would assault people about whose conduct he had no certain knowledge, beat them mercilessly, and smash vessels—performances all due to ignorance. When a man who has knowledge censures, you are quite safe with him. The ancients used to show delicacy in censuring. Silah b. Ashyam[15] seeing a man talking to a woman said: Verily God shields; may He shield us and you!— Passing by some people he said: My brethren, what say ye of a man who, meaning to travel, sleeps all night and plays games all day? When will he do his travelling?—The attention of one of them was aroused and he said: Friends, this man means us.—So he and his companions repented.

The people who have the best right to be censured with delicacy are princes. The proper way to speak to them is as follows: Truly God has exalted you, so recognize the extent of His benefits, for gratitude ensures their continuance, and they ought not to be requited with transgressions.

The devil deludes some devout persons so that when they see wrong they fail to censure it, saying: Enjoining and forbidding are for saints; I am no saint, so how can I command anyone else?—This is a mistake, for it is his duty to enjoin and forbid, even if he were guilty of the same offence; only when a person who is innocent of an offence censures it, his censure is effective, whereas if he be not innocent, it is ineffective. Hence the censor ought to keep himself innocent in order that his censure may have effect, Ibn Aqil said: We have seen in our time Abû Bakr al-Aqfali in the days of al-Qa'im, who when he set about censuring wrongdoing took with him a number of shaikhs who supported themselves entirely by the labour of their hands, such as the saintly Shaikh Abû Bakr al-Khabbâz (the baker),

---

[15] The story of his devoutness is told by Tabari, ii, 393 (A.H. 61).

who was taken from his inspection of the oven and followed him, with others, no one of whom accepted alms, or soiled himself by taking presents, men who fasted all day and kept vigil all night, shedders of tears. If any dishonest man tried to follow him, he would be rejected. Al-Aqfali would say: If we meet an army with untrustworthy troops, we shall be routed.

CHAPTER IX

The Way Wherein the Devil Deludes Ascetics and Devotees

An ordinary man may hear the condemnation of the world in the Glorious Qur'ān and the Tradition, and hold that salvation lies in abandoning it, not knowing what the world which is condemned is. The devil will delude him, saying: You cannot be saved in the next world except by abandoning this, and such a man will go off headlong to the mountains, where he will be away from the congregation and the company and from knowledge, becoming like a wild beast, imagining that this is genuine asceticism. How could it be otherwise when he has heard that one person wandered away and another took to devotion on a mountain, though he may have had a family which went to ruin; or a mother who wept over his departure, and may not be acquainted with the rules of prayer, or have inflicted injuries on others which he has not made good. The devil can only succeed in deluding such a man by reason of his ignorance, to which is due his complacency with the amount which he knows. Had he had the good fortune to associate with a jurist who understood, the realities, such jurist would have shown him that the world is not condemned on its own account—how indeed can condemnation fall on a gift of God and an institution which is necessary for the continuance of the human species, and a means of aiding him to procure knowledge by furnishing him with food, drink, clothing and a sanctuary wherein he can pray? What is condemned is the taking of things from illicit sources or handling them extravagantly, not according to need, and disposing of them capriciously, not as the Code permits. Such jurist would have shown him too that going out to lonely mountains is forbidden; for the Prophet forbade spending the night alone; and that his venturing to abandon company and congregation is loss not gain; and that distance from knowledge and the learned strengthens the power of ignorance. Further that desertion of father and mother in such a case is unfilial, and unfilial conduct is a capital offence. Those who have been reported to have gone out to a mountain may well have been persons who had neither families nor parents, and went out in company to some place to practise devotion; those whose condition admits of no sound explanation yet do this are in error whoever they may be. One of the ancient said: We went out to a mountain to practise devotion, then Sûfyan al-'Thauri came and brought us back.

Among the delusions which he practises on the ascetics is his diverting them from learning while occupying themselves with asceticism. They thereby take the worse in exchange for the better; for the profit of the ascetic does not go beyond his own threshold, whereas that of the savant does go beyond. Many a devotee has been brought back to the right path.

He further deludes them by making them fancy that asceticism means abstension from lawful things. Some of them therefore will not go beyond barley bread; some will not taste fruit; some reduce their food to such an extent that the body dries up, torture themselves by wearing wool, and abstaining from cold water. This was not the way of the Prophet nor of his Companions nor their followers. They hungered indeed when they found no food, but ate when they found it. The Prophet ate meat and liked it, and poultry and liked it; he also liked sweets, and enjoyed the taste of water, which he preferred stale, holding that flowing water injured the stomach and did not slake the thirst.

A certain man said: I cannot eat date and almond paste, since I cannot be adequately grateful for it. Al-Hasan said: The man is a fool; can he be adequately grateful for cold water?

Sufyan al-Thauri when he travelled used to take with him as provision roast meat and almond and honey paste.

A man ought to know that his soul[1] is his mount, which he must treat gently in order that it may bring him to his destination. So he had better take what benefits it and eschew what harms it, such as satiety and excessive gratification of desires. For this injures both body and religion.

---

[1] His body would be more appropriate.

Further, people differ in nature, so when the Bedouin wear wool and restrict themselves to milk as a drink, we do not blame them, the mounts of their bodies can endure this. Similarly when the inhabitants of the Black Country[2] wear wool and eat unleavened bread, we do not blame them either nor do we speak of them as having burdened themselves, since such is their custom; only when the body is fastidious, being accustomed to delicacies, we forbid its owner to make it endure what will harm it. If such a man is ascetically inclined and prefers to abstain from desirable things either because what is lawful does not admit of luxury, or because delicious food involves frequent meals with much sleep and idleness, such a person should know what it will injure him to give up and what he can give up without injury, and so take as much as is good for his health without causing himself pain. Some people suppose that plain bread is sufficient for the maintenance of the body; even if this were so, restriction thereto would be injurious, inasmuch as the humours of the body require the sour and the sweet, the hot and the cold, the astringent and the aperient. There is implanted in nature an inclination towards what suits it, and sometimes it inclines to the sour but at others to the sweet, and for this there are reasons, *e.g.*, paucity of phlegm which is indispensable for its maintenance, whence there is a desire for milk, or there may be an excess of yellow bile so that it has an inclination for sourness; one who restrains it from following its natural craving for what benefits it injures it, unless indeed he restrain it from surfeit and greed and what may have dangerous consequences, for such will ruin it. Mere abstinence is an error; you should know this and take no notice of the sayings of al-Hārith al-Muhasibi and Abû Tālib al-Makki concerning exiguity of food and combating the soul by abstinence from what is lawful for it. It is better to follow the Legislator and his Companions Ibn 'Aqil[3] used to say: How extraordinary it is that pious people should harbour caprices to be followed or new fangled monasticism, trailing the skirts of licentiousness in love and sport, or neglecting their duties, deserting their families, and retiring to the corners of mosques! Why cannot they serve God reasonably and legitimately?

---

[2] The fertile lands of Irak.

[3] 'Alî b. Aqil, died 513.

One of the delusions which he casts upon them is making them fancy that asceticism means contentment with a minimum of food and clothing. Contenting themselves therewith, in their hearts they aspire to leadership and seek for honour, so that you may see them looking out for visits from princes, and to be honoured as the poor are not; when they meet people they assume a devout attitude as though they had just been experience a vision. Such a man often refuses money for fear it should be said that he has changed his mind about asceticism whereas they open the door widely to worldly advancement in the matter of receiving visits and having their hands kissed—worldly, since leadership is the summit of worldly ambition.

The commonest delusion which the devil casts on devotees and ascetics is secret, hypocrisy. Manifest hypocrisy, such as display of emaciation, paleness of face, and matted hair, does not come within this form of delusion. The same is the case with hypocritical praying and almsgiving, for such acts are not hidden. We are referring to secret hypocrisy; the Prophet said: Acts are by their intentions.—When the purpose of an act is not God's approval, it is not accepted. Malik b. Dinar said: Tell the person who is not sincere not to trouble himself.

You should know that the Believer in his conduct is thinking of God only, but he is liable to secret hypocrisy through delusion, and from this escape is hard. There is a Tradition going back uninterruptedly to Yasar[4] according to which he said: Yûsuf b. Asbat[5] said to me: Learn to distinguish sound conduct from unsound; it took me twenty-two years to learn. There is a Tradition going back uninterruptedly to Ibrāhim al-Hanzali according to which he said: I heard Bāqiyyah b. al-Wālid[6] say that he had heard Ibrāhim b. Adham say: I learned the meaning of knowledge from a monk named Sam'an, whose cell I entered. I asked him how long he had been in his cell.—Seventy years, he replied.—What, I asked, is your food?—He said: What makes you ask that, Hanefite? I said: I should like to know.—One chick-pea a night was his reply.—What emotion, I asked, does it stir in your heart so that this chick-pea can suffice you?—He asked me whether I saw the people in front of him.—

---

[4] Date of death not ascertained.
[5] Died 195.
[6] 115-97.

I replied that I did.—They, he said, come to me one day in each year, deck my ceil, make circuit of it, and pay me honour in this way. Whenever I feel weary of my devotions I remind myself of that hour; and I can endure the strain of a year for the glory of an hour; endure therefore, Hanefite, the strain of an hour for the glory of eternity.— This furnished my heart with copious knowledge. He then asked whether he should add more?—I bade him do so.—He told me to descend from the cell, which I did, and then he let down to me a bucket containing twenty chick-peas. He bade me enter the monastery, as the people had seen what he had let down to me.— When I entered it, the Christians collected and said: Hanefite, what did the old man let down to you?—Some of his food, I replied.— What, they said, will you do with it? We have the better right to it. Ask your price.—Twenty dinars, I said.—-They gave me the money. I went back to the old man, who said: You have made a mistake. Had you asked for twenty thousand, they would have given them to you. This is the glory of one whom you do not worship ; think what will come of the glory of Him Whom you do worship; Hanefite. Turn your face to your Lord!

I would observe that for fear of hypocrisy the saints have concealed their doings, giving them the appearance of the contrary, Ibn Sirin used to laugh during the day and weep during the night. Ayyûb al-Sakhtiyani used to wear a robe with a somewhat lengthy skirt; when Ibn Adhām was ill, food fit for the healthy was to be found set before him. There is a Tradition going back to 'Abdallah b. al-Mûbarak[7] after Bakkar b. 'Abdallah according to which the latter heard Wāhb b. Munabbih say: There was a certain man, one of the best of his time, whom people used to visit and honour. One day they gathered round him and he said: We have left the world, abandoning family and goods for fear of impiety, yet I am afraid that more impiety has befallen us in this condition than befalls the wealthy in their wealth. I find we like people to render us services; if we make a purchase, to get easy terms on account of our piety: if we are met, to be greeted and made much of on account of our piety.—This speech was noised abroad till it reached the king, who marvelled thereat and rode out to salute the man and gaze upon him. When the man saw him, he was told that it was the king who had come to

---

[7] 118-81.

salute him.—What is he going to do? asked the man.—It is on
account of your sermon, they said.— He asked his attendant whether
he had any food, and was told that there was some of the fruit
whereon he ordinarily breakfasted. He ordered that this should be
brought on a mat and set before him. He began to eat, though it was
his practice to fast during the day and eat nothing. The king
approached him and saluted him. He replied in a low voice and
proceeded to eat. The king asked where the man of whom he had
heard was, and was told that this was he. The man who is eating?
asked the king.—Yes, they said.—There is no good in him, said the
king, who turned away.—The man said: Praise be to God Who has
caused you to depart by this expedient.

According to another report Wahb said that when the king came
forward the man made large mouthfuls of the vegetables, dipped
them in oil, and began to eat voraciously. The king said to him: How
are you, whoever you may be?— The man said: Like other people.—
The king then turned away the rein of his mount, saying: There is no
good in him. The man said: Praise be to God Who has sent him
away from me with censure.

There is a Tradition going back to 'Ata[8] according to which he
said: al-Walid b. 'Abd al-Mālik[9] wanted to appoint Yāzid b. Marthad to
an office and when Yazid heard this, he put on a fur with the skin on
his back and the wool outside; in his hand he took a loaf of bread,
and some Arack, and started out without cloak, hood, sandals, or
shoes. He ate as he walked in the street. Al-Walid was told that
Yazid had lost his reason, and was informed of his proceedings. So
he let him alone.

There are ascetics who practise asceticism both outwardly and
inwardly, yet such a man, being aware that his friends or his wife will
certainly talk about his abandoning the world, will find this easy to
endure as the monk whose encounter with Ibrāhim b. Adham we
have recorded found it. If such a man were sincere in his asceticism
he would eat with his family such quantity as would win no reputation
for sanctity and cause talk about him to stop. Dawûd b, Abi Hind[10]

---

[8] Ibn Abi Rabah, 27-114.

[9] Umāyyad Caliph, 86-96.

[10] Died about 139.

fasted twenty years without letting his family know. He would take his food, go out into the street and give it away. So the people in the street thought that he had eaten at home, whereas his household thought he ate in the street. Such were people then!

There are besides ascetics whose sustenance is retreat in a mosque or monastery or on a mountain, and whose pleasure consists in people knowing of their isolation. Such a man may plead in defence of his retirement that he is afraid of seeing something of which he disapproves if he came out. He has, however, various ends in view; among them pride and contempt of other people, fear lest they should not pay him sufficient attention; preservation of his dignity and leadership, which would be impaired by mixing with people, whereas he is anxious that his credit and reputation should remain intact. At times indeed his object is the concealment of his faults and failings, and general ignorance, which might be seen; and he desires to be visited and not have to pay visits; and takes delight in princes coming to him, and commoners crowding at his door and kissing his hand. So he neglects visitation of the sick, and attendance at funerals, and his friends say: Excuse the shaikh, this is his custom (he had better not have had a custom which violates the Code!) Should such a person be in want of food and have no one with him to buy it, he would endure hunger so that he might not have to go out to buy it himself, and so lose dignity by walking among the populace. If he were to go out and buy what he wanted, his reputation would be at an end! His inner purpose is maintenance of his dignity. Yet the Prophet used to go out into the street, buy what he needed, and carry it himself. Abû Bakr used to carry clothes on his shoulder and sell and buy. There is a Tradition going back to Muhammad b. al-Qasim who stated that it was reported on the authority of 'Abdallâh, b. Hanzalah[11] how 'Abdallâh b. Sâlam[12] was seen walking with a bundle of firewood on his head. People said to him: What induces you to do this, when God has enriched you? He said: I wanted to keep off pride thereby, for I heard the Prophet say: He in whose heart there is an atom's weight of pride shall not enter paradise.

I would observe that the practice which I have mentioned of

---

[11] Died; 63.

[12] Convert from Judaismi, died. 43.

going out to buy what is required and similar sacrifices of dignity were customary with the ancients; the practice has changed like conditions and fashions in dress. I should not advise a learned man in our time to go out to buy what he wants, since such a proceeding would eclipse the light of learning in the eyes of the ignorant, who are bound to respect it. Regard for their sentiments in this matter would not degenerate into hypocrisy, and employment of such measures as will enforce respect is not to be forbidden. Not every proceeding whereby men of old time avoided changing people's sentiments can be practised in our time. Al-Aûza'i said: We used to laugh and make merry, but when we find that pecple follow our example I do not think this proper for us. It is reported how one day the friends of Ibrãhim b. Adhãm were making merry, when a man knocked at the door and bade them be quiet and dignified. They said to him: You would teach us hypocrisy.—He said: I do not wish God to be disobeyed through you.

This man, I would observe, was afraid of what the ignorant would say, *viz.*, See what these ascetics are doing!—For the populace cannot endure such conduct on the part of professed devotees.

Among these people there are those of whom if one were asked to don soft raiment, he would decline, for fear of loss of dignity; he would rather expire than be seen eating. He would restrain himself from smiling, not to speak of laughing. The devil makes him fancy that this is for the improvement of his character; in reality it is hypocrisy, a means of maintaining his prestige. So too you may see him with bowed head, showing the signs of grief. When he is by himself, there is no knowing what he would look like.

The men of old time used to keep off anything which would bring them into notice; they would flee from any place in which they might be pointed at. There is a Tradition traced to 'Abdallãh b. Khãfif,[13] according to which Yûsuf b. Asbat said: I started on foot from Manbij and reached Missisah (Mopusuestia) with my wallet on my neck. Then one man rose up from his booth and saluted me, and another, so I threw down my wallet and entered the mosque, where I made a prayer of two inclinations. People surrounded me, and one man gazed on my face. So I said to myself: How long will my heart endure

---

[13] Perhaps Abû 'Abdallãh Muhammad b. Khãfif, died 371.

this?—So I took up my wallet, and returned sweating and tired to Manbij, and for two years my heart did not return to me.

There are ascetics who wear tattered garments and do not stitch them neither adjust their turbans nor comb their beards, to let people see that they know nothing of mundane matters. This is a form of hypocrisy; for if the man be sincere in his neglect of externals, as when Dawud al-Ta'i[14] was asked why he did not comb his beard, he replied "I have other things to think of"—he should know that he is off the high road; for this was not the procedure of the Prophet or of his Companions. He combed his hair, looked in the mirror, used ointment and perfume, though more occupied with the next world than any other creature. Abū Bakr and 'Umar used to dye their hair with henna and phyllirea; yet they were the most scrupulous and most ascetic of the Companions. No attention should be paid to one who claims rank which surpasses the Sunnah and the practice of the chief men.

There are ascetics who maintain continual, silence and isolate themselves from the society of their families, whom they annoy by their unamiability and excessive moroseness, forgetting the saying of the Prophet "You have a duty to your family." The Prophet used to be of good humour, play with children and talk to his wives, run races with 'A'ishah, and do other amiable things. This devotee who makes his 'wife into a widow and his children orphans by his unamiability and isolation, supposing that different conduct will distract him from the next world, is so ignorant as not to know that cheerfulness with one's family is an aid to the next world. In both the *Sahih* there is a Tradition that the Prophet, said to Jabir: Why not marry a virgin so that you could play together—Such an ascetic often neglects his conjugal duty, and so violates an ordinance for an improper act of supererogation.

There are ascetics who are pleased with their conduct and if anyone were to tell them they were the pillars of the earth, would regard it as the truth. Some of them watch for the occurrence of miracles in their honour, and such an one fancies that if he were to come to water he could walk upon it. If occasion comes for him to pray and he is not answered, he feels indignation, as though he

---

[14] Abû Sālaiman Dawûd b. Nusair, pupil of Abû Hānifah. See *Kashf,* p. 109.

were a hireling demanding payment for his work. Had he been favoured with intelligence he would have known that he is a bond-servant who earns no thanks for his labour. Had he considered how he had been divinely guided to his work, he would have seen cause for gratitude and been afraid of falling short therein. His fear of such shortcoming might well have kept him from thinking about his work, as Rabi'ah said: I ask God's forgiveness for the want of veracity in my speech.—She was asked whether she had performed any act which she thought would be accepted of her. She said: If there be any, it is my fear of its rejection.

One of the delusions which the devil practises on certain ascetics whom he approaches through their ignorance is their acting according to their own imaginings without attending to what the jurist says. Ibn 'Aqil said: Abû Ishaq al-Kharraz was a saintly man, and the first person who taught me the Book of God. It was his practice to abstain from speech in the month of Ramadan, only uttering phrases from the Qur'ân when occasion demanded speech. Thus for the admission of visitors he would say (v. 26) *Enter unto them the gate,* and to his son at the evening of the fast (ii. 58) *of its greens and its cucumbers* as an order to buy vegetables.

I said to him: This is a thing which you believe to be a pious act, whereas it is a sin.—This grieved him; and I went on to say: This Glorious Qur'ân was revealed for the explanation of the ordinances of the Code, and should not be used for mundane purposes. You might as well wrap your soap in leaves of the Sacred. Volume, or make of it a pillow for your head.—He cut me and would not listen to the argument.

At times (I observe) an ignorant ascetic hears something from the laity and gives a legal opinion according to it. I was told by the jurist Abû Hakim Ibrâhim b. Dinâr how a man had asked him for an opinion on the following question: If a woman after a third divorce gives birth to a male child, can she lawfully be taken back by her husband? I answered No, he said. There was present with me al-Shârif al-Dhhali, a man renowned for his asceticism, and highly esteemed by the populace. He said to me: On the contrary, she may be taken back.—I said: No-one has taken that view.—He said: I assure you I have given this opinion from here to Basrah.

So see the effect which ignorance has on those who suffer from it, and how there is added thereto the maintenance of dignity for fear lest the ascetic be regarded as an ignorant man. Men of old time used to disapprove of an ascetic giving legal opinions even though he possessed much learning, on the ground that he did not possess all the qualifications for doing so. What then would they say if they were to see the devotees of our time giving wrong opinions out of their imaginations? There is a Tradition going back to Ismā'il b. Shabbah according to which he said: I entered the presence of Ahmad b. Hanbal, when Ahmad b. Harb[15] had arrived from Makkah. Ahmad asked me: Who is this man of Khurasan who has arrived?—I proceed to tell him about the man's asceticism and integrity. He said: A man who professes what he does ought not to meddle with legal opinions.

Among the delusions which he practises on ascetics is their contempt for and vituperation of the learned. They assert that the object to be aimed at is action; not knowing that knowledge is the action of the heart. If they understood the rank of the learned in memorizing the Code, and that it is the rank of Prophets, they would regard themselves as dumb brutes by the side of correct speakers and blind by the side of the seeing. The learned are the guides of the path, with the rest of mankind behind them, and one of them, if he be fit, can walk alone. In the two *Sahih* there is a Tradition of Sahl b. Sa'd[16] that the Prophet said: By Allāh that He should guide any man by you is better for you than ruddy camels.

Among the faults which they find with the learned is that the latter allow themselves certain liberty in things permitted, to gain strength therewith for the prosecution of study; and similarly they find fault with one who amasses wealth. Had they understood the meaning of the word "permitted" they would have known that no blame attaches to the person who practises it. The utmost that can be said is that those who do not are better than those who do. Would it be proper for one who prays the whole night to find fault with one

---

[15] He was of Nisabûr, died 234. The story is told in *Kitāb Baghdād*, iv, 119.

[16] Died about go: The last of the "companions" who died in Madinah.

who performs the obligatory prayer and then goes to sleep? There is a Tradition going back to Muhammad b. Jā'far al-Khaulani[17] according to which he said: The following was told me by Abû 'Abdallāh al-Khāwwas who was a companion of Hātim al-Asamm:[18] We entered Rayy with Hātim al-Balkhi who was accompanied by three hundred and twenty followers and was on his way to the pilgrimage. They all wore wool, with tunics of the same material, not one of them bringing wallet or food. We stopped at the house of a devout trader, who entertained us. The next morning he said to Hātim: Abû 'Abd al-Rāhman, do you need anything? For I wish to visit one of our jurists who is ill.—Hātim said: If there is a sick jurist among you, visiting such a person is highly meritorious, and indeed to gaze upon a jurist is a pious act. I will come with you.—Now the sick man was Muhammad b. Mûqatil, qadi of Rayy. The trader bade him come with him. They came to the door of the sick man's house, and there was a door-keeper. Hātim kept thinking and saying: O Lord, is the house of a learned man of this style!—Permission was then given them to enter, and they found it to be a spacious mansion with fine furniture, hangings, carpets and curtains. Hātim kept thinking and staring till they entered the room wherein Muhammad b. Mûqatil was, and there they found him lying on a soft, handsome couch, with a flyflap at his head, and men standing. The trader from Rayy sat down, but Hātim remained standing; Muhammad b. Mûqatil with a gesture bade him take a seat.—Hātim said: I will not sit down.—Ibn Mûqatil asked him whether he wanted anything. He said: Yes.—What is it? asked Ibn Mûqatil. He said: I wish to ask you a question.—Ask me, he said.—Hātim said: Rise and sit up that I may ask you about it.—Hātim ordered his servants to prop him up. Then Hātim said: Whence did you procure this knowledge of yours? He replied: By instruction from trustworthy persons who had it from others who were trustworthy who had it from the founders of the Science. —From whom, asked Hātim, did they obtain it?—From the epigoni[19] he answered.—And from whom did the epigoni obtain it?—From the Companions of the Prophet, he replied.—And whence did the Prophet procure it? he asked.—From Gabriel, who had it from God Almighty, he replied.—

---

[17] In the *Kitāb Baghdād* al-Hasan b. Muhammad (viii. 242).

[18] Notice of him in *Kāshf al-Mahjub*, p. 115. He was from Balkh.

[19] Generation which came after the companions.

Then Hātim said: In the matter conveyed by Gabriel from God Almighty to the Prophet, by the Prophet to his Companions, by his Companions to the epigoni, by the epigoni to the founders by the founders to trustworthy persons, and by those trustworthy persons to you, have you heard that the finer a man's house, the softer his bedding, and the more copious his decoration in this world, the higher will be his rank with God? —He said: No.—Ther. what he asked, have you heard?—He said: I have heard that the man who is averse to mundane things, has his affections fixed on the next world, loves the poor, and makes preparation for the future life, is of higher rank with, and nearer to, God.—Hātim said: And whom have *you* taken for your model? The Prophet, his Companions, the epigoni who followed, the saints who trod in their footsteps?—or Pharaoh and Nimrod? They were the first to build with gypsum and brick. O ye that are learned in mischief! The ignorant man who is passionately attached to the world will say: This man of learning lives in this style; shall I not do the like?

Hātim departed from his presence; Muhammad b. Mûqatil's illness became worse. The people of Rayy heard what had passed between Hātim and Ibn Mûqatil, and told Hātim that Muhammad b. 'Ubaid al-Tanafisi in Qazwin was yet more luxurious than Ibn Mûqatil. So Hātim went to him, entered his house, and found a number of people with him to whom he was discoursing. Hātim said to him: God have mercy on you, I am a foreigner who has come to learn from you the elements of my religion, and the preliminaries of prayer: how should I wash for prayer?—Muhammad b. 'Ubaid said: Most certainly; slave, bring a vessel with water.—One was brought, Muhammad b. 'Ubaid squatted down, washed himself three times, and said: This is the way you should wash.—Hātim said: Please wait till I wash in your presence, in order to enforce my point.—So al-Tanafisi rose, and Hātim squatted down in his place and began to wash. He washed his face three times, but when he got to his arm he washed that four times. Al-Tanafisi said: You have been too lavish.—Hātim asked wherein? He said.: Washing your arm four times.—Hātim said: Good heavens! I have been too lavish with a handful of water, and have you not been too lavish in all this that I see?—Al-Tanafisi understood that Hātim's intention was to rebuke him, entered his house, and did not appear in public for forty days.

Hātim departed for the Hijaz. When he got to Madinah, he wanted to dispute with the savants of that city. Entering it, he said: Ye people, what city is this?—They said: The City of God's Prophet.—Where, he asked, is the palace of God's Prophet that I may go and offer there a prayer of a couple of inclinations?—They said: The Prophet of God had no palace, he had only a low hut.—Where then, he proceeded to ask, are the palaces of his family, his Companions, and his wives?—They said: They had no palaces, but only low huts.— Then, said he, this is Pharaoh's city!—They reviled him (says the narrator) and brought him to the governor, saying: This foreigner calls this Pharaoh's city.—The governor asked him why he had said that.—He replied: Prince, do not be hasty with me. I am a stranger, and entering this city asked what city it was. They said: The city of God's Prophet. I then asked for the palace of God's Prophet and the palaces of his Companions. They told me that they had only low huts. Now I have heard God Almighty say: (xxxiii. 21) *Ye have had in God's Prophet a good model;* now whom have you taken for your model? God's Prophet, or Pharaoh?

Here I would observe: Woe to the learned from the ignorant ascetic who is satisfied with his knowledge and thinks obligatory that which is supererogatory. For that which he disapproves is permitted, and that which is permitted has the assent of the Code; the Code would not assent to an act and then remonstrate on its account. Such ignorance is disgraceful. Had Hātim said to them: Might you not have moderated your style of living so as to give an example to others, it would have been more fitting. What too would the man have said had he heard that 'Abd al-Rāhman b. 'Auf, al-Zubair b. al-'Awwam, 'Abdallāh b. Mās'ud, and many more of the Companions left huge fortunes? Tamim al-Dari gave a thousand dirhams for a cloak in which he used to keep vigil.

It is the duty of the ascetic to learn of the learned, and if he has not learned, he had better keep silence. There is a Tradition traced to Malik b. Dinār according to which he said: Satan plays with the Readers as boys with nuts. The same Tradition is traced to Habib al-Farisi.

"Readers," I would observe, here mean ascetics; it is an old and well-known name for them. God is the Guide to what is correct, and to Him is recourse and return.

CHAPTER X

The Way Where Devil Deludes the Sûfis

The Sûfis belong to the ascetic group, and we devote a fresh section to them, although we have described the manner wherein the devil confuses the ascetics, because the Sûfis are distinguished from other ascetics by certain qualities and states and bear certain badges. Sûfism is a system which commences with general asceticism, whose adherents afterwards permitted themselves music and dancing. They have won the favour of seekers of the next world from among the multitude by reason of the asceticism which they exhibit; and by seekers after this world owing to the comfort and amusement which they find these persons enjoy. It is necessary to dispel the delusions which the devil introduces into their system, and this can only be done by revealing the system with its branches, and explaining its methods.

In the time of the Prophet men took their appellations from Belief and Islam, calling themselves Believer and Muslim. Then there came into use the names Ascetic and Devotee; then there arose persons who attached themselves to asceticism and devotion, separated themselves from the world and gave themselves up to devoutness, adopting therein a system of their own and conforming themselves to a certain character. They supposed that the first person to isolate himself for the worship of God in His holy house was a man called Sufah, whose name was al-Ghauth b. Murr; so they named themselves Sûfis after him, as they resembled him in separating themselves to serve God.

I was told by Muhammad b. Nāsir after Abû Ishaq Ibrāhim b. Sa'id al-Habbal that the following had been said by Abû Muhammad 'Abû al-Ghani b. Sa'id the Hafiz:[1] I asked, he said, Walid[2] b. al-Qāsim

---

[1] Died 229.

[2] Died 183.

from what did the Sûfis take their name?—He replied: There were certain people in the days of paganism called Sufah, who separated themselves for the worship of God and inhabited the Ka'bah; those who imitate them are the Sûfis, 'Abd al-Ghâni added: the people known as Sufah were the children of al-Ghauth b. Murr, brother's son to Tamim b. Murr. According to a Tradition going back to al-Zûbair b. Bakkar[3] he said: The conducting of the pilgrims from 'Arafah was committed to al-Ghauth b. Murr b. Tabikhah and continued among his descendants who were called Sufah. When the time arrived for such conducting the Arabs said, Conduct, Sufah!— Al-Zûbair added: Abû 'Ubaidah asserted that the name Sufah or Sufan was given to anyone who was in-charge of any business connected with the House, not being one of its chief officials, or who looked after any part of the ceremonial. Zûbair also said: I was told by Abû'l-Hasan al-Athram after Hisham b. Muhammad b. al-Sa'ib al-Kalbi that according to this last al-Ghauth b. Murr was called Sufah because his mother, finding that all her children died, vowed that if he lived she would attach a piece of wool to his head and make him bound to the Ka'bah. She carried this out, and in consequence, he and his descendants were called Sufah; Al-Zûbair further states that he was told by Ibrâhim b. al-Mundhiri[4] after 'Abd al-'Aziz b. Imran[5] that this last had been told by 'Aqqal b. Shabbah[6] that the mother of Tamim b. Murr having given birth to a number of girls promised Allâh that if she bore a boy she would make him a slave of the House. She gave birth to al-Ghauth b. Murr and when she attached him to the House he felt the heat. Passing by him when he had fallen down and was in a state of collapse she said: This boy of mine is no better than a piece of wool, whence he was called Sufah. Sufah had charge of conducting the pilgrims from 'Arafah to Mina and from Mina to Makkah. This right continued with the descendants of Sufah till it was taken by 'Udwan, who also held it till it was taken by Quraish.

Some people, I would observe, take the views that Sûfism is traceable to the "people of the Suffah" (the bench in the Prophet's Mosque). Their reason for this opinion was that they found the people

---

[3] Died 256.

[4] Died 236.

[5] Died 197.

[6] Contemporary of al-Mahdi (158-69).

of the Suffah agree with our description of Sufah in devotion to God and the practice of poverty; for these were poor people who came to the Prophet, having neither families nor possessions, and a bench was built for them in the Prophet's mosque, whence they were called People of the Bench. There is a Tradition traced to al-Hāsan as having said: A Bench was built for the weak Muslims, and the other Muslims used to bring them any charity they could. The Prophet would come to them and say, Peace be upon you, ye people of the Bench; to which they would reply, And on thee, O Prophet of God!—He would ask them how they were and they would reply, Well, O Prophet of God.

There is a Tradition traced to Nu'aim b. al-Mu'jammir after his father after Abû Dharr; according to which the last of these said: I was one of the people of the Bench, and when evening came, we used to present ourselves at the Prophet's door, who would order each of us to go off with some man, until only ten or fewer of the people of the Bench remained; the Prophet would sacrifice his own supper to us, and when we had supped would bid us go and sleep in the mosque.

These people, I would observe, only sat in the mosque of necessity and only fed on charity out of necessity. When God bestowed victory on the Muslims they could dispense with this state and went away. Moreover the derivation of Sûfi from Suffah is erroneous, since the form would have been Sûfi. There is an opinion that the name is derived from *Sufanah,* which is a soft and stumpy vegetable; the people according to this were called from it because they were satisfied with the herbs of the field. This also is erroneous, because the form should have been *Sufani.* Others derive it from the *sufah* of the nape of the neck, *i.e.,* certain hairs which grow on the back of it; the idea being that the Sûfi turns away from creatures and swerves towards God. Others derive it from the word for wool, which is admissible; only the first derivation is the correct one.

The name came into use before the year 200, and when the first of these people proclaimed it, they talked about it, expressing its import in various ways; whereof the gist is that according to them Sûfism means disciplining of the soul, and resistance to nature by restraining it from vices and impelling it to virtues such as asceticism, gentleness, patience, sincerity, veracity, etc., such as earn praise in this world and reward in the next. There is a Tradition going back to al-Tusi according to which he said: I heard Abû Bakr b. al-Muthaqif say: I ask Junaid b. Muhammad about Sûfism, and he replied: It is departure from all evil qualities and entrance into all noble qualities.— There is a Tradition going back to 'Abd al-Wahid b. Bakr according to which he said: I heard Muhammad b. Khafif[7] say: Ruwaim[8] said: All mankind are seated on semblances, save this sect which is seated on realities. All mankind demand of themselves the externals of the Code, whereas these people demand of themselves the reality of chastity, and constancy in veracity.

I would observe that the first Sûfis carried this out; the devil however deluded them in certain ways, and yet further deluded their successors. As a century elapsed his hopes for the next century increased, and he deluded them still further, and obtained complete control over the later generations.

He started deluding them by diverting them from knowledge, making them suppose that the object to be aimed at is action. When he had extinguished the lamp of knowledge which they had, they floundered in darkness. He persuaded some that the purpose of their system was complete abandonment of the world; hence they discarded what was good for their bodies; compared wealth to scorpions, forgetting that it was ordained for useful purposes; imposed all sorts of penances on themselves, so that some of them would never lie down. The aims of these people were indeed good, only they were off the right path. Some of them through want of knowledge used to act according to fabricated Traditions of which they got hold, not knowing them to be fabrications.

Then came persons who discoursed to them about hunger, poverty, suggestions and insinuations, and composed works on the subject like al-Hārith al-Muhasibi. Others arose who systematized Sûfism, and gave it certain distinguishing characteristics, such as the patched garment, music, erotic sentiment, dancing, clapping of the hands: they further distinguished themselves by excessive purity and cleanliness. Then the process continued, and their shaikhs made continual inventions, and discoursed of their imaginations. So the

---

[7] An account of him in *Kashf al-Mahjub*, p. 61.

[8] *Ibid.*, p. 135.

gulf between them and the learned widened, nay, they came to regard their own system as the most complete knowledge, which they called "the inner knowledge," whereas they made knowledge of the Code "the outer knowledge." Some of them were led by hunger into false fancies, professing to be enamoured with God and to rave about Him: imagining Him to be an individual of beautiful form, about whom they raved. These were something between unbelievers and innovators; and then the paths of some branched out, and their beliefs were corrupted. Some of them adopted the doctrine of incarnation, others of union; and the devil continued to encompass them with various heresies so that they even made for themselves laws. There arose Abû 'Abd al-Rāhman al-Sûlami[9] who composed for them a Book of *Sunan,* and collected for them *The Realities of Interpretation,* in which he mentioned extraordinary ways that they have of interpreting the Qur'ān according to their fancies without finding support for them in any scientific principles, but merely accommodating it to their doctrines. Strange indeed that they should be so scrupulous in the matter of food and take such liberties with the Qur'ān! The following was told us by Abû Mansûr 'Abd al-Rāhman al-Qazzaz after Abû Bakr al-Khātib. The last said[10] he had been told by Muhammad b. Yusuf al-Qattan al-Naisaburi that Abû 'Abd al-Rahman al-Sulami was untrustworthy, only having heard a little from al-Asamm; yet, when al-Hakam Abû 'Abdallāh b. al-Bay' died, he taught on the authority of al-Asāmm the history of Yāhya b, Mu'in and many things besides. He was also in the habit of fabricating Traditions for the Sûfis.

Further Abû Nāsr al-Sārraj composed a book to which he gave the title *Flashes of Sûfism*[11] wherein he set forth wrong beliefs and vicious utterances, of which we shall presently produce some specimens, if God will. Abû Tālib al-Makki composed for them *The Provision of the Hearts*[12] wherein he set forth false Traditions, continuous fastings for days and nights supported by no authority, with other fictions and erroneous doctrines. He frequently employs

---

[9] Died 412. Sam'ani has an account of him *(Ansab,* pp. 20-21).

[10] The passage is in the *Kitāb Baghdād,* ii, 248. Al-Sulami's name was Muhammad b. al-Hāsain.

[11] Edited by R. A. Nicholson.

[12] Printed Cairo, 1310, etc.

the phrase *One of those favoured with revelations says,* which is meaningless, and recounts on the authority of Sûfis that God appears in this world to His saints.

I was told by Abû Mansûr al-Qazzaz after Abû Bakr al Khātib[13] that Abû Tahir Muhammad b. 'Alî al-'Allaf[14] said: Abu Tālib al-Makki came to Basrah after the death of 'Abûl Hāsan[15] b. Salim, and professed to be one of his followers. Then he went to Baghdād, where people gathered to the room in which he preached, and his speech was confused; he was remembered, to have said *There is naught more injurious to the creature than the Creator.* He was charged with heresy and shunned and spoke no more in public after that. Al-Khātib added: Abû Tālib al-Makki composed a book which he called *The Provision of the Hearts,* in the language of the Sûfis, wherein he sets forth many things which are to be disapproved, and abominable concerning the attributes.

Then (I would observe) came Abû Nu'aim al-Isfahani, who composed for them a book called *The Ornament*[16] in which he sets forth very disgraceful things within the bounds of Sûfism, and is not ashamed to mention among Sûfis Abû Bakr, 'Umar, 'Uthman, 'Alî, and the chief Companions, about whom he records marvellous things. Among them too he mentions Suraih the qadi, al-Hasan al-Basri, Sûfyan al-Thauri, and Ahmad b. Hanbal. Likewise al-Sulami[17] in his *Classes of Sûfis* mentions al-Fudail, Ibrāhim b. Adhām, and Ma'ruf al-Karkhi, whom he makes out to have been Sûfis by pointing out that they were ascetics.

Sûfism is a well-known system, which goes beyond asceticism; the difference between the two is indicated by the fact that no-one has ever found fault with asceticism, whereas Sûfism, has been censured as will presently be recorded. A treatise called *The Epistle* was composed for them by 'Abd al-Karim b. Hawazin al-Qushairi[18] wherein he gives marvellous accounts of *extinction, persistence,*

---

[13] See *Kitāb Baghdād,* iii, 89.

[14] Died 442 : *ibid,* iii. 104.

[15] His name was Ahmad b. Muhammad. See the *Luma'.*

[16] Printed Cairo, 1351. The author died 430.

[17] Abû 'Abd al-Rāhman Muhammad b. al-Husain, died 412.

[18] Often printed.

contraction, expansion, time, state, emotion, existence, combination, separation, sobriety, intoxication, taste, drink, erasure, confirmation, revelation, conversation, unveiling, perceptions, arisings, flashings, fashioning, empowering, the Code, the reality, etc., all baseless illusions, with yet more marvellous comments. Then there arose Muhammad b. Tahir al-Maqdisi'[19] who composed for them *The Quintessence of Sûfism,* wherein he recounted things which a man of sense would be ashamed to mention. We shall give such specimens as it will be suitable to mention in their places, if God will.

Our Shaikh Abû'l-Fadl b. Nâsir the Hafiz used to say: Ibn Tâhir held the doctrine of Licence, and wrote a book dealing with the lawfulness of gazing on beardless lads, into which he introduced a story of Yâhya b. Mu'in,[20] who said: I saw a pretty girl in Egypt, God be gracious to her!—People said to him: What, do you invoke a blessing on her!—He said: God be gracious to her and everyone who is beautiful—Our Shaikh Ibn Nâsir added: Ibn Tâhir is not a person to be employed as evidence. Then arose Abû Hamid al-Ghazzali, who composed for them the work *Revival*[21] according to their system which he filled with fictitious Traditions, not knowing them to be fictions; he also discoursed on Unveiling, and transgressed the rules of jurisprudence. He asserts that what is meant by the stars, sun, and moon, which were seen by Abraham (vi. 76-78) were lights which veiled God Almighty, and not the objects known. This is a comment in the style of the Esoterists. In his work called *Clear Account of States,* he asserts that the Sûfis in their waking hours witness the angels and the souls of the Prophets, hear their voices, and acquire information from them; then their "state" ascends from witnessing forms to stages too grand for language.

I would observe that the cause which led these people to compose these things was their ignorance of the laws, of Islam, and of Tradition, and the attraction which they felt for parts of the system which they approved; their approval being due to their conviction of

---

[19] Died 507. A long account of him in *Tabaqat al-Huffaz* xv, 21.

[20] Famous Traditionalist, died 233.

[21] Its content is being reproduced in Spanish by M.A. Palacios.

the merit asceticism, and to their regarding no condition as in form than that of these people, and no language as more affecting than theirs. Then the biographies of the men of old display a sort of roughness. Further these people enjoy popular favour to a high degree because their system is outwardly one of cleanness and devotion, and involves quiet and music, which people naturally favour. Besides, the original Sûfis used to keep away from kings and princes, which made people friendly.

Now the bulk of the works composed for them are based on no authority, being merely fancies which one has learned from another, and which they have compiled and called esoteric science. There is a Tradition going back to Abû Ya'qûb Ishaq b. Hayyah according to which he said: I heard Ahmad b. Hanbal say on the subject of "suggestions" and "occurrences" that neither the Companions nor the Epigoni talked of them.

At the beginning of this book we have recorded a similar Tradition traced to Dhu'l-Nun, and one traced to Ahmad b. Hanbal to the effect that, having heard the language of al-Hârith al-Muhasibi he told one of his followers that he thought he had better not associate with them. There is another of this going back to Sa'id b. 'Amr al-Barda'i[22] according to whosoever said: I was in the presence of Abû Zur'ah[23] when he was ash flesh about al-Hârith al-Muhasibi and his books, and he warneisi the questioner against them. These books, he said, are innovations and misleading; go to the Tradition, wherein you will find what will enable you to dispense with these books.—He was told that these books contained warning. He said: Whoso does not find warning in the Book of God will not find it in these books. Have you ever heard that Malik b. Anas, Sufyan al-Thauri, al-Auza'i, and the early authorities composed such works on Occurrences and Suggestions, etc? These are people who oppose the men of knowledge, citing to us at one time al-Hârith al-Muhasibi, at another 'Abd al-Rahim al-Dabili[24] at another Hâtim al-Asamm, at another Shaqiq.[25]—He went on to say: How ready people are to innovate!

We have been told by Muhammad b. 'Abd al-Baqi after Abû

---

[22] Died 290. Account of him in *Tâbaqat al-Huffaz* x. 88.

[23] His name was 'Abd al-Rahman b. 'Ami', died 281.

[24] Mentioned by Sam'ani.

[25] An account of him in *Kashf al-Mahjub*, p. 111.

Muhammad Rizq Allah b. 'Abd al-Wâhhab al-Tamimi after 'Abd al-Rahim al-Sûlami a Tradition according to which the last of these said: The first person who discoursed in our town on the order of States and the Stages of sainthood was Dhu'l-Nun al-Misri.—His statement was disapproved by 'Abdallâh b. 'Abd al-Hakam who was a leading man in Egypt[26] and a follower of Malik's system. Accordingly al-Sulami was shunned by the savants of Egypt when it had got abroad that he had invented a science about which the men of old had not spoken. They went so far as to charge him with atheism.—Al-Sulami says that Abû Sulaiman al-Darani[27] was expelled from Damascus, it being said that he asserted that he saw the angels, and that they talked to him. Some persons attested that Ahmad b. Abi'l-Hawari[28] regarded the saints as superior to the Prophets, and had to flee from Damascus to Makkah. The people of Bistam so strongly disapproved of the sayings of Abû Yazid al-Bistami[29] who was reported to al-Hûsain. They have [30] gone so far as to say that he had an Ascent and the Prophet had an Ascent, that they expelled him Ibn Bistam. He remained in Makkah for two years, then returned to Jurjan, where he remained till the death of al-Hûsain b. Isa, when he returned to Bistam. Al-Sûlami says: A certain man reported that Sahl b. 'Abdallah al-Tustari[31] declared that the angels, the Jinn, and the demons visited him and that he discoursed to them. This was disapproved by the populace, who went so far as to attribute evil acts to him, so that he fled to Basrah, where he died. He also states that al-Hârith al-Muhasibi talked about some theological matters, including the Attributes; and was shunned by Ahmad b. Hanbal, in consequence of which he went into hiding till he died.

Abû Bakr al-Khâlla[32] also states in his work *'The Sûnnah* that Ahmad b. Hanbal bade people beware of al-Hârith to the utmost of

---

[26] See Guest's *Al-Kindi*.
[27] 'Abd al-Râhman b. 'Atiyyah. Account of him in *Kashf al-Mahjûb*, p. 112.
[28] Account of him, *ibid*, p. 118.
[29] His name was *Taipur b. Isâ* died about 264. See ibid., 106.
[30] Probably the governor.
[31] Died 283. See *ibid*, 139.
[32] Died 311 (Brockelmann).

their ability. Al-Hārith, he asserted, is the root of trouble;—with reference to the results of *their learning* the theology of Jahm.[33] One person and another associated with al-Hārith and he perverted them to the opinion of Jahm. He has always been the resort of the metaphysicians. Hārith is like a lion on the watch; look out for the day when he will spring on people!

Now the first Sûfis used to acknowledge that reliance was to be placed on the Book and the Sunnah, only owing to their ignorance the devil was able to delude them. There is a Tradition going back to Jā'far al-Khuldi'[34] according to which he said: I heard Junaid say that he had heard Abû Sûlaiman al-Darani say: Often I am impressed for days by some point that the people (the ascetics) make, only I do not accept it without two trustworthy witnesses, the Book and the Sunnah. There is a Tradition going back to Tāifur al-Bistami[35] according to which he said: I heard Mûsa b. 'Isa say that his father had told him that Abû Yazid said: If you see a man endowed with such miraculous powers that he can elevate himself into the air, do not be deceived by him; but first see how you find him in the matter of enjoining and forbidding, and observance of the rules. According to another Tradition the father of Musa I heard Abû Yazid al-Bistami say: Which I neglects the reading of the Qur'ān, mortification of their attendance at public worship, attendance at funerals, and visitation of the sick, and professes to be a Sûfi is a heretic. A Tradition which goes back to 'Abd al-Hamid al-Hubli records that he said: I heard Sari say: Whosoever professes esoteric knowledge which contradicts a manifest rule commits an error. Junaid is reported to have said: This doctrine of ours is limited by the foundations, the Book and the Sûnnah. And again: Our science depends on the Book and the Sûnnah. No-one is to be imitated who has not memorized the Qur'ān, written Tradition, and studied Law. And again: We have not taken Sûfism from people's talk but from hunger, abandonment of the world, and parting from what is familiar and admired; for Sûfism has its name from purity of dealing with God Almighty, and its basis is self-knowledge in this world, as Hārithah says: I got to know myself in this world, kept awake at night, and thirsted during the day. There is

---

[33] Ibn Sāfwan, Murjite doctor.

[34] Died 348. Account of him in *Kashf al-Mahjub* p. 154.

[35] Evidently the younger ascetic of the name.

a Tradition that Abû Bakr al-Shaqqaq[36] said: Whosoever violates the rules of enjoining and forbidding in externals forfeits internal communication of the heart. Al-Hûsain al-Nûri[37] said: Have nothing to do with anyone who claims that he has in his dealings with God a state which takes him outside the bounds of knowledge of the Code. Suspect the religion of one whom you see claiming a state for which there is no evidence and which is unattested by any clear text that can be remembered. Al-Jurairi[38] is recorded to have said: Our whole system can be comprised in one article, *viz.*, that you should compel your heart to watchfulness, while kno wledge governs your external conduct. Abû Ja'far is recorded to have said: Reckon no man in the register of men who does not weigh his words, deeds, and states by the Book and the Sûnnah, and is not suspicious of his thoughts.

If these be ascertained sayings of their leading men, then some of them too have committed errors owing to their want of knowledge; if such sayings be genuinely theirs, then the refutation falls on them, since there can be no respect of persons in dealing with the truth; if the sayings are not theirs, then let us be on our guard against similar sayings and similar doctrine from whomsoever it proceeds. As for those who do not belong to these people but only imitate them, their errors are numerous; we will record some of those which have come to our knowledge; God knows that our purpose in exposing such errors is only to keep the Code pure, and anxiety to see that it is not corrupted. We are not concerned with the personality of the speaker; we are only discharging the obligation which knowledge imposes. The learned have always exposed each other's errors, their purpose therein being to bring the truth to light, not to show up the failing of the delinquent. No attention need be paid to the question of some ignorant person: How can such an ascetic who brings luck be refuted?—For obedience is due to the content of the Code, not to individuals. A man may be a saint, deserving Paradise, and yet commit errors; his station does not exclude their exposure.

You should know that one who looks at the honour paid to an individual and does not look at his procedure and what is to be inferred from it is like one who looks at the miracles performed by

---

[36] A notice of him in Sam'ani, p. 336.

[37] Probably Abû'l-Hâsan Ahmad al-Nûri is meant See *Kashf al-Mahjub*, p. 130.

[38] Abû' Mãs'ud Sa'id b. Iyas, died 144.

Christ without studying his person, and so claims divinity for him; had he studied his person, seeing how he was sustained by food, he would not give him what he does not deserve. We have been told by Isma'il b. Ahmad al-Sāmarqandi with a chain of authorities going back to Yāhya b. Sa'id that the latter said: I asked Shu'bah, Sufyan b. 'Uyainah, and Malik b. Anas whether a man who had not memorized the Qur'ān was suspect in Tradition. They all said: His case is clear.[39] The Imam Ahmad b. Hanbal would praise a man excessively and then mention a series of mistakes which he had committed. He would say: An excellent man, were it not that he has a certain failing. Of Sari al-Sāqati he said: He is the shaikh who is renowned for his taste in food.—Presently he was told that Sari had said that when God created the letters, the B prostrated itself. He then said; Keep the people away from him!

Enumeration of the false doctrines which are recorded of a number of them

Abû 'Abdallāh al-Ramli narrates that Abû Hāmzah[40] discoursed in the mosque of Tarsus and was favourably received. One day when he was discoursing a raven, croaked on the roof of the mosque. Abû Hāmzah cried out "I obey thee" twice. He was charged with heresy and supposed to be a believer in Immanece.[41] His horse was sold at the gate of the mosque by auction, as the heretic's horse. There is a Tradition going back to Abû Bakr al-Farghani according to which he said: Abû Hāmzah was generally supposed to be a believer in Immanence, because when he heard any sound he used to say I obey thee! Abû 'Alî however stated that Abû Hāmzah only supposed the sound to be a summons from God to arouse him to devotion. Abû 'Alî al-Rudhbari[42] said that Abû Hāmzah was generally supposed to be a believer in Immanence because when he heard a sound like the whistling of the wind, the rush of water, the singing of birds, he would cry out I obey thee! twice. This was the reason for the charge. Al-Sārraj says: I have been told that Abû Hāmzah entered the dwelling of al-Hārith al-Muhasibi once when a sheep bleated; Abû Hāmzah groaned and said: I obey thee, my Lord !—Al-Hārith al-

---

[39] Apparently the meaning is "of course he is suspect".
[40] Al-Bazzaz. See *Kashf al-Mahjub,* p. 154.
[41] *i.e* in dwelling of the Deity in individuals.
[42] Muhammad b. Ahmad, died 323. Notice of him in Sam'ani.

Muhasibi was angry, took up a knife, and said: If you do not repent of your practice, I will cut your throat.—Abû Hâmzah replied: If you cannot listen, decently to this practice of mine, why do you eat bran mingled with ashes?

Al-Sârraj proceeds: Some men of learning disapproved and attributed to infidelity certain phrases which they found in *The Book of Mystery* composed by Abû Sa'id Ahmad b. 'Isâ al-Kharraz,[43] among them the saying: *A servant obedient in what was permitted to him, for which God should be glorified,* and *God sanctify his soul*[44] Likewise infidelity and atheism were attributed to Abû'l-'Abbâs Ahmad b. 'Ata[45] Many a time too Junaid with all his learning was arrested and his infidelity and atheism attested. Al-Sârraj further asserts that it was reported, that Abû Bakrah[46] Muhammad b. Mûsa al-Farghani al-Wasiti said: Whoso makes mention *of God* fabricates, and whoso endures is audacious: beware, lest thou glance at friend or interlocutor or companion when thou canst find a means of glancing at God.—He was asked: May I not then pray for them?—He said: Pray for them without solemnity, and let the prayer have no importance in thy heart.

Al-Sârraj proceeds: I have been told that a number of the believers in Immanence maintain that God Almighty has chosen certain bodies to abide in with the concepts of Lordship, having removed from them the concepts of humanity.[47] Some of them maintain this by looking at the evidences of God's power which win admiration. Some of them say: He abides in those things which win admiration.

He proceeds: I have also been informed that certain Syrians claim vision with the heart in this world similar to vision with the eyes in the next. Further that Ghulam al-Khalil[48] testified that he had heard Abû'l-Hûsain al-Nûri say: I am enamoured of God and He is enamoured of me—al-Nûri said: I hear God say (v. 59) *He loves*

---

[43] Died about 277. Notice of him in Sam'ani, p. 191 and *Kashf* p. 143

[44] It is not clear where the impropriety lies.

[45] Many references to him in *Kashf*

[46] In the *Lumá* Abû Bakr.

[47] See the *Lumá*, ed. Nicholson, p. 428. The author's citations are so abridged as to be unintelligible.

[48] Died 275.

them and they love Him, and "to be enamoured of" is no more than "to love." So, said Abû Ya'la the qadi, God in the opinion, of the believers in Immanence can be enamoured.

I would observe that this is a case of ignorance from three aspects. One in regard to the name; for "to be enamoured" according to authorities on the language is only applied to the marriageable. The second is that the attributes of God are known bv communication, whence we know that He loves, but we may not say He is enamoured, and He is loved, not enamoured of. Just as it is said that He knows, but not that He cognizes. The third—whence has the man the right to say that God loves him? This is a claim without evidence. The Prophet said: A man who says he is in Paradise is really in Hell.

It is recorded that Abû 'Abd al-Rāhman said: It is related that 'Amr al-Makki said: I used to walk with al-Hûsain b. Mansûr[49] in some of the streets of Makkah, while I recited the Qur'ān; hearing my recitation he said: I could myself say the like of that. I left him in consequence.—Muhammad b. Yāhya al-Razi is recorded to have said: I heard 'Amr b. 'Uthman cursing al-Hallāj and saying: Were I able, I should kill him with my own hand.——I said: How has he angered the shaikh ?—He replied: I recited a text of God's Book and he said I could say or compose and utter the like of this.

There is a Tradition going back to Abû'l-Qāsim al-Razi according to which he said: Abû Bakr b. Mimshad related as follows: There was a man present with us in Dinawar with a sack froni which he would not part night or day; the sack was examined and there was found therein a letter of al-Hallāj addressed from the Merciful the Clement to So-and-so son of So-and-so. It was sent to Baghdād, and Hallāj was summoned and shown it. He admitted that it was his script and that the letter had been written by him. They said: You used to claim prophethood and now you claim divinity.—He said: I do not claim divinity; only this is the essence of the mystic state according to us.[50] Is the writer any but God, while he hand therein is an instrument?—He was asked whether there were any people with him. He said Yes, Ibn 'Atā', Abû Muhammad al-Jûrairi, and Abû Bakr al-Shibli. The second and the third are in hiding, so if there be anyone,

---

[49] Better known as Hāllaj.
[50] For the phrase in the text see Massignon *Lexique Technique.*

it will be Ibn 'Atā'. Al-Jārairi was produced and asked; he said: The man who says that is an Unbeliever, and should be put to death.

Shibli was asked and said: He who says that should be stopped,— Ibn 'Atā' was asked about al-Hallāj's assertion and adhered to it; this was the cause of his execution.

There is a Tradition going back to Ibn Bākuyah according to which he said: I heard 'Isa b. Bardal narrate: when Abû 'Abdallāh bin Khāfif[51] was asked about the sense of the following verses.

Praise be to him whose manhood here displays

The secret of His Godhead's piercing rays;

Plainly Himself He manifested then

As one who eats and drinks like other men.

So that His creatures glancing at His sheen

Their dazzled vision with their eyelids screen,

he said, The Curse of God be on their author. 'Isā b. Furak said they were the verses of al-Hûsain b. Mansûr. He added: If this be his belief, then he is an infidel; only the verses may be falsely attributed to him.

There is a Tradition going back to the qadi' 'Alî b. al-Muhassin[52] after Abû'l-Qāsim Isma'il b. Muhammad b. Zanji after his father according to which the daughter of al-Samarri being brought before the vizier Hamid and asked by him about Hallāj said: My father brought me to him, and he said: I marry you to my son Sulaiman, who resides in Nisabûr. If any act on his part displeases you, fast for the rest of the day, at the end of it mount the roof, stand on the ashes, and breakfast off them and coarse salt. Then turn your face in my direction, tell me what displeases you, and I will hear and see. One night, she said, I was asleep on the roof and felt him approaching me. I woke up in a fright at his procedure. He said: I have only come to wake you up for prayer.—When we had descended his daughter told me to prostrate myself before him. I asked her whether prostration should be performed to anyone but God.—He heard what I said and said: Yes, there is a God in heaven and a God on earth.

I observe that the doctors of the time agreed that the life of al-

---

[51] Notice of him in *Kashf* p. 158.

[52] *Eclipse,* 1-78.

Hallāj was forfeit. The first who gave his opinion to that effect was the qadi Abû 'Umar the others agreed. Only Abû'l-'Abbâs Suraij kept silence on the subject, alleging that he did not know what al-Hallâj said. Consensus is an infallible guide. There is a Tradition traced to Abû Hûrairah according to which he said: The Prophet said: God guarantees you against general agreement in error. There is also one going back to Abû'l-Qâsim Yûsuf b. Ya'qûb al-Nû'mani according to which he said: I heard my father say that he had heard the jurist of Ispahan Abû Bakr Muhammad b. Dawûd say: If what God revealed to His Prophet be true, then what al-Hallâj says is false. He was vehemently opposed to him

A number of the Sûfis take the part of al-Hallâj out of ignorance and carelessness about the consensus of the jurists. There is a Tradition traced to Muhammad b. al-Hûsain al-Nisaburi according to which he said: I heard Ibrahim b. Muhammad al-Nasrabadi[53] say: If there was ever a monotheist after the Prophets and the saints, it was al-Hallâj. The same view, I may say, is taken by most of the story-tellers and Sûfis of our time, being due in all cases to ignorance of the Code, and unacquaintance with Tradition. I have myself composed a work on the life of al-Hallâj in which I have set forth his tricks and deceptions with what has been said about him by the learned. God aid us in suppressing the ignorant!

There is a Tradition going back to the Hafiz Abû Nu'aim according to which he said: I heard 'Umar al-Banna al-Baghdadi in Makkah narrating how, when there was the trouble of Ghulam al-Khalil[54] and the ascription of atheism to the Sûfis, the Caliph ordered their arrest. Al-Nûri was taken with a number of others, they were brought before the Caliph and he ordered them to be decapitated. Al-Nûri pressed forward to the executioner for decapitation. Why this haste? asked the executioner. He said: I prefer that my comrades should live for this short space rather than I.—The matter was brought before the Caliph, who referred it to the qadi of qadis Isma'il b. Ishaq who ordered their release. There is further a Tradition going back to Abû'l-'Abbas Ahmad b. 'Atâ' according to which he said: Ghulam al-Khalil used to bring charges against the Sûfis in Baghdâd to the Caliph, saying, There are atheists here. There were arrested Abû'l-Hûsain al-Nûri,

---

[53] Died 367. Account of him in Sam'ani, p. 561.

[54] Abû 'Abdallâh Ahmad b. Muhammad, died 275.

Abû Hãmzah the Sûfi, Abû Bakr al-Dãqqaq, and a number of their companions. Al-Junaid b. Muhammad alleged in his defence that he followed the juridical system of Abû Thãur. The others were brought before the Caliph who ordered their decapitation. Abû'l-Hûsain al-Nûri hastened to be first. The executioner asked why he hurried in front of his fellows and felt no fear. He said: I prefer that my comrades should live for this short period. The Caliph referred their case to the qadi and they were released.

One of the causes which led to this affair was al-Nûri's saying: I am enamoured of God and He is enamoured of me. This was testified against him. Then al-Nûri pressed forward to the executioner to be killed, 'assisting in his own death—which also is an error.

There is a Tradition going back to Ibn Bãkuyah according to which he said: I heard Abû 'Amr, disciple of al-Rãqqi,[55] say: I heard al-Rãqqi say: We had a guest-house ; there came to us a poor man clad in a couple of rags, whose patronymic was Abû Sulaiman. He requested entertainment, and I bade my son take him to the house. He stayed with us nine days, eating once in three days. I asked him to stay one more, but he said "entertainment is for three days." So I asked him not to withhold news about himself. He was away for twelve years and then returned. I asked him whence he came, and he said: I saw a shaikh called Abû Shu'aib al-Mûqaffa who was afflicted; so I stayed with him for a year to minister to him, when it occurred to me to ask him what had been the cause of his affliction. When I approached him, before I had asked he anticipated me, saying; Why ask about what is no concern of yours? So I restrained myself till three years were completed; when the fourth had begun he said I suppose you must. I said, If you please. Then he said: while I was praying one night there appeared a light from the niche; I said; Avaunt, accursed one! My Almighty Lord has no need to appear to His creatures. Three times I said this; then I heard a voice from the niche: Abu Shu'aib!—I said I obey. It said: Wouldst thou that I take thee now that we should reward thee for what has passed, or try thee with affliction whereby we shall raise thee *in excelsis?*—I chose the trial, and my eyes, feet, and hands fell away.—So (said the narrator). I stayed and ministered to him for full twelve years. One day he bade me approach him, which I did. I heard his members

---

55 Ibrãhim b. al-Muwallad, died 342.

say to each other Come out, and they did all come out in front of him, which he gave praise and glory, after which he died.

I would observe that this narrative suggests that the man saw God Almighty, and was punished because he refused to believe it. We have already mentioned that some say that God is seen in this world. Abû'l-Qāsim 'Abdallāh b. Ahmad al-Balkhi in his book *Discourses* states that certain anthropomorphists record that they allow that God may be seen with the eyes in this world, and do not reject the idea that He may be someone who meets them in the street. Further that some besides allow that He may be embraced, touched, and held in contact. They profess to visit Him and receive His visits, and are called in Iraq Esoterists, or followers of hallucinations or fancies.

This I may observe, is more than atrocious. We implore God's protection from abandonment by Him.

CHAPTER XI

The Way Wherein the Devil Deludes the Sûfis in the Matter of Purification

We have mentioned his delusion of the devotees in the matter of purification, only in the case of the Sûfis he goes beyond all bounds. To such an extent has he strengthened their hallucination concerning the use of a great quantity of water that I have been told how when Ibn 'Aqil[1] entered a monastery he was ridiculed for the small amount of water which he used. They did not know that one *ratl* of water constitutes an adequate ablution. We have also been told that Abû Hamid al-Shirazi asked a *faqir* whence he got the water for ablution. He said: "From the river. I have a hallucination on the subject of purification." Abû Hamid said: I remember the time when the Sûfis mocked Satan; now Satan mocks them.

Some of them walk in sandals on the matting; there is no harm in this, only a beginner looking for a model might suppose this to be a rule, whereas the best men of old did not do it. Well may one wonder at a man who goes to such a length in precaution and describes himself as a cleanser of his outside, when his inside is crammed with filth and foulness! God is our guide!

Account of the way wherein the devil deludes them in prayer

We have mentioned, how he deludes the devotees in prayer, and he practises the same delusions on the Sûfis, only to a greater extent. Muhammad b. Tãhir al-Maqdisi states that among the practices in which they stand alone, and from which they take their name[2] is a prayer of two inclinations said after donning the patched cloak and

---

[1] Abû'l-Wafa 'Alî, author of a work in 400 volumes. Died 513.

[2] Probably with referennce to the derivation of the name Sûfi from a verb signifying "to be pure."

repenting. The ground alleged for this is a Tradition of Thumamah b. Uthal that when he became a Muslim he was ordered by the Prophet to wash.[3]

I would observe that when an ignorant person meddles with what is not his concern he is very reprehensible. Thumamah was an Unbeliever, and when an Unbeliever becomes a Muslim it is incumbent on him to wash, according to a number of jurists, among them Ahmad b. Hanbal. But no man of learning has enjoined a prayer of two inclinations on one who becomes a Muslim, neither is there any mention of a prayer in the Tradition of Thumamah which could furnish an analogy. Is this then anything in fact but an innovation which they term "a practice." Further his assertion that the Sûfis have practices wherein they stand alone is most reprehensible. For if these practices are to be referred to the Code, then all Muslims are alike in respect of them, and the jurists know best about them; how then do the Sûfis stand alone in observing them? If on the other hand the practices are according to their own ideas, then they are alone in observing them because they invented them.

Account of the way wherein the devil deludes the Sûfis in the matter of dwellings

As for the building of hermitages it is true that some of the earlier devotees took to them in order to practise devotion in isolation. The Sûfis, however, if their purpose be sincere, are in error from six points of view.

1. They have invented this sort of building, whereas the Islamic building is the mosque.

2. They have produced a rival to the Mosque, reducing the size of the congregation.

3. They fail to see, that they transfer the error to the mosques.[4]

4. They imitate the Christians by isolating themselves in monasteries.

5. They practise celibacy though they are young, and most of them are in need of matrimony.

---

[3] According to Ibn Hishām ed. Wûstenfeld, p. 997. he did so of his own initiative.

[4] _i.e.,_ if it is right to build hermitages, it is wrong to build mosques.

6. They make a sign which proclaims that they are ascetics, which causes them to be visited and is supposed to give good luck.

If however their purpose be insincere, then what they build are gaming-houses, abodes of idleness, and modes of parading asceticism. We have seen a number of the modern Sûfis reposing in their hermitages from the labour of earning their living; and occupied with eating, drinking, music and dancing. They seek this world's goods from every rogue and have no scruple in accepting the gift of the tax-gatherer. Most of their hermitages have been built by tyrants, who have endowed them with ill-gotten gains. The devil has deluded them with the suggestion. "What comes to you is your provision, so do not worry about temperance." Their concern is the proper working of the kitchen, food and iced water. Where is the hunger of Bishr, the abstinence of Sari, the industry of Junaid? These people, spend most of their time with amusing conversation or visiting the great ones of the earth. If one of them is in luck, he sticks his head into his tunic and becomes melancholy, and says: "My heart tells me from my Lord." I have been told that a man who read the Qur'ān in a hermitage was forbidden to do so, and that some people who read Tradition in one were told that it was no place for that.

Account of the way wherein the devil deludes the Sûfis in the matter of giving up their property

The devil used to delude the early Sûfis, who were genuine ascetics, showing them the evil of wealth and warning them of its mischief; in consequence they used to give up their property, and sit on the carpet to poverty. Their aims in this matter were saintly, though their actions were erroneous owing to inadequate knowledge. At the present day the devil is spared such trouble, for if one of them has any money he squanders and wastes it. There is a Tradition going back to Muhammad b. al-Hûsain al-Salimi according to which he said: I heard Abû Nāsr al-Tusi[5] say that he had heard a number of the shaikhs of Rayy state that Abû 'Abdallāh al-Muqri[6] had inherited from his father 50,000 *dinārs*—besides estates and houses; he gave the whole up and expended it on the poor.

---

[5] Died 344. He is highly praised by Sam'ani, p. 373.

[6] Died 366. His name was Muhammad b. Ahmad b. Muhammad.

Similar stories are told of a great number; I should not blame the person who acted in this way provided he kept a hoard sufficient for his wants or was master of some craft which would render him independent, or if the wealth came from a suspected source; so that he gave it away, in charity. The case which is reprehensible and to be forbidden is that of a man giving away the whole of his legal property, and then being in need of other people's possessions, and impoverishing his family; making himself an object of the charity or alms of his friends or taking from persons guilty of robbery or suspected thereof. I am not indeed surprised at ignorant devotees doing this; the wonder is that men of intelligence and learning should have recommended and even enjoined this course; which conflicts with both reason and the Code.

Al-Hārith al-Muhasibi has a long discourse on this subject, which is confirmed and supported by Abû Hamid al-Ghazali. To my mind al-Hārith is more excusable than Abû Hamid for the latter was the more skilled in jurisprudence; only his adoption of Sûfism led him to support his adopted system.

The following is a specimen of al-Hārith al-Muhasibi's discourses.[7] "O thou that art deceived, if thou holdest that the amassing of lawful wealth is nobler and more honourable than the discarding of it, thou art contemning the blessed Muhammad and the Apostles, and dost hold that the blessed Muhammad gave bad advice to his nation when he forbade them to amass it, well-knowing that amassing it was for their good. And thou dost hold that God was inconsiderate of His servants when He forbade them to amass wealth, well knowing that amassing it was for their 'good; it will not profit thee to allege the wealth of the Companions, Ibn 'Auf will wish on the Day of Resurrection that he had been given no more than enough to sustain him in this world. And indeed (he proceeds) I have been told that when 'Abd al-Rāhman b. 'Auf died, some of the Prophet's Companions said they were afraid about 'Abd al-Rāhman on account of the estate which he had left. Ka'b, however, said; Good heavens! why need you fear for 'Abd al-Rāhman, who acquired virtuously and spent virtuously?—The news reached Abû Dhārr who came out in anger, and wanted Ka'b; passing by the jaw of a camel he took it into his hand and went off in search of Ka'b. Ka'b was told that Abû Dhārr

---

[7] The passage is given by Ghazali. *Ihyā' 'Ulum al-din*, iii. 199.

was looking for him. So he fled and came to 'Uthman to implore his protection. He told 'Uthman the story; Abû Dhārr followed the trial of Ka'b till he tracked him to "Uthman's dwelling. When he entered Ka'b rose up and seated himself behind 'Uthman out of fear of Abû Dhārr. The latter said to him: Away with you, son of a Jewess! You hold that there is no harm in the estate left by 'Abd al-Rāhman b. Auf! The Prophet one day came out and said: On "the Day of 'Resurrection the most shall be the least save one who says thus and thus;[8] then he said: O Abû Dhārr, thou art desirous of the most, whereas I am desirous of the least.— Of that then the Prophet was desirous, whereas thou, O son of the Jewess, dost say There is no harm in the estate which was left by 'Abd al-Rāhman b. 'Auf! Thou liest and whosoever says the same lies.—Ka'b did not utter a word in reply till he had gone.

Al-Hārith proceeds: So this 'Abd al-Rāhman notwithstanding his eminence is to be detained in the Resurrection-court because of the wealth which he acquired honourably and in order to live temperately and do good works; he is to be prevented from running into Paradise with the poor Refugees, and instead will have to creep after them. The Companions rejoiced when they were destitute, and you hoard wealth and amass it in fear of poverty. This is to hold a bad opinion of God and to have no confidence in His guarantee, which is of itself sufficiently criminal. Perhaps too thou amassest the wealth for the comforts, vanities, and pleasures of this world, whereas we have been told that the Prophet said: Whoso laments over worldly fortune which he has missed comes a whole year's journey nearer Hell. And you grieve over what you have missed, not troubling about your proximity to God's punishment! Consider, canst thou find in thy lifetime lawful wealth to the amount which the Companions found? Where is the lawful wealth which thou canst amass? I give thee good counsel I would have thee contended with a minimum, and not amassing wealth for charitable purposes. A certain man of learning was asked concerning one who amasses wealth for charitable purposes and replied that it is yet move, charitable to abstain therefrom. We have also been told that one of the best of the Epigoni being asked concerning two men, one of whom sought fortune by honourable means, won it, helped his relations and benefitted himself,

---

[8] Apparently explained in what follows.

and another who disregarded fortune, neither sought it nor gave it away—which of the two was the better? He replied that there was a vast difference between them; the one who disregarded fortune was the better by a distance as great as that between East and West. This is the language of al-Hārith al-Muhasibi, quoted by Abû Hamid, who confirms it and supports it by the Tradition of Tha 'labah, who was given wealth and declined to give alms.[9] Abû Hamid goes on to say: Whoso[10] observes the circumstances of the Prophets and saints and their sayings will not doubt that the absence of wealth is better than its presence, even if it be employed on good objects; the least of its evils is that its possessors are diverted by care of it from the thought of God. The neophyte should give up his wealth, only reserving what is absolutely necessary. So long as a *dirhām* remains to him, to occupy his mind; he will be screened from God Almighty.

Now all this, I observe, is country to the Code and to reason and is misunderstanding the meaning of wealth.

Refutation of the above view

To begin with the nobility of wealth, God Almighty has magnified it and commanded its conservation, inasmuch as He has made it the support of man, and that which has been constituted the support of the noble creature man is itself noble. He says (iv. 4) *Give not unto the fools your goods which He has made a support for you,* forbidding the surrender of property to one who is not of discretion. And again (iv. 5) *And if ye have ascertained that they have discretion, then hand over to them their goods.* Further it is certain that the Prophet forbade the waste of money. He said to Sa'd: It is better that thou shouldst leave thy heirs wealthy than that thou shouldst leave them poor to beg of people.—And again: No money ever helped me like that of Abû Bakr.— There is a Tradition going back by a sound chain, to 'Amr b. al-'As according to which he said: The Prophet sent to me, saying: Put on thy garments and thy armour and come to me. So I came to him, and he said: I wish to send thee in command 'of an army, and may God keep thee safe and give thee spoil. I would fain

---

[9] He urged the Prophet to pay that he might be enriched and when his wealth increased, neglected his religious duties.

[10] *Ihyā 'Ulum al-din,* iii. 205.

have thee acquire wealth.—I said: O Prophet of God, I did not accept Islam for the sake of wealth, but for its own sake.—He said: O 'Amr, a good fortune is a fine thing for a good man!—There is also a Tradition going back to Anas b. Malik according to which the Prophet invoked various blessings upon him, saying at the end of his petition: O God, multiply his wealth and his offspring and bless him!—There is also a Tradition going back to 'Abd al-Rāhman b. Ka'b b. Malik according to which 'Ubaidallah b. Ka'b b. Malik said: I heard Ka'b b. Malik telling the story of his repentance, in which he said: I said: O Prophet of God, part of my repentance is my denuding myself of my wealth as an offspring to God and His Apostle.—He said; It will be better that thou retain part of it.

These Traditions, I would observe, are produced in the collections of sound Tradition, and they are opposed to the belief of the Sûfis that the increase of wealth is a screen and earns punishment, and that the saving of it is inconsistent with reliance on God. It is not to be denied that it is a dangerous temptation and that many people have kept clear of it for fear of that; that it is difficult to amass it in the right way, and that it is rare that a heart is safe from its temptation: and rare too that the heart of its possessor is occupied with the thought of the next world. Hence its temptation is feared. As for the acquisition of wealth, he who restricts himself to the acquisition of a minimum from lawful sources is only doing what he is obliged to do. Where a man purposes to amass it in quantities, we must consider his object. If that be merely ostentation and vainglory, it is a bad object; but if it be to preserve the honour of himself and his family, to lay by against accidents which may befall himself or them, to deal generously with friends, enrich the poor, and do good works, he will be rewarded for his endeavour, and his amassing with this intent will be better than many an act of piety. The intentions of many of the Companions (God's favour be with them all!) in the amassing of wealth were sound, owing to the good objects which they had in view: hence they were anxious for it and asked for increase. There is a Tradition going back to Ibn 'Umar according to which the Prophet offered al-Zûbair in fief as much land as his horse could gallop over in a region called Tharthar. Al-Zûbair made his horse gallop till it stopped, when he threw his whip, and the Prophet said: Give him as far as the whip reaches.—Sa'd b. 'Ubaidah used to say in a prayer:

O God, give me plenteously.

What is even more striking than these is that Jacob (on whom be favour and peace!) agreed to his sons' proposition when they said (xii. 65) *We shall have the extra measure of a comel-load,* and sent his son Benjamin with them, and that Shu'aib wanted an addition to what he was to get and said (xxviii. 27) *And if thou wilt make it up to ten, it will be of thine own accord;* [11] and that when Job (on whom be peace!) was healed, there was sprinkled on him a swarm of golden locusts, and he began to gather them in quantities into his garment. He was asked: Art thou not satisfied? He replied: O Lord, who can be satisfied with thy bounty?[12] This is a matter implanted in men's nature, and is absolutely good when what is intended by it is good.

The language of al-Muhasibi displayed ignorance of what he ought to have known and his assertions that God forbade His servants to amass wealth and that the Prophet laid the same prohibition on his community are absurd. The Tradition of Ka'b and Abû Dhârr which he narrates is an absurd fabrication by some ignorant persons into whose category al-Mûhasibi is brought through his failure to perceive the fact about it.

Something of this sort is indeed narrated, though the line of Tradition is uncertain. There is a Tradition going back to Malik b. 'Abdallāh al-Ziyadi to the effect that Abû Dhârr asked to be admitted to the presence of 'Uthman, and was admitted, having a staff in his hand, 'Uthman said: O Ka'b b. 'Abd al-Rāhman is dead and has left a fortune, what thinkest thou thereof?—Ka'b replied: There is no harm, if he have been paying therein the dues of God.—Abû .Dhârr lifted up his staff and smote Ka'b, saying: I heard the Prophet say: I should not like to have this mountain all gold to spend and to be accepted of me. Throw behind me six ounces!—I adjure thee by God, 'Uthman, didst thou hear this?— three times?—'He said Yes.

I would observe that this Tradition cannot stand; Ibn Lahi'ah (the reporter) is of damaged reputation; Yahya[13] says that his Traditions cannot be used as evidence. The historical fact is that Abû Dhârr

---

[11] *i.e.,* if Moses would work ten years instead of only eight.

[12] The story is told al-Kisai'i's *Tales of the Prophets,* ed. Isenberg, i. 189.

[13] Yāhya b. Sa'id quoted by Bûkhari. Ibn Lahi'ahs name was Abdallāh.

died in the year 25 whereas 'Abd al-Rāhman died in the year 32, surviving Abû Dhārr by seven years! Further the expressions employed in their narrative show that it is a fabrication. Besides how could the Companions say We fear for 'Abd al-Rāhman? Is there not a consensus of opinion that the amassing of wealth from lawful sources is permitted? What then have they to fear when there is this permission? Can the Code 'give licence for a proceeding and then punish it? This is want of intelligence and of legal knowledge. Then can Abû Dharir have censured 'Abd al-Rāhman, who was immeasurably his superior? Further his laying hold of 'Abd al-Rāhman only is evidence that he had not studied the lives of the Companions; for Talhah left 300 *buhar* each of them equal to 3 *qıntar*.[14] A *buhar* means a load. The fortune of al-Zubair was 50,200,000 *dirhāms*. Ibn Mās'ud left 90,000. Most of the Companions acquired and left fortunes, and none of them found fault with another.

His assertion that 'Abd al-Rāhman will creep on Resurrection-day shows that he does not know the Tradition. Or was this a dream, the man not being awake? God forbid that 'Abd al-Rāhman b. 'Auf should creep on Resurrection-day! Who then will go in front if 'Abd. al-Rāhman has to crawl, when he was one of the Ten assured of Paradise, one of the fighters at Bādr to whom pardon was promised, one of the Committee![15] Besides, the Tradition is narrated by 'Umarah b. Zadhan, of whom Bûkhari asserts that his Traditions are often confused, Ahmad that he told on the authority of Anas stories which are to be rejected, Abu Hātim al-Razi that he must not be used as evidence, D raqutni that he is weak. We have been told by Ibn al-Hāsin by a sound chain which goes back to 'Umarah b. Thabit after Anas that the last said: One day when 'A'ishah was in her house she heard a noise in Madinah and asked what it was. She was told that it was a train of camels belonging to 'Abd al-Rāhman b.'Auf coming from Syria laden with all sorts of goods, and consisting of 700 beasts. Madinah shook with the noise.'A'ishah said: I heard the Prophet say that he had seen 'Abd al-Rāhman b.'Auf entering Paradise crawling,— The story came to the ears of 'Abd al-Rāhman b. 'Auf, who said: If I can, I shall, enter it erect. So he devoted the camels with their saddles and their loads to the service of God.

---

[14] A large sum, variously explained.

[15] The committee appointed by 'Umar to choose a successor.

With regard to his assertion that the abandonment of wealth lawfully acquired is better than amassing it, that is not so. If the object be a sound one, amassing it is on the contrary better according to the learned. The Tradition which he quotes as a saying of the Prophet Whoso laments over worldly fortune that he has missed, etc., is absurd: the Prophet never said this. With regard to his question: Canst thou find in thy lifetime lawful-wealth, etc., he may be asked: What is the matter with wealth lawfully acquired? The Prophet says: The lawful is clear and the unlawful is clear.—Do you suppose he means by the lawful a grain which from the time when it was extracted from the mine has been handled in no doubtful, transaction? That is unlikely, and is not, demanded of us. Nay, if a Muslim sells a Jew, the price which he obtains is lawful without a doubt. Such is the doctrine of the jurists, and I am astonished at the silence of Abû Hamid and still more at his corroborating what he quotes. How too can he assert that absence of wealth is better than its presence, even if it be employed in good objects? It would be correct to claim consensus of opinion to the contrary of this. How- ever his adoption of Sûfism altered his judgment. There is a Tradition that al-Mārwazil[16] said: I heard a man say to Abû 'Abdullāh I have a competence. Abû 'Abdallāh said: Stick to the market, you will help your relations and visit the sick.

With, regard to his statement, that the neophyte ought to give up his fortune, we have already explained that if that fortune be unlawfully acquired, or be suspected of being so or if the man can be satisfied with a little or earn his maintenance, he may give it up; otherwise there is no justification for the act. As for Tha'labah, his fortune did him no harm, only his unwillingness to pay his dues.

As for the Prophets: Abrāham had fields and goods; likewise Shu'aib and others. Sa'id b. al-Musayyib used to say; There is no good in a man who does not make money, wherewith he can pay his debts, protect his honour, help his relatives, and when he dies make bequest to his successors, Ibn al-Mûsayyib left 400 *dinārs*. We have recorded the sums left by the Companions. Sufyan al-Thaûri left 200. He used to say: Money in our age is a weapon. The men of old were always eulogizing wealth, amassing it against an evil day, and to help the poor. If certain of them abstained from doing so it was

---

[16] Mentioned in the *Luma'*.

only because they preferred to occupy themselves with devotion and to be free from distraction, if our author had said that it was better to do it sparingly, it would have been near the truth. As he states it, he comes near incurring guilt.

You should know that poverty is a disease, and one who is patient under it will be rewarded for his patience. And this is why the poor will enter Paradise five hundred years before the rich; it is the reward for their endurance of misfortune with patience. Wealth is a boon, for which gratitude is due. The rich man, though he toils and risks, is like the Mufti (one 'who delivers legal opinions) and the fighter in the holy war, whereas the 'poor man is like the anchorite. Abû 'Abd āl-Rāhman al-Sûlami in his book *Practices of the Sûfis* has a section *Disapproval of a poor man leaving anything* in which he cites a Tradition that one of the People of the Beach when he died left two *dinārs*, and the Prophet said "Two burnings!"

I would observe that this is the reasoning of one who does not understand the circumstances. The poor man of the anecdote jostled other poor men to receive alms, while retaining his own property; for this reason the Prophet said: Two burnings. Had the objection been to the simple act of leaving property, the Prophet would not have said to Sa'd: it is better that you should leave your heirs wealthy than that you should leave them poor begging alms of people. Neither would any of the Companions have left property. 'Umɑr b. al-Khāttab said: The Prophet exhorted to almsgiving and I brought half my fortune. The Prophet said: And what have you saved for your family?—I replied: The same amount.—The Prophet made no objection, Ibn Jārir al-Tabari[17]says: This Tradition shows the fallacy of the assertion of ignorant Sûfis that a man may not hoard anything today for the morrow, and that whoso does this has a bad opinion of his Lord, neither places full reliance on Him. Likewise (he goes on to say) the shying of the Prophet "Take to yourselves sheep for they are a blessing" proves the falseness of the assertion of certain Sûfis that no man's reliance on his Lord is sincere unless he is to be found morning and evening without either coin or other goods. Remember that the Prophet hoarded a year's provision for his wives.

Some persons have given away their lawful possessions and

---

[17] The historian and commentator.

come to picking up filth and begging; this is because a man's wants do not stop. A wise man prepares for the future. These people who give away their possessions at the commencement of their Sûfism are like one who provides himself with water for the journey to Makkah and then pours it away. There is a Tradition going back to Jabir b. 'Abdallāh according to which he said: Abû Hûsain al-Sûlami brought some gold from their mine,[18] paid a debt and had a surplus about the size of a hen's egg. He took it to the Prophet and said: O Prophet of God, place this where God shows thee, or where thou thinkest fit.—He approached the Prophet from his right, and the Prophet turned away: then from his left and again he turned away: then from the front, and the Prophet lowered his head. As the man insisted, the Prophet took it from his hand and flung it at him; had it hit, it would have wounded him. Then the Prophet turned to him and said: One of you people takes his money, gives it away in charity, and then sits down and begs of the people. Charity should come out of wealth, so begin with those whom you have to support.—This story is told by Abû Dawûd in his *Sunan* as a Tradition of Mahmud b. Labid after Jabir b. 'Abdallāh. He said: We were with the Prophet when there arrived a man with a thing like an egg of gold. He said: O Prophet of God, I got this out of a mine; take it, it is for charity, and I possess nothing else.—The Prophet turned away from him; the man then approached him from his right side and said the same: the Prophet, again turned away. Then the man approached him from his left side, and again the Prophet turned away. Then he approached the Prophet from behind. This time the Prophet took it and flung it at him: had it hit, it would have killed or wounded him. The Prophet then said: One of you people brings his property and says this is for charity, and then sits down and begs of people. The best charity is that which comes out of wealth.—According to another account the Prophet said: Take your property back, we have no need of it.—Abû Dawûd also records a Tradition according to which Abû Sa'id al-Khûdari said: A man entered the Mosque and the Prophet ordered clothes to be put out which was done; and he ordered two garments to be given to the man. He then exhorted to almsgiving, and the man came and laid down one of the two garments. The Prophet cried out: Take your garment!

I copied the following from the manuscript of Abûl-Wâfa b. 'Aqil[19]

---

[18] *i.e.*, that of the Banu Sulaim.

He says: Ibn Shãdhan reports that a number of Sûfis came to visit Shibli, who sent to a rich man asking him for money to spend upon them. The man sent the messenger back with the reply: You, Abû Bakr, know the Truth (the Deity); have you asked Him?—Shibli said to the messenger; Go back to .him and say: Worldly goods are base, so I seek them of the base like you; I ask for Truth of the Truth. —Ibn 'Aqil observes: If the man sent him a hundred *dinãrs* to ransom himself from foul language of this kind, then Shibli himself fed from a foul source and entertained, his guests with the same.

Some of them having marketable goods expended them,[20] saying "I would not have my confidence in anything but God." This is want of intelligence, these people supposing that "reliance" means doing away with means and giving wealth away. We were informed by al-Qazzãz after al-Khãtib after Abû Nû'aim 'the Hãfiz that Jã'far al-Khuldi stated in his book that he had heard Junaid say: I with a number of our comrades knocked at the door of Abû Ya'qûb al-Zayyat: He said: Had you no business with God which would distract you from coming to me?—I replied: If our coming to you be part of our business with Him, why should we abstain from it?—I then asked him a question about Reliance. He threw away a *dirhãm* which he had, and then gave me an answer which did full justice to Reliance. Then he said: I was ashamed before God to answer you while I had anything in my possession.

I would observe that if these people understood the sense of Reliance, that it means confidence of the heart in God, not giving up different forms of wealth, they would not have used this language. Only they do not understand. Now the leaders of the Companions and the Epigoni used to trade and amass wealth, none of them saying this. It has been told us that when Abû Bakr al-Siddiq was told that he must give up earning owing to his being occupied with the Caliphate, he said: Then whence shall I support my family?— This language is disapproved by the Sûfis, who declare that one who utters it is not Reliant. Similarly they disapprove of anyone saying: This food will harm me. On this subject they narrate a story of Abû Tãlib al-Razi. I was present, he said, in a certain place with

---

[19] See above. Accounts of him in *Shãjarat al-dhahab*, iv. 35, and *Hisan al-Nizãm*.

[20] Apparently this means realized them and gave away the proceeds.

our comrades, who produced some *leben*[21] I will not eat it, I said, for it does me harm. Forty years later I was praying one day behind the *Maqam*[22] and said in my orison: O God thou knowest that I have associated none with Thee even for the twinkling of an eye—I heard a mysterious voice saying: Not even on the day of the *leben*?

God, I would observe, knows best about the accuracy of this story. You should know, however, that the man who says: "This will harm me "does not mean that the thing will work the mischief of itself: his meaning is merely that it is a cause of mischief, as when Abraham said (xiv. 39) *O Lord, verily they have misled many of the people.* It is ascertained that the Prophet said: No wealth has helped me like Abû Bakr's. His phrase *has not helped me* corresponds with that of one who says *has not harmed me.* It is also ascertained that he said: My meal at Khaibar has not ceased revisiting me till now till it has severed my aorta.[23] It is certain that there is no rank higher than that of Prophet, and he ascribed help to wealth and harm to food. To feel scruples about following his path is to attack the Code. No attention should be paid to the chatter of this person on such a subject.

We have explained how the original Sûfis gave up their property out of indifference to it, and have stated that they did this with a good intention only they were mistaken in so doing, as we have said, as they went against the Code and reason. The later Sûfis favour worldly prosperity and the amassing of wealth from any source whatever, being auxious for comfort and gratification of their desires. Some of them, though able to earn, decline to work, sit down in a hermitage or a mosque and rely on people's charity, constantly listening for a knock at the door. Now it is well-known that charity is unlawful for the rich or able-bodied. They care not who sends to them; the sender may be an oppressor or a tax-gatherer, but they do not refuse him. They have invented a vocabulary of their own for this matter, designating the procedure as "opening" or "our maintenance must of necessity come to us,"or "it is from God, so we shall neither send it back nor thank for it." All this is contrary to the Code, and ignorance of it, and the reverse of what the pious of old time used to practise. For the Prophet said:

---

[21] Probably curds.

[22] Stone which retains the impress of Abraham's foot.

[23] Ibn Hishām, ed. Wûstenfeld, p. 765.

The licit is manifest and the illicit is manifest between the two are doubtful matters which many men do not know; whoso is on his guard against doubts secures his religion and his honour. Abû Bakr al-Siddiq vomited when he had eaten, something that was doubtful. The pious would not accept the gift of an oppressor or of one the source of whose wealth was doubtful. Many of the men of old would not accept presents from friends out of conscientiousness and scrupulousness.

It is recorded of Abû Bakr al-Marwazi that he said: I mentioned a certain Traditionalist to Abû 'Abdallāh and he said: What a man he would be for a certain quality! He paused, and then proceeded: A man cannot be perfect in every quality.—I said to him. Was he not an expert, in the Sûnnah?—He replied: Assuredly; I have taken down Traditions from him, but he had one quality: He did not care from whom he accepted.

We have been informed how a certain Sûfi visited a tyrannical prince, and preached to him; the prince then gave him something, which he accepted. The prince said: We are all hunters, the only difference, is in the nets.[24] Where then do these come in respect of their supposed repugnance to worldliness? For the Prophet said: The upper hand is better than the lower (the upper meaning that which gives, as the learned interpret it, which is correct, whereas some suppose the upper hand to be that which takes, Ibn Qûtaibah observes that in his opinion this must be the view of persons who approve of mendicity).

The original Sûfis used to examine the source of wealth, and scrutinize their food. Ahmad b. Hanbal was asked about al-sari al-saqati and replied: The shaikh who is celebrated for the excellence of his food.—Al-sari said: I accompanied a raiding party; we hired a house and I set up an oven therein. My Companions, however, had scruples about eating the bread baked in that oven.[25]

Now one who sees how the newer type of Sûfis in our time care not whence they take may well be amazed. I myself entered a hermitage and asked for its shaikh; I was told that he had gone off to congratulate a prince on the robe of honour which had been conferred on him. This prince was a notorious oppressor. I said: Alas, you are

---

[24] Table-talk of a Mesopotanian Judge, i. 281.

[25] He does not explain what their objection was.

not satisfied with opening a shop, but must needs hawk your wares on your heads! Though you could earn your living you decline to do so and depend on alms and gifts but that is not enough, so you take from anyone; whoever he may be. And even that is not enough, but you must needs go the round of the oppressors, soliciting presents, and congratulating them on raiment which they have no right to wear, and magistracies wherein no justice will be administered. Assuredly you do more injury to Islam than anyone else.

Some of their shaikhs combine to collect money from doubtful sources and then divide it between them. Some make profession of asceticism while owning much money and amassing it with avidity, their profession being in conflict with the facts. Some while amassing wealth make a show of poverty; these make things harder for the real poor by taking the alms, which they have no right to do. Abû'l-Hasan al-bistami; Shaikh of the heritage of Ibn al-Majyan (?), used to wear wool in both summer and winter, and receive visits from people who supposed that this would bring them luck. When he died, he left 4,000 *dinârs*.

This, I would observe, is more than disgraceful. It is ascertained that when one of the People of the Bench dying left two *dinârs*, the Prophet said: Two burnings!